How to Stop School Rampage Killing

"*How to Stop School Rampage Killing* makes a major contribution to our understanding of how school violence schemes are developed and provides insight about core recurring themes in the planning of rampage violence across a range of cases. This book provides a rich source for anyone interested in how school violence in general and rampage school violence in particular unfolds. Dr. Madfis is masterful at telling the story through the words of his subjects while remaining analytical and never losing sight of the key issues facing schools."
—Stuart Henry, *Professor of Criminal Justice and Director of the School of Public Affairs at San Diego State University, USA*

"On the subject of assessing and preventing acts of extreme violence in schools, this book sets the standard as the forefront of rigorous knowledge. In a topic that often abounds with hype and emotion, no other volume presents such a steadfastly researched, sober discussion of what effectively prevents and thwarts school rampages. This book is essential reading for anyone with the desire to understand evenhanded social scientific perspectives on the risks and prevention of school rampages."
—Glenn W. Muschert, *Professor of Sociology at Khalifa University of Science and Technology, Abu Dhabi, United Arab Emirates*

"How can you stop a student armed with firearms, explosives, and murderous intent—before he ever sets foot on campus? Madfis skillfully answers this question and more, based on his interviews with principals, teachers, counselors, and police officers who have successfully prevented nearly a dozen school shootings since Columbine."
—Adam Lankford, *Professor of Criminology and Criminal Justice at the University of Alabama, USA*

"This important book by Dr. Madfis provides an updated and in-depth perspective on school shootings and ways to prevent them."
—Atte Oksanen, *Professor of Social Psychology, Tampere University, Finland*

Eric Madfis

How to Stop School Rampage Killing

Lessons from Averted Mass Shootings and Bombings

Eric Madfis
School of Social Work and Criminal Justice
University of Washington Tacoma
Tacoma, WA, USA

ISBN 978-3-030-37180-7   ISBN 978-3-030-37181-4 (eBook)
https://doi.org/10.1007/978-3-030-37181-4

1st edition: The Risk of School Rampage, © Eric Madfis, published by Palgrave Macmillan, 2014
2nd edition: © The Editor(s) (if applicable) and The Author(s), under exclusive license to Springer Nature Switzerland AG 2020
This work is subject to copyright. All rights are solely and exclusively licensed by the Publisher, whether the whole or part of the material is concerned, specifically the rights of translation, reprinting, reuse of illustrations, recitation, broadcasting, reproduction on microfilms or in any other physical way, and transmission or information storage and retrieval, electronic adaptation, computer software, or by similar or dissimilar methodology now known or hereafter developed.
The use of general descriptive names, registered names, trademarks, service marks, etc. in this publication does not imply, even in the absence of a specific statement, that such names are exempt from the relevant protective laws and regulations and therefore free for general use.
The publisher, the authors and the editors are safe to assume that the advice and information in this book are believed to be true and accurate at the date of publication. Neither the publisher nor the authors or the editors give a warranty, expressed or implied, with respect to the material contained herein or for any errors or omissions that may have been made. The publisher remains neutral with regard to jurisdictional claims in published maps and institutional affiliations.

Cover illustration: ND700/shutterstock

This Palgrave Macmillan imprint is published by the registered company Springer Nature Switzerland AG
The registered company address is: Gewerbestrasse 11, 6330 Cham, Switzerland

For Lucille Rose and Violet Ember—
You deserve to live in a world with safe and supportive schools and in a society that has the courage to tackle difficult issues and make real change.

Foreword by Jack Levin

In response to high-profile rampage school shootings, Professor Madfis offers a promising research-based alternative to the fear-based approach promoted by many politicians, media pundits, and misinformed professionals. In this groundbreaking work, he examines characteristics of school shootings and bombings that have somehow been averted. Professor Madfis asks, "What does it take to *prevent* a tragic school rampage?" Readers may be surprised to find little evidence for increasing security measures on school and college campuses. Instead, his answer shines a bright light on effective alternative practices that deserve to have a prominent place in the literature of public criminology.

Those who seek to reduce school rampages tend to focus on protecting potential victims—the locked doors and metal detectors, enlarged presence of resource officers, security cameras, student drills, harsh zero-tolerance policies, and guns for teachers. Some commentators have suggested assigning each student a hockey puck which they might aim at a menacing intruder. What is too often missing in this conventional analysis are the short- and long-term variables that come into play before a killer decides to plant a bomb or open fire—planning and preparation, encouragement from peers, outsider status, failures in life, collection of weapons, internet behavior, and victimization at the hands of other students.

Efforts to prevent school violence need to begin when students are troubled and long before they become troublesome. There are many youngsters who are being chronically bullied and harassed by their schoolmates on a regular basis. These are the students who tend to remain socially isolated and unable to cope with the many frustrations they face every day in the classroom, in the cafeteria, and on the playground. After they graduate, such troubled young people have only the most depressing and angry memories of their years in school. They continue to suffer losses at home, in personal relationships, and at work; they are reduced to feeling worthless on the Internet, and they lack any significant places to turn for effective guidance and assistance. A few of them seek some semblance of personal justice by inflicting multiple casualties at home or in a public setting.

Once youngsters turn from troubled to troublesome, they are—for the first time, possibly able to locate individuals in their lives who are willing to intervene to lend a helping hand. Sadly, however, the motivation for intervention may arise not out of any sense of altruism but out of fear. The troublesome individual may now be regarded as a threat to the safety of the public, someone who is simply too dangerous to be ignored. Still, even the most threatening youngster may remain without a source of companionship or advice. Or, it may simply be too late to avert a tragedy.

Thanks to the code of silence existing in schools across the country as described by Professor Madfis, there are numerous youngsters whose preparations for violence are known but totally ignored by their peers. Madfis emphasizes the importance of having credible authority figures at school and at home to whom a student is willing to go with information about a likely catastrophe. He also recognizes that a school climate based on retribution and fear only encourages bystander apathy and supports the persistence of a code of silence. This outstanding book provides the ingredients necessary for transforming this code of silence into a culture of caring and peace.

Boston, MA, USA

Jack Levin, Ph.D.
Professor Emeritus and
Co-Director of the Brudnick
Center on Violence and Conflict
at Northeastern University

Foreword by Kristina Anderson

My awakening to the importance of school safety and violence prevention occurred on the college campus of Virginia Tech on April 16, 2007. On a cold Monday morning, alarming bangs—gunfire—came into the hallway and classrooms of Norris Hall, the engineering building I sat in. Within seconds, a student, aiming two handguns, barged into my classroom. For the following eleven minutes, my emotions progressed from confusion, shock, to extreme fear and quiet panic. Thirty-two members our community lost their lives that day; my classmates and I were severely injured, physically and psychologically impacted. Joining a small, and growing, group of mass shooting survivors who have channeled their tragic experiences into helping others, I formed a school safety nonprofit, The Koshka Foundation, to help communities prevent similar events, and also recover over the long-term.

I first met Dr. Eric Madfis, trying to understand the scope of school safety research and literature, as his work is uniquely focused on averted attacks. A significant amount of energy and time is focused on studying the intimate details of a rampage killing, or mass shooting, after a tragedy has already happened, and yet Dr. Madfis' research offers an important proposition and incredible opportunity: we may be able to more efficiently glean information and better understandings from the attacks that were in the earlier planning and preparation stages.

Media coverage and government after-action reports are sources that often singularly focus on the final acts and terrible actions of attackers. I appreciate Dr. Madfis' discussion, in this text and in his other research, on the importance of the role of media portrayal in potentially glorifying the attackers themselves. Media coverage rarely includes accurate analysis of the preceding months, or even years, before an attack. A fuller background portrait of how school mass shooting plots progress or are stopped can significantly aid prevention efforts.

By adding to this missing knowledge of averted attacks, Madfis broadens our view of the possibility of overall prevention by providing us insight into effective interventions. Schools can reach out sooner to students before punitive measures are the only option, ask more insightful questions about their behaviors, and provide resources and assistance that seek to keep the student in school. The interviews that this text shares with the reader, words from principals and others who helped to intervene, are a human perspective we rarely see in contrast to graphic and re-traumatizing reports of mass killings. I hope the case studies serve as learning opportunities for us all to be reminded of our self-efficacy and community capacity to work together to prevent school violence. I am deeply grateful for Madfis' work and dedication, as one of the early pioneers in understanding and vocalizing the importance of learning from the near-misses, and for his continued research in mass shootings and school violence prevention.

As Madfis shows us through his discussion of the cultural impact of zero-tolerance policies and physical security measures, school policies are often questioned or scrutinized, especially in the wake of recent violence. In our experience, Virginia Tech endured numerous and long-lasting investigations and inquiries from families of victims, lawyers, the media, and many other entities. It is important to remember that rampage shootings are still very rare, and, on the daily level, maintaining safety within a school is a multi-layered and collaborative process. The tasks sometimes needed to help ensure an issue does not escalate—managing a disruptive student or parent, responding to writing that has frightened a teacher, deciphering a social media post—all require thoughtful analysis, nuance, and a researched method and process.

Shortly after the Sandy Hook Elementary Shooting in 2013, the state of Virginia became the first to legislatively mandate, and fund, training for the creation of multi-disciplinary behavioral threat assessment and management teams within K-12 and colleges and universities. These teams (made up of members of counseling, law enforcement, student affairs, legal, and other areas) meet on a weekly basis, and address potentially concerning behavior by providing resources, outreach, and support before an individual may cause harm to themselves, or others. Madfis stresses the need for continued research in this area of violence prevention, as school districts across the nation use different risk assessment rubrics and instruments and are not always effectively training in threat management. While it may be tempting to rely heavily on one solution or surveillance technology, Madfis reminds us that assessing potentially violent behavior is an "imminently complicated issue." We must always remember to consider how the actions we take to provide safety, with good intentions, also impact a student's level of connection and perceived support from the school.

Our personal thresholds for what constitutes "dangerous behavior" or "threatening" varies based on culture, previous experiences, and many other factors. We do not want to overreact, and yet the fear of the *possibility* of a school rampage, felt heavily through graphic media coverage and other means, has allowed for the existence of unbalanced and punitive policies. Dr. Madfis' research informs our misunderstandings about the reality of prevention—that multiple variables, decisions by various stakeholders, and proactive conversations helped attacks be stopped. Therefore, we must also be open to the understanding that it may be a counselor, a parent, or a teacher who plays a crucial role in either bringing information forward or intervening when someone is speaking about a violent attack or suicide. Madfis reminds us that each individual within the school is important for ensuring safety and helping to build a school climate that values mutual respect, empathy, and kindness.

As we look toward a future that continues to increase focus on positive school climates and safety, the hope is that we have more teachers, principals, school law enforcement, and parents working together to evaluate and implement policies that benefit the well-being of all students. While it is difficult to fully measure what we have averted, Madfis' gift to us, through this text, serves as an inspiration and guidebook that prevention is not only possible, it is a critical conversation for each school to address the issues that strict security practices fail to avert. To the individual reader, may you share the lessons learned throughout the following chapters directly with your communities, so this knowledge may be sustained. During our recovery in Virginia, the university motto of *Ut Prosim*, "That I May Serve," became an important marker of our strength and resilience. Thank you to those that dedicate their time to serving and educating our communities with the ultimate goal of peace, words will never adequately describe our gratitude.

Seattle, WA, USA

Kristina Anderson
Virginia Tech Shooting Survivor,
School Safety Advocate, and
Executive Director of the Koshka
Foundation for Safe Schools

Preface

My interest in school rampage attacks and the reaction to them began back when I was still in high school. I directly experienced the changing school climate that arose in the wake of one of our nation's most publicized and feared mass shootings. The tragedy at Columbine High School in Jefferson County, Colorado occurred on April 20, 1999 which was during my junior year of high school. Afterwards, students, parents, and school staff were genuinely terrified that these types of massacres were going to start happening with great frequency in schools everywhere around the country (Gallup, 1999; Madfis, 2016). Certainly, there were numerous copycat attempts and attacks and the number of mass school shooting incidents did increase in the coming years (Blair & Schweit, 2014; Follman et al., 2019; Langman, 2018), but in many respects, the United States underwent a full-scale moral panic, where the subjective fervor and fear of school shootings went far beyond the objective reality or frequency of the problem. As a result, schools reacted with a series of "get tough" on crime disciplinary policies, mechanisms to secure and surveil the school and those in it, and a zealous desire to locate broad warning signs among potential school shooters. Part of this entailed propagating false stereotypes that cast the Gothic subculture (and many other vaguely associated cultural phenomenon such as black trench coats or "alternative" music) as disproportionately if not exclusively made up of future school shooters (Griffiths, 2010; Merelli, 2018; Muzzatti, 2004; Ogle et al., 2003).

In this post-Columbine environment, I was a teenage punk rocker from Framingham, Massachusetts with brightly dyed spikey hair who wore steel-toed boots and spikes, patches, and metal studs on his jacket. I hung out with punks, goths, anti-racist skinheads, hardcore kids, metal heads, and other kids generally seen as misfits and outcasts. Roughly a year after the Columbine attack, during the Spring of 2000, I was in my senior year of high school. School officials were alerted to some graffiti that had been written on a stall in one of the boy's bathrooms. The graffiti, we were told, stated something to the effect of "Columbine could happen here" on a particular date during the upcoming month. This fact was then widely circulated around the school community—and administrators, teachers, and parents all discussed what should be done. Ultimately, school officials decided to proceed with the school day as normal. However, the vast majority of students still chose not to attend school on that day. During my various classes throughout that day, I noticed that only about a quarter of my classmates were in attendance.

Why did I go to school that day? Just like everyone else, I had read about the incident at Columbine High School and heard various pundits proclaim that the shooters had been the victims of bullying who had mainly targeted those people who had victimized them. As I saw it, I had nothing to fear for I had never bullied any of my peers. In retrospect, I confess that this wasn't really the best rationale for feeling secure, as I know now that, while rampage school shooters may often target certain people, they also frequently seek to attack symbolic targets and/or merely go for volume in pursuit of killing as many random people as possible (Lankford, 2016; Madfis, 2017).

After my last class of the school day, I started walking to my locker with one of my good friends at the time. He was a skate punk who looked and dressed not unlike I did at the time. He was not the best student—or even the least truant student—but he was a genuinely nice kid with a good sense of humor. He was certainly not a violent person and he had no history of such behavior either in or out of school. As he and I walked down the hallway toward our lockers to pack up for the day, my friend turned to me and said the following: "Boy, today sure was disappointing!"

Unfortunately, he made this comment as we turned around a corner, and at that same exact moment, one of the Vice Principals (the one most infamous in the school for being tough with student discipline) turned this corner from the other direction and overheard his comment. He was then sent immediately to her office and subsequently given a lengthy out-of-school suspension. As a result of this incident, he was made to feel wholly unwelcome at the school and passively if not actively discouraged from coming back. He ultimately did then drop out of high school, never to return. That weird day when nearly everyone stayed home was his last day of high school.

Did he write the graffiti on the bathroom wall? I am certain that he did not. Did he mean by his comment that he thought the day was disappointing because there weren't enough people there on that day for him to kill? Of course not. Was he perhaps making a dark sarcastic comment about the disappointing lack of excitement on a day that so many people had hyped up and expressed fear about? Maybe—and, to be perfectly honest, that was how I took his meaning at the time. We were cynical teenagers who thought we were just talking to one another. But it is equally plausible that he was just expressing annoyance at a complete waste of a school day in which we had to sit through classes where teachers couldn't teach anything as a result of the unusually high number of absences. Regardless of the many ways that one could interpret that comment, the school administration decided to interpret his comment as a threat which needed to be harshly punished.

As this book will discuss, this was during the height of a new era of zero tolerance in school disciplinary policy, where strict punishments are uniformly applied to everyone, regardless of individual intentions, contexts, or circumstances. In the wake of Columbine, the United States experienced a serious panic and overreaction in schools over the fear of horrifying yet rare instances of school shootings. This ultimately resulted in a dramatic expansion of the school-to-prison pipeline and in the adoption of extreme penalties and increased justice system involvement for what would previously have been perceived as minor infractions. This experience with my friend in high school helped to spark my initial interest in school shootings—and particularly the significance of understanding more reasonable, measured, and effective ways to respond to and prevent the genuine risks of mass shootings, bombings, and other rampage attacks in American schools. It is my hope that today, through rigorous empirical research like that of mine and many others, we can start to implement the types of policies and procedures which have proven to effectively thwart these potentially tragic incidents—without unduly harsh discipline, without stereotyping kids who happen to look different, and without sacrificing students' rights or positive pedagogical environments in the process. School rampage killings are profoundly disturbing and destabilizing events, rare though they may be. We must resist the impulse to view these tragedies as part of "the new normal" for society (Edwards, 2018; Graham, 2018) and instead acknowledge the fact that far more can be done to prevent and stop these attacks and to lessen their deadly impact. This book will provide numerous recommendations about just how this could be done, as it is a far more achievable goal than many believe it to be. That said, much work needs to be done to transform sound evidence-based policy into real change on the ground, and it will take far more advocacy and activism from the public and far more political will from lawmakers to accomplish what should be an obvious common goal of all Americans—no more rampage killings in our schools.

Over the last few decades, school rampage attacks have taken multiple lives and caused widespread fear throughout the United States. During this same period, however, dozens of potential incidents have also been averted wherein student plots to kill multiple peers and faculty members came to the attention of authorities and thus were thwarted. This book investigates how such successes occurred, utilizing data gleaned from in-depth interviews conducted with 32 school and police officials (administrators, counselors, security and police officers, and teachers) who were directly involved in assessing and preventing what many perceived to be potential rampages at eleven public middle and high schools across the Northeastern United States. A multi-tiered method was employed to examine the process by which threats of rampage violence are assessed by school and police officials as well as how previous school rampage plots have been averted. Interview data about the eleven averted incidents were triangulated via news media reporting and legal documentation (such as court transcripts, arrest reports, and legal briefs) in order to verify concordance with and inconsistencies among the interviewees' accounts of their threat assessments and crime prevention practices.

The resultant data provide insight into the institutional cultures and practices that were involved in determining the magnitude of school rampage risks and ultimately enabling various potential attacks to be foiled. In addition, the findings also serve as a means through which to better understand contemporary perspectives on the fear, risk assessment, and criminalization of American youth. The way in which school authorities have reacted to the school rampage phenomenon reveals a great deal about our current justice mindset, which often views the identification, surveillance, and management of potentially dangerous individuals as the best approach to what is understood as the inevitability of crime. Subsequently, this research reveals the significant shortcomings and sometimes harmful consequences of contemporary risk assessment, violence prevention, and punishment practices prominent in American schools. By examining averted incidents, this work addresses problematic gaps in school violence scholarship and reveals both practical implications for the assessment and prevention of school violence and significant theoretical insight regarding the causes and consequences of enhanced school discipline and security.

Broadly, this book explores perceptions of and reactions to threats of rampage school violence. In Chapter 1, readers will be introduced to the phenomenon of school rampage killing, the literature on the causes and reactions to prior incidents of school violence, and the field of violence risk assessment. This chapter will also situate the American reaction to school rampage in the broader social context of contemporary school disciplinary and security practices and will provide theoretical background for explaining recent developments though insights from the sociology of risk, actuarial justice, and neoliberal penality. The second chapter illustrates how school and police officials engage in violence risk assessment by examining the forms of evidence present when claims are made that a school rampage threat has been averted. After categorizing the forms of risk assessment that have been utilized, chapter three addresses the extent to which and under what circumstances officials express confidence in their use of risk assessment. The fourth chapter covers the manner in which student threats of rampage violence have come to the attention of parents, police, and school authorities in order to be averted and considers the extent to which students have actually broken through a code of silence which discourages them from informing on their peers. In addition, as many contemporary school violence prevention practices (such as enhanced discipline and increased security and surveillance) were not found to play a decisive role in preventing these incidents, alternative approaches from restorative justice are suggested to improve school climates, and accordingly, to increase positive bystander behavior on the part of students. Chapter 5 presents a discussion of the findings as a whole along with the policy and theoretical implications that may be drawn from them, provides a review of emerging policies and scholarship on new ways to prevent rampage killing, and suggests areas for future research. Finally, Chapter 6 serves as a methodological appendix and addresses the research design of the project as well as the benefits and potential limitations of the study's methods.

Tacoma, WA, USA   Eric Madfis

Contents

1	**Introduction**	1
	Research Questions and Background Information on Averted School Rampage Incidents	2
	Explaining and Reacting to School Rampage Killing	7
	Responding to Rampage—Current School Disciplinary and Security Practices	15
	Understanding School Criminalization and Risk Assessment as Actuarial Justice	24
	Questions for Discussion	29
	References	30
2	**Assessing the Substance and Risk of Student Rampage Threats**	43
	Distinguishing Threats, Risks, Plots, and Genuine Aversion	46
	The Assessment of Evidence in Averted Rampage Violence	52
	Conclusion	79
	Questions for Discussion	80
	References	80

3 Confidence and Doubt in Assessing Averted Rampage Violence — 87
Variations in Confidence and Doubt by Risk Assessment Type — 88
Conclusion — 97
Questions for Discussion — 100
References — 100

4 Preventing School Rampage Violence Through Student Bystander Intervention and Positive School Environments — 103
School Rampage Violence Prevention and the Student Code of Silence — 104
Perceiving a Diminished Student Code of Silence Since Columbine — 109
Weakening the Code of Silence Through Positive School Climate — 110
Breaking the Code of Silence—Interventions Through Leakage — 113
Following the Code of Silence—The Persistence of Bystander Inaction — 119
Implications of Findings — 122
Conclusion — 126
Questions for Discussion — 131
References — 131

5 Summary of Findings, Policy Implications, and Future Research — 139
Summary and Implications of Findings — 140
Other Emergent Areas to Help Prevent and Stop School Rampage Killing — 144
Suggested Areas for Future Research — 155
References — 159

6	**Methodological Appendix**	167
	Operationalizing School Rampage and Averted Threat	168
	Research Design and Sample	172
	Complications of Relying on the News Media to Build a Sampling Frame	176
	On Qualitative Methodology	178
	Generalizability in Qualitative Research	179
	References	181
References		185
Index		215

About the Author

Eric Madfis, Ph.D., is an Associate Professor of Criminal Justice at the University of Washington Tacoma, where his research focuses on the causes and prevention of school violence, hate crime, and mass murder. As a nationally recognized expert on mass/school shootings, he has spoken to audiences across the country and around the world about his research, including at the United States Congressional Briefing on School Safety and Violence Prevention and to the Washington State Legislature's House Education Committee. He received his Ph.D. in Sociology from Northeastern University in Boston, where he was a Research Associate at the Brudnick Center on Violence and Conflict. His work has been published in *American Behavioral Scientist, Behavioral Sciences & the Law, Critical Criminology, Homicide Studies, The Journal of Contemporary Criminal Justice, The Journal of Hate Studies, The Journal of Psychology, Men and Masculinities, Social Justice, The Social Science Journal, Sociological Focus, Violence and Gender, Youth Violence & Juvenile Justice*, and in numerous edited volumes. He served as co-editor (along with Dr. Adam Lankford) of the February 2018 special issue of *American Behavioral Scientist* on "Media Coverage of Mass Killers." Dr. Madfis has been interviewed by and/or has had his research featured on *ABC News,*

The BBC, MSNBC, NBC, NPR, The Australian Broadcasting Corporation, The Canadian Broadcasting Corporation, The Boston Globe, The Los Angeles Times, Money Magazine, The New York Times, Newsweek, Politico, The Seattle Times, Slate, Time, Vice, The Washington Post, and many other local, national, and international outlets. In 2018, he won UW Tacoma's Distinguished Research Award.

1

Introduction

Over the last twenty years in the United States, there have been hundreds of school rampage plots that have successfully been averted (Daniels, 2019; Madfis, 2014a). During this same period, however, American schools have prioritized discipline and security in a manner which has exaggerated the extent of school violence as a social problem and dramatically transformed public education as a social institution. In the wake of numerous highly publicized multiple-victim school homicides that occurred during the 1990s, American schools responded with massive changes to their disciplinary policies and security apparatuses. With the intention of preventing future rampage attacks, such as mass shootings and bombings, schools implemented increased security through school resource officers (hereafter, SRO's), cameras, locked doors, and lockdown procedures, and expanded discipline via zero-tolerance policies with mandatory arrests and school exclusions (King and Bracy, 2019). This cluster of practices, which Hirshfield and Celinska (2011) have collectively referred to as "school criminalization," represent the fairly recent but pervasive incursion of law enforcement personnel, ideology, and technology into the school setting. In addition, many school officials and academics responded with a risk assessment approach by focusing upon the identification of potential school shooters through warning sign checklists, behavioral profiles, and threat assessments.

Whatever failures or successes these varied approaches have had with regard to fighting school crime or violence more generally, no prior scholarship has looked at the numerous cases of rampage plots which have actually been averted in order to discern if and when any of these developments have actually played a preventative role. In fact, with the exception of a few recent studies (Daniels, 2019; Daniels et al., 2007, 2010; Langman & Straub, 2019; Larkin, 2009; Madfis, 2014a; Madfis & Cohen, 2018; Pollack, Modzeleski, & Rooney, 2008), social scientists and the public at large possess next to no systematic information on the rampage attacks which have been plotted and planned, yet never came to fruition. Through their exploration, this study endeavors to understand not only how schools assess violent threats and construct risk generally and at times problematically, but also what social and individual forces have been at work in practice to prevent instances of school rampage violence from taking place.

Research Questions and Background Information on Averted School Rampage Incidents

Averted incidents of school rampage offer a unique opportunity for social scientific investigation. As there has been little empirical research on how previous rampage plots have been thwarted, most of the rhetorical arguments regarding how future attacks are to be prevented amount to mere speculation and rely on far too many problematic assumptions about the unlimited benefits and minimal consequences of enhanced school criminalization and risk assessment.

First, this book will explore the process by which schools engage in the risk assessment of their students. To what extent are school officials aware of various forms of violence risk assessment and what are their perspectives regarding the utility of these techniques? Which approaches are utilized for what purposes? What criteria do police and school officials deem most important in the assessment of student threat? How do school officials manage student threats and maintain a sense of safety in the school community? The second goal of this research was to ascertain how student threats of rampage violence have been successfully averted. In particular, how have these threats come to the attention of authorities? What role did risk assessment and the criminalization of schools play in the prevention of the rampage plots? What additional factors, policies, or procedures permitted the rampage to be averted?

My data reveal that, between the years 2000–2009, there were at least 195 averted incidents where student plots to kill multiple peers and faculty members came to the attention of authorities and thus were thwarted. I conducted in-depth interviews with thirty-two school and police officials (administrators, counselors, security and police officers, and teachers) directly involved in assessing and preventing potential rampages at eleven middle and high schools located across the Northeastern United States.

All of the eleven schools that granted me permission for interviews were public institutions. Nine were high schools, one was a middle school, and one was a junior/senior high school. Two were located in Pennsylvania, one was in New York, two were in New Jersey, three were in Massachusetts, and three were in Connecticut. All eleven schools were located in communities where the vast majority of residents were white. Seven of these schools were located in suburban predominantly middle-class communities, three of them were located in very affluent suburban areas, and one school was in a lower middle-class rural community. In order to preserve the anonymity of participants, pseudonyms have been used for all individuals and schools, and no sources (whether news media reporting or legal documentation on specific cases) can be explicitly referenced or cited. This is consistent with how Daniels and his colleagues (2007, 2010, 2011) presented their findings on incidents of averted school rampage killings.

In the first case at Adams High School, a 16-year-old male student, who later admitted to making and exploding more than 40 bombs in the woods near his suburban home, sent videos of himself firing his father's guns and using the homemade explosives to a friend. The friend's mother notified the police, and numerous weapons, including two assault rifles, and detailed plans to commit a rampage attack at his school were seized from the teenager's bedroom.

The second case occurred at the affluent Blane High School, where several students came forward to inform administrators that one of their peers had brought explosives to school with him. When school officials searched this student's backpack, they discovered tennis balls filled with explosives. Later, police found four additional explosive devices at the student's home.

In the third incident, a 15-year-old student at Courtside High School stole three handguns and hundreds of rounds of ammunition from his father's safe. According to the best friend he entrusted to hold onto these weapons for him, he intended to use them in his plan to attack the school.

The fourth incident ended when three teenagers were arrested while walking down a street carrying an arsenal of weapons and thousands of rounds of ammunition, after failing in their attempt to steal a car. They intended to use the vehicle to embark on a killing spree throughout their town, including a massacre at Donovan High School of students who had teased them.

The fifth case involved three teenage students at Everton High School creating very detailed and threatening profiles on a social networking website. These profiles featured, among many other disturbing images and words, a digital countdown clock ticking down to the anniversary of the Columbine massacre and several communications and videos expressing the desire to kill lots of people.

Four students at Finley High School, in the sixth incident, were involved in elaborate planning and extensive training to commit a rampage attack at their school. Despite many attempts, these students were never able to attain their own firearms, but they did acquire BB guns, knives, axes, gunpowder, and several homemade explosives. When one of the conspirator's dedication to carrying out their deadly plans became in question, the other three plotters went to school authorities and blamed everything on their reluctant friend, though the complicity of the whole group was eventually revealed to the police.

In the seventh case, several students at the affluent Greenvale High School expressed serious concern to school administrators about one of their peers having what they perceived to be a hit list of the names of his current and former teachers written in his notebook. The student ultimately left the school voluntarily rather than facing expulsion.

The eighth incident entailed five students at a rural combined middle and high school, Hastings Jr./Sr. High School, who made death threats against various members of the football team and other students on a social networking website. One of the threatened students informed his parents about the threats, and this parent, in turn, called the President of the School Board to express concern. The school was shut down for the remainder of the week, and several students were suspended.

In case nine, a teacher and several students at affluent Iverson High School noticed threatening messages scribbled onto walls in a boys' bathroom stall and informed the school principal. An 18-year-old student was arrested and charged with threatening with a deadly device and disturbing a school assembly.

In the tenth case, a teacher at Jefferson Middle School saw one of her students, a 13-year-old girl, writing out a list of people she disliked on a piece of paper at the girl's desk and subsequently notified the school principal. As the paper was interpreted as a hit list, she was charged with making terrorist threats against her classmates, suspended indefinitely, and forced to undergo psychiatric evaluation.

In the final incident, the eleventh case, students at Kranston High School noticed a threatening message written on a wall in one of the boys' bathroom stalls. These students then informed teachers who in turn told the school principal and SRO about the written threat, but no one was ever found responsible.

See Table 1.1 for basic information on the eleven schools, their communities, the perpetrators, and the substance of the threats. Consult Chapter 6 for additional demographic information about these schools and their communities.

Through the detailed investigation of these cases of averted rampage violence, my research explores how officials explain their concerns about violent threats, the process by which threats are assessed and notions of safety are maintained, and how previous school rampage plots have been averted. The resultant data provide insight into the school cultures, policies, and procedures that enabled rampage attacks to be foiled, but also

Table 1.1 Background information on schools, perpetrators, incidents, and communities

School name	Perpetrator(s)	Basic offense info	Location of school
Adams High School	16-year-old male student	Detailed school rampage plot and weapons cache	Middle-class suburban community
Blane High School	Teenage male student	Explosives brought to school	Affluent suburban community
Courtside High School	15-year-old male student	Weapons stolen with stated intent to commit school rampage	Lower middle-class suburban community
Donovan High School	3 male teenage students (ages 18, 14, and 15)	Rampage attack caught in progress while attempting to steal a car to carry out attack	Middle-class suburban community
Everton High School	3 male teenage students (ages 15, 16, and 16)	Detailed school rampage plans posted on social media site	Middle-class suburban community
Finley High School	4 male teenage students (all ages 16 or 17)	Detailed school rampage plot	Middle-class suburban community
Greenvale High School	Teenage male student	Written list of disliked current and former teachers perceived to be a hit list	Affluent suburban community
Hastings Jr./Sr. High School	5 male teenage students (all ages 15 or 16)	Death threats made against members of football team and other students on social media site	Lower middle-class rural community

(continued)

Table 1.1 (continued)

School name	Perpetrator(s)	Basic offense info	Location of school
Iverson High School	18-year-old male student	Threatening messages written on boys' bathroom stall	Affluent suburban community
Jefferson Middle School	13-year-old female student	Written list of disliked students perceived to be a hit list	Middle-class suburban community
Kranston High School	Unknown student	Threatening message written on boys' bathroom stall	Middle-class suburban community

are a means through which to better understand contemporary perspectives on the fear, risk assessment, and surveillance of American youth. Therefore, the way in which school authorities have reacted to the school rampage phenomenon reveals a great deal about our contemporary justice mindset, which often views the identification, surveillance, and management of potentially dangerous individuals as the best approach to the inevitability of crime. As such, this research contains both practical implications for the assessment and prevention of school violence and significant theoretical insight regarding the causes and consequences of enhanced school discipline and security.

Explaining and Reacting to School Rampage Killing

School Rampage Killing as a Social Problem

A dramatic series of mass killings took place in the late 1990s at several rural and suburban public middle and high schools across the United States. These events were highly publicized as they shocked the American public not only for their brutality, but because of the prior belief that such schools were "safe havens, free of the dangers of street crime" (Lawrence, 2007, p. 147). That such violence could be perpetrated in middle and upper class school districts away from the plight of urban areas was seen as especially perplexing (Kimmel & Mahler, 2003). Perhaps unsurprisingly, a great deal of empirical research has since been conducted on the phenomenon.

While the term school shooting has been defined and operationalized in almost countless ways by many different scholars, Newman, Fox, Roth, Mehta, and Harding (2004, p. 50) can be credited with delineating the fairly new phenomenon as "rampage school shootings" which "take place on a school-related public stage before an audience; involve multiple victims, some of whom are shot simply for their symbolic significance or at random; and involve one or more shooters who are students or former students of the school." While only a portion of school gun violence fit all of these criteria, many of the most publicized attacks during the last two decades (such as those at Colorado's Columbine High School in 1999, Connecticut's Sandy Hook Elementary School in 2012, and Florida's Marjory Stoneman Douglas High School in 2018) conform to these specifics. In addition to the aforementioned rampage shootings, Muschert (2007, p. 62) has filled in this typological picture to form the accompanying school shootings categories of "mass murders" committed by older nonstudents perpetrators, "terrorist attacks" engaged in by individuals or groups to advance their political or ideological goals, "targeted shootings" that involve only specific preplanned victims, and the "government shootings" of student protesters.

Many scholars (Aitken, 2001; Best, 2002; Burns & Crawford, 1999; Killingbeck, 2001; Madfis, 2016; Muschert & Peguero, 2010), have asserted that the recent American response to rampage school attacks has constituted a moral panic, in that the reaction has been based on an exaggerated perception of their pervasiveness, prevalence, and threat to social order bred by excesses in media coverage (Cohen, 2011). True as this may be, mass shooting incidents at schools and other public places have genuinely occurred with greater frequency since the turn of the twenty-first century (Blair & Schweit, 2014; Follman, Pan, & Aronsen, 2019; Fox, Levin, & Quinet, 2019; Fox & Savage, 2009).

There has been a great deal of debate in the media and among academics recently about the extent to which mass and school shootings are becoming increasingly common (see, for example, Blair & Schweit, 2014; Everytown for Gun Safety, 2014; Follman et al. 2019; Fox & DeLateur, 2014; Lott, 2014). Much of the disagreement here lies with how school shootings are defined and operationalized. Often it is the case that these numbers are politicized with gun control advocates favoring broad definitions so that the size of the problem is amplified and gun control opponents favoring far more specific criteria so as to minimize the extent of the problem. The broadest definition (Everytown for Gun Safety, 2014) includes all shooting incidents on school grounds regardless of whether shooters have any connection to the schools they attack, irrespective of how many people are killed or injured. Such an expansive operationalization typically includes suicides and gang-related violence, Such an expansive operationalization typically includes suicides and gang-related violence, which are certainly consequential incidents worthy of quantification and concern as components of the school violence problem, but they are qualitatively distinct in most ways from school rampage shootings.

Recent studies (Blair & Schweit, 2014; Follman et al., 2019) conclude that mass killings more generally are on the rise, though Fox and DeLateur (2014) point out that this increase only holds for attacks in public places, as the growth largely disappears when domestic mass killings in private homes are included. However, schools are typically public locations, and distinct data analyzed by *Mother Jones* (Follman et al., 2019) and the FBI (Blair & Schweit, 2014) both conclude that American school shootings (and public mass shootings more generally) have increased in recent years. Further, dozens of plots to commit such heinous crimes continue to be revealed and preempted every year in the United States (Daniels, 2019; Madfis, 2014a). Likewise, since the April 1999 Columbine massacre, school shooters in nations around the world from Brazil to Finland have turned to this infamous American case for homicidal inspiration (Larkin, 2009; Madfis & Levin, 2013; Martins, 2019).

Rare as these events may be, such incidents warrant serious concern, for when they do occur, they not only cause multiple casualties, but leave many survivors and bystanders with post-traumatic stress (James, 2009; Schwarz & Kowalski, 1991) and create extensive fear among the larger public (Altheide, 2009; Burns & Crawford, 1999; Harding, Fox, & Mehta, 2002; Madfis, 2016). In the literature review to follow, the extant scholarship on completed and averted school rampages will be discussed, followed by a review of the current state of discipline, security, and surveillance that has become so widely pervasive in American public schools since the turn of the twenty-first century and which has resulted, at least in part, as a reaction to the problem of school rampage killings.

The Causes of School Rampage Killing

Due to the prolific fear and extensive publicity which school rampage killings have typically received since the late 1990s, the bulk of social science research has focused on this particular form of school shooting (Mushert, 2007). The etiology of school rampage killings has been explored by a vast array of academics ranging from sociologists and criminologists to anthropologists, social workers, psychologists, and psychiatrists. Often, scholars have brought one particular causal factor to the fore, whether it is an individual deficiency, interpersonal conflicts, the school or community context, or the larger sociocultural background.

At the individual level, some have focused upon the depression, mental illness, and personality disorders of said killers (Langman, 2009a, 2009b; McGee & DeBernardo, 1999). Others have stressed the role played by negative relationships with peers, such as victimization through bullying (Burgess, Garbarino, & Carlson, 2006; Kimmel & Mahler, 2003; Klein, 2012; Larkin, 2007; Leary, Kowalski, Smith, & Phillips, 2003; Meloy, Hempel, Mohandie, Shiva, & Gray, 2001; Newman et al., 2004). Both the exclusionary nature of teenage cliques (Larkin, 2007; Lickel, Schmader, & Hamilton, 2003) and the cohesion of intolerant homogeneous communities (Aronson, 2004; Newman et al., 2004) have been implicated in previous rampage attacks. Finally, at the macro-sociological level, various researchers have clarified the role that masculinity (Farr, 2019; Kimmel & Mahler, 2003; Madfis, 2014b; Mai & Alpert, 2000), a desire for fame in an increasingly globalized and profit-centered media environment (Lankford, 2016; Lankford & Madfis, 2018; Levin, Fox, & Mazaik, 2005), and the widespread accessibility and acceptance of gun culture (Glassner, 2010; Haider-Markel & Joslyn, 2001; Lawrence & Birkland, 2004; Webber, 2003) play in reinforcing and legitimizing violent solutions. Of late, scholars (such as Henry, 2009; Hong, Hyunkag, Allen-Meares, & Espelage, 2011; Johnson, 2019; Levin & Madfis, 2009; Muschert & Peguero, 2010) have attempted to fuse these disparate etiological concerns to achieve a more multifaceted, holistic, and cross-disciplinary understanding of the causes of school rampage across the micro, meso, and macro levels of analysis.

Averted School Rampage Killing

Despite the breadth of research and theorizing on school rampages, far fewer studies have addressed attacks which have been planned yet have not come to fruition. Whereas incidents of school violence that have resulted in multiple fatalities and injuries are often extensively investigated by numerous parties in the government, the justice system, and the media, far less information exists about "near misses" (Verlinden, Hersen, & Thomas, 2000, p. 28). Pollack et al. (2008, p. 9) pointed out that:

> few [schools] track threats made against other students or the school (especially if the event did not result in official law enforcement intervention). The result of this failure to collect and maintain records regarding threats is that very little is known about the extent or nature of the problem.

Some academics have tried to make up for the lack of a comprehensive database by gathering their own samples. O'Toole (2000) first noted the importance of studying averted school rampages, and several scholars (Larkin, 2009; Newman et al., 2004) have since compiled incidents of averted rampages but only tangentially discussed them. Those interested in advancing the field of violence risk assessment (Borum, Cornell, Modzeleski, & Jimerson, 2010; Cornell, 2003; Cornell & Sheras, 2006; Cornell et al., 2004; Fein et al., 2002; Jimerson, Brock, & Cowan, 2005;

O'Toole, 2000; Pollack et al., 2008; Randazzo et al., 2006; Reddy et al., 2001) have focused energy upon understanding averted school attacks as have Agnich (2015), Langman (2005), and Madfis (2014a, 2018); Madfis and Cohen (2018), but much of the foundational scholarship on the topic to date has been conducted by Jeffrey Daniels and his colleagues (Daniels, 2019; Daniels & Bradley, 2011; Daniels et al., 2007, 2010).

Daniels and his colleagues' (2007) first completed a content analysis of 30 school rampages which were thwarted in 21 states sometime between October 2001 and October 2004. From newspaper accounts, the authors reported data on the details of the plot, how the plot was discovered, what steps were taken by the school and law enforcement once the plot was revealed, and the legal outcomes of the incidents. They discovered that the majority of violent schemes had planned for the attack to occur in public high schools, though several targeted public elementary and middle schools and one was aimed at a private school. In half of the incidents, one student acting alone was implicated, while two to six students were accused in the other half. Guns were the most frequent intended weapon for plotters, though bombs, knives, and swords were mentioned in the reporting of other incidents. The majority of plotters, 65%, communicated their fatal plans to others, with 30% doing so via email or paper notes, 20% verbally informing others, and 15% admitting guilt when questioned by police. Rampage plots were uncovered in a variety of ways. The most common method was other students coming forward to inform school or police officials. This was often a result of plotters informing, and in some cases unsuccessfully recruiting, their peers, but students who had overheard rumors or themselves been personally threatened also came forward. Other plots were averted by alert school administrators whose suspicions were aroused by rumors or irregular student behavior, and in some cases, school staff overheard the conversations of plotters. Still others were prevented by police who were alerted to rumors or found notes or emails which revealed the threat. Two events were avoided when the plots were discovered as a result of the students being investigated for other crimes and one well-developed plan was preempted only thirty minutes before it was to be carried out. Schools responded to discovered plots in numerous ways. Students involved in plots were frequently suspended or expelled and also often arrested. Schools also responded by notifying parents and students, making counseling available, conducting internal investigations, calling the police, enhancing school security, and evacuating, searching, and/or closing down the school. Less common school responses were to consider banning trench coats and to avoid doing anything to change the school's normal routine.

In his next stage of scholarship on this topic, Daniels and his colleagues (2010) conducted interviews with school personnel at four American schools where shooting rampages were averted. The goal of this research was to better understand what roles school officials felt they played in preventing the rampage incidents, what reasons they attributed to the successful outcome, and what advice they would offer to other schools. The research design for this project was ostensibly qualitative and, while the authors categorized respondents' interview data into helpful domains and core ideas, they then quantified the prevalence of these themes in a manner which subsequently sacrificed what could have been a more in-depth understanding of these themes. The study revealed that the most dominant domains represented in interviews were descriptions of school conditions that focused on: (1) securing safety and optimizing learning, (2) intervention descriptions about how plots were discovered, (3) discussions about crisis planning and preparation, (4) conversations regarding interpersonal relationships between staff and students, (5) debates about the relative merits of violence prevention efforts, and (6) problematic issues at the school which made dealing with the crisis more difficult. In their analysis, Daniels and his colleagues (2010, p. 88) concluded that anti-bullying programs were perceived to be the "most salient" method of preventing future rampages. Many school officials also believed that supportive and strong relationships between school staff and students encourage people to come forward with knowledge about threats, and that formal crisis planning that dictates specific roles helps to both prevent and respond to such potentially dangerous incidents.

In a recent report for the Office of Community Oriented Policing Services, Daniels (2019, p. vii) studied 51 averted incidents of school violence, defined as "a violent attack planned with or without the use of a firearm that was prevented either before or after the potential perpetrators arrived on school grounds but before any injury or loss of life occurred." These incidents took place in 27 states throughout the United States. He found that 48 (94.1%) of averted violent incidents occurred in public schools, two (3.9%) occurred in faith-based schools, and one (2%) took place at a charter school (ibid., p. 6). High schools were where the most violent incidents occurred (68.6%), followed by middle and junior high schools (15.7%), colleges and universities (11.8%), and elementary schools (3.9%) (ibid., p. 8). Most averted incidents occurred in suburban communities (68.6%), while rural communities accounted for 25.5% of incidents and only 5.9% of incidents occurred in urban areas (ibid., p. 9). This report (ibid., p. 10) also concluded that most (58.8%) of the schools where an averted incident of school violence took place had a security or police officer, few had security cameras (27.4%) or locked entrance and exit doors (9.8%), and none had metal detectors.

In terms of the plotters themselves, Daniels (2019, pp. 11–12) found that most attacks (58.8%) involved only one plotter, 23.5% of attacks involved 2 plotters, 5.9% of attacks involved 3 plotters, and 11.8% entailed four or more plotters. The vast majority of would-be attackers were male (94.1%), non-Hispanic Caucasian (86.4% of those where race/ethnicity was known), young (60.8% were under age 18—ages ranged from 12 to 47, with an average age of 18.1 years old), and current students of the school they targeted (76.5%).

The scholarship of Daniels and his colleagues contributed significant original knowledge about foiled school rampages through content analyses and interviews with school personnel. Little research, in contrast, has been conducted by interviewing the failed perpetrators themselves. Such a deficit similarly exists in research on completed school rampage killers and on mass murderers more generally, those who have killed numerous people in a single episode at one or more closely related locations (Fox, Levin, & Fridel, 2018). Very few researchers have attained multiple interviews with successful mass killers, as Mullen (2004) and Vossekuil, Fein, Reddy, Borum, and Modzeleski (2002) constitute the only examples. However, Langman (2005, p. 25) wrote about his experiences with "potential school shooters in a locked psychiatric hospital." In this brief article, Langman described the differences between deniers, admitters, and intenders of school shootings. Deniers refute that they ever intended to do harm to others and minimize or contest any evidence which suggests otherwise. Admitters acknowledge their violent thoughts and sometimes quite detailed plans, but state that they never had any intention to carry them through. Intenders admit that they desire to, or may be at risk for carrying out a homicidal episode, though they may lack any semblance of a plan. This preliminary typology speaks to both the difficulty in assessing seriousness and the complexity inherent in predicting what people, especially teenagers, may do in the future.

Responding to Rampage—Current School Disciplinary and Security Practices

The current state of school discipline, security, and surveillance does not resemble the American public schools of even a few decades ago. A regime of tighter social control has manifested itself in schools across the country through punitive zero-tolerance disciplinary policies, the proliferation of police officers and surveillance cameras, and various forms of school security designed to prevent crime through environmental design. As a result, students are increasingly exposed to prison-like regimes of control (Hirschfield, 2008; Kupchik, 2010; Kupchik & Monahan, 2006; Madfis, 2016; Monahan & Torres, 2010; Morris, 2016; Nolan, 2011).

Zero-Tolerance Disciplinary Policies

One of the most frequently cited reactions to the various school shooting massacres of the late 1990s was the implementation of various zero-tolerance disciplinary policies, which mandate strict penalties for student misbehavior, regardless of individual or situational circumstances. Though the original formulation took the form of the 1994 Gun Free Schools Act which required schools to expel, for a minimum of one year, any student caught carrying a firearm in school, various states and individual school districts broadened the scope to include zero-tolerance policies for aggressive behavior, possession of other objects deemed weapons, and various controlled substances (Ayers, Ayers, & Dohrn, 2001;

Welch & Payne, 2018). As a result, schools have expelled, suspended, or sent to alternative schools large numbers of students for sharing over-the-counter medications with their peers, for bringing utensils and toy weapons to school, some made of paper or plastic, to school grounds, or for making relatively questionable gestures or comments which have been deemed violent or threatening (Welch & Payne, 2018).

Skiba and Peterson (1999) documented several of the more egregious examples that showcased the "dark side of zero tolerance" spawned by fear of Columbine and other similar shootings. One particularly egregious incident involved the suspension of an 8-year-old child for pointing a chicken finger at a teacher and saying "Pow, pow, pow" (Times Wire Reports, 2001). In 2009, a 6-year-old boy from Newark, Delaware was suspended for bringing his Cub Scouts camping utensil to lunch (Urbina, 2009), and, in 2010, a 13-year-old female honor roll student in Houston, Texas was expelled and labeled a "terrorist" by the school's principal for pointing a "finger gun" in the general direction of one of her teachers ("Student Suspended," 2010). Though zero-tolerance policies have been widely condemned by various academics (Ayers et al., 2001; Casella, 2003; Skiba, 2000), the American Bar Association (2001), and the American Psychological Association (APA Zero Tolerance Task Force, 2008), these punitive policies persist in various forms.

Recent research (such as Hirschfield, 2018) suggests that zero-tolerance policies are now on the decline overall, though some forms of them remain in full force, particularly at the local level, in districts that serve high proportions of poor and/or minority students, in special education programs that serve students with disabilities, and in charter schools (Curran, 2017; Rafa, 2019; Welch & Payne, 2018). During the second term of the Obama administration, United States Secretary of Education Arne Duncan created and promoted new guidelines seeking to reduce harsh school discipline, such as zero-tolerance policies and other forms of exclusionary punishment, emphasizing the disproportionate impact these practices have borne upon students of color. Since that time, several states, cities, and school districts have implemented policy reforms limiting the breadth of offenses under which zero-tolerance policies may be applied, reducing the length of such punishments, or even banning them outright (Hirschfield, 2018; Welch & Payne, 2018). However, the Trump administration under Education Secretary Betsy DeVos rescinded the Obama era guidance on school discipline in favor of "maintaining order in the classroom," a directive which seeks to reassert the role of zero-tolerance discipline and punitive punishment more generally throughout the United States (Devos, Nielsen, Azar, & Whitaker, 2018, p. 14).

Surveillance Through the Proliferation of School Resource Officers and Security Cameras

The last few decades have seen a massive increase in the surveillance of school students, whether that means through additional SRO's officially stationed as police liaisons or security cameras which record student movements through school hallways and egresses. Whereas there were less than one hundred police officers in American public schools at the end of the 1970s (Brady, Balmer, & Phenix, 2007), there were more than 17,000 SRO's working in public schools nationwide in 2007, the last year this data was officially collected (NASRO, n.d.; Thurau & Wald, 2010). There are no formal databases that keep track of how many SRO currently work in schools, as police departments and school systems are not required to report this information, but The National Association of School Resource Officers estimates that "between 14,000 and 20,000 SROs are currently in service nationwide, based on DOJ data and the number of SROs that NASRO has trained" (NASRO, n.d.). One report (Public Agenda, 2004) found that 60% of teachers in American high schools—and 67% of teachers in majority Black or Hispanic schools—reported armed police officers working at their schools. Further, the National Center for Education Statistics found that 42% of public schools reported having at least one SRO present at least one day per week during the 2015–2016 academic year (NASRO, n.d.). After recent school shootings in Maryland and Florida in 2018, both states have issued laws requiring that law enforcement officers (or armed safe-school officers) be stationed in every single school throughout the state

(Kinnally, 2018; Wamsley, 2019; Winn, 2018), while California is currently considering also adopting this measure (Jenkins, 2019).

Not unlike police officers in schools, security cameras were a rare sight thirty years ago anywhere but in prisons and retail establishments. They did not arrive in schools until the 1990s and, while urban school districts were the first to implement cameras, wealthy suburban schools are now usually the proud owners of the most sophisticated and expensive surveillance technology (Casella, 2006). During the 1999–2000 school year, only 19% of all public high schools used security cameras to monitor their students (Dinkes, Kemp, Baum,& Snyder, 2009, p. vii). By the 2007–2008 school year, 55% of all public schools—and 76.6% of all public high schools—possessed security cameras (Addington, 2013; Ruddy et al., 2010). While cameras may have numerous security and monitoring benefits, as well as the potential for various invasions of personal privacy, the security industry markets technological surveillance as an inevitable "way of the future" (Casella, 2003, p. 88).

School Security Designed to Prevent Crime Through Environmental Design

Part of a larger field referred to as Crime Prevention through Environmental Design (CPTED) influenced by Routine-Activities Theory (Felson, 1994), attaining school safety via the use of architectural designs such as large windows, skylights, and straight hallways to increase visibility has become extremely lucrative. The advent of gates, specialized door locks, and the limiting of entry and exit to one location during school hours have similarly been adopted to secure areas in numerous school buildings (Casella, 2006). Typically affluent communities prefer these environmental designs (as well as surveillance through police and cameras) to the daily use of metal detectors and random weapon searches. These latter invasive security measures are more commonly found in urban schools with predominantly minority students (Hirschfield, 2010).

Responding to Rampage—Violence Risk Assessment

According to scholars documenting its origins, the field of violence risk assessment has advanced from early empirical studies in the 1970s that attempted to predict violence to a more complex, multidisciplinary research literature which deals not only with the estimation and assessment of future violence potential, but also how best to manage and intervene with high-violence risk individuals (Andrade, 2009). Knowledge gleaned from this field is frequently used by numerous practitioners, from "adult and juvenile courts, parole and probation departments, and correctional facilities, as well as for child protective services agencies, school departments, community mental health centers, and more" (Andrade, O'Neill, & Diener, 2009, p. 3). While all methods of risk assessment engage in the "scientific effort to identify ways to improve estimates of future violence," the approaches vary substantially (Grisso, 2009, p. xvi). Reddy and colleagues (2001) codified and categorized these varied approaches as profiling, guided professional judgment, automated decision-making, and threat assessment.

Profiling

Profiling, often qualified as criminal profiling (Douglas, Ressler, Burgess, & Hartman, 1986; Kocsis, 2007; Turvey, 2008), behavioral profiling (Petherick, 2006), or offender profiling (Canter & Youngs, 2009; Keppel, 2006; Palermo & Kocsis, 2005), is practiced in a number of diverse forms but broadly refers to investigative techniques or assessment strategies used to identify current and potential offenders. In its original form developed by the FBI's Behavioral Science Unit, hypotheses regarding offenders' behavioral, demographic, and personality characteristics were generated from data left at crime scenes (Douglas et al., 1986). The realm of profiling has expanded, however, to include the "prospective identification of would-be criminals" wherein "the typical perpetrator of a particular type of crime – such as serial murder or school shootings – is compiled from characteristics shared by known previous perpetrators" (Reddy et al., 2001, p. 161). This prototypical profile is then used to both identify the types of individuals likely to become perpetrators and to assess an individual's likelihood of future offending. To this end, the FBI (Band & Harpold, 1999, p. 14) created a prospective profile of the school shooter which included characteristics such as being an isolated white male who dresses sloppily, has a history of mental health treatment, violence, alcohol, and/or drug abuse, and is influenced by "satanic or cult-type belief systems" or violent song lyrics. Similarly, psychologists McGee and DeBernardo (1999) generated their own profile of the classroom avenger as a socially immature and isolated middle-class white male who has no prior history of serious school misbehavior and has been rejected and teased by his peers. Many features of these two widely circulated profiles overlap (especially the focus upon isolated White males), but they also directly contradict one another on numerous points.

While various profiling techniques have gained some measure of empirical support for other types of perpetrators (Homant & Kennedy, 1998; Kocsis, Irwin, Hayes, & Nunn, 2000; Pinizzotto & Finkel, 1990), the profiling of young students has proved particularly problematic. Many students who fit general profiles never commit school violence of any kind, while numerous students who have planned and even completed attacks at their schools did not closely match prior profiles (Sewell & Mendelsohn, 2000). Such student profiles have recently fallen out of favor, and a systematic investigation of targeted school shooting incidents revealed that there simply "is no accurate or useful 'profile' of students who engaged in targeted school violence" whether demographic, psychological, or social (Vossekuil et al., 2002, p. 11).

Guided Professional Judgment and Warning Signs

Another technique used to appraise students' violence risk is guided professional judgment, which has also been referred to as structured clinical assessment (Reddy et al., 2001). This approach entails evaluation through the use of checklists of risk factors or warning signs for violence (Borum, 2000; Otto, 2000). Such assessment is sometimes conducted by licensed mental health professionals (Reddy et al., 2001), though school and law enforcement officials have also utilized the various checklists which have been publicized over the years by the Justice and Education Departments (Dwyer, Osher, & Warger, 1998), the International Association of Chiefs of Police (1999), and the collaboration between MTV and the American Psychological Association (American Psychological Association, 1999). As some of these checklists featured general warning signs such as a "minimal interest in academics," this approach has been criticized for utilizing criteria that are vague and broad enough to apply to the majority of any student body (Fox & Burstein, 2010, p. 69). While standardized psychological tests and instruments used by mental health professionals have been found to be somewhat accurate in certain contexts with violence in general (Reddy et al., 2001), there is no empirical evidence which suggests that they are successful in predicting targeted school violence with preselected victims (Arluke, Lankford, & Madfis, 2018; Arluke & Madfis, 2014; Borum, 2000; Borum et al., 2010).

Automated Decision-Making

Risk assessment approaches classified as automated decision-making have been broken into two camps, actuarial formulas and artificial intelligence, both of which "produce a decision…rather than leaving the decision to the person conducting the assessment" (Reddy et al., 2001, p. 166). The actuarial form of automated decision-making is based on purportedly objective algorithms utilizing empirically based criteria which produce outcome scores to determine judgments about the future likelihood of violence (Vincent, 2009). Though the use of actuarial measurements has shown some success (Borum, 2000), their accuracy is somewhat questionable (Mossman, 1994).

The use of artificial intelligence programs represents the other automated approach to risk assessment. Computer programs render decisions in a manner thought to reduce human error and bias. One such technology developed by a California company for the Bureau of Alcohol, Tobacco, and Firearms, the MOSAIC Threat Assessment System, is frequently used on the campus of Yale University even though it remains extremely controversial (Fox & Burstein, 2010; Sachsman, 1997). Both types of automated decision-making have been criticized for not being sufficiently malleable or flexible (Reddy et al., 2001; Sewell & Mendelsohn, 2000; Vincent, 2009) and for an inordinate focus upon statistical associations or objective conclusions over complex understandings of causality and etiology (Grubin & Wingate, 1996).

The Threat Assessment Approach

The threat assessment perspective is a prolific approach utilized to advance understanding about the causes and manifestations of targeted school violence, a term which refers to "situations in which an identifiable (or potentially identifiable) perpetrator poses (or may pose) a threat of violence to a particular individual or group" (Fein, Vossekuil, & Holden, 1995, p. 1). Initially developed as a "set of investigative and operational techniques that can be used by law enforcement professionals to identify, assess, and manage the risks of targeted violence and its potential perpetrators" (ibid., p. 1), the last two decades have seen a multitude of school violence research conducted under the threat assessment rubric (Cornell, 2003; Cornell & Sheras, 2006; Cornell et al., 2004; Deisinger, Randazzo, O'Neill, & Savage, 2008; Fein et al., 2002; Jimerson et al., 2005; Meloy, 2015; O'Toole, 2000; Randazzo et al., 2006; Rappaport & Barrett, 2009; Reddy et al., 2001; Strong & Cornell, 2008; Twemlow, Fonagy, Sacco, O'Toole, & Vernberg, 2002; Vossekuil et al., 2002).

The threat assessment approach differs from previous attempts to discern dangerousness due to its focus upon the substantive analysis of existing threats rather than predicting the future behavior of people based on typical personality profiles, warning signs, or other aggregate data pertaining to individual characteristics. This approach argues that people who perpetrate acts of targeted violence lack a single homogeneous profile, but the evaluation of offenders' backgrounds, personalities, lifestyles, and resources may aid in determining the gravity of threats (O'Toole, 2000).

Perhaps most significantly, this perspective asserts that not all threats are equivalent—that is, "there is a distinction between making a threat…and posing a threat…Many people who make threats do not pose a serious risk of harm to a target. Conversely, many who pose a serious risk of harm will not issue direct threats prior to the attack" (Reddy et al., 2001, p. 168). Critical details, such as how direct, detailed, developed, and actionable the threat is, help to further assess seriousness. O'Toole (2000) classified threats into four categories: direct, indirect, veiled, and conditional. A direct threat, announced in a plain and unambiguous manner, specifies that a certain action will be taken against a specific target. An indirect threat with tentative phrasing is less clear and definitive. A veiled threat implies but does not overtly intimidate so that there is some question as to how the threat could be interpreted. A conditional threat warns that violence will occur unless certain demands are met. In addition to forming a typology of threats, O'Toole (2000) differentiated between low, medium, and high risk levels. Low-level threats, which pose minimal risk, are vague, implausible, and lack realism. Medium-level threats, which may be carried out but are not wholly realistic, show evidence that the person threatening others has thought through the plan, indicated potential locations and times, but lacks any indication that he/she has taken preparatory steps to act on the threat. Finally, high-level threats, which pose an imminent danger to the safety of others, are direct, detailed, conceivable, and show evidence that concrete steps have been taken toward carrying it out.

Cornell and Sheras (2006) have similarly distinguished between transient and substantive threats. Transient threats are "statements that do not express a lasting intent to harm someone. Transient threats either are intended as figures of speech or reflect feelings that dissipate in a short period when the student thinks about the meaning of what he or she has said" (Cornell & Sheras, 2006, p. 21). In contrast, substantive threats are "statements that express a continuing intent to harm someone…they also indicate a desire to harm someone that extends beyond the immediate incident or argument when the threat was made" (Cornell & Sheras, 2006, p. 22). These scholars further separate substantive threats into serious and very serious threats based on the intended harm to be committed, where a serious threat is a threat to physically assault someone and a very serious threat is to kill, sexually assault, or severely injure someone (Cornell & Sheras, 2006).

While the assessment of violence risk is a diverse and developing field, there are numerous issues and unanswered questions regarding their application in practice at schools around the country. Verlinden et al. (2000, p. 27) noted that there is a total lack of "data at this point to assist a clinician in selecting the 'best' strategy for risk assessment for violent school assaults." Similarly, Reddy et al. (2001, p. 160) pointed out that "[i]t is not currently known how many schools use which type of assessment" and that no data exist which "describe the prevalence of any of these three approaches (or others) schools may currently use, nor of their effectiveness-perceived or actual." Though the pressing need for such knowledge was pointed out more than a decade ago, scholars and practitioners still lack this vital data.

Thus, while the threat assessment approach arguably has attained the most positive evaluations via empirical testing (see Cornell, 2013 for a review), the other forms of risk assessment (not to mention the zero-tolerance approach that presumes no need for risk assessment at all) may still be preferred or more frequently utilized by school and police officials. Specifically as it relates to this research, nothing is known whatsoever about the role that any of these various risk assessment techniques played during the numerous school rampage attacks which have been averted during the last decade.

Understanding School Criminalization and Risk Assessment as Actuarial Justice

There has been a dramatic transformation of school discipline and security in American public schools since the turn of the twenty-first century. Not unlike assertions that contemporary culture represents a post-9/11 era, many school officials refer to a post-Columbine era in public education in which everyone must now think about school safety in an entirely new manner (Madfis, 2016; Muschert, Henry, Bracy, & Peguero, 2013). As just discussed, this new way of thinking entails expanded zero-tolerance policies that dictate mandatory suspensions, expulsions, and arrests of students, surveillance through the proliferation of police officers and security cameras in schools, and school security which is designed to prevent crime through the environmental design of the school building itself. These developments represent a swift and widespread "penetration of law enforcement personnel and technology into urban, suburban, and rural schools" (Hirshfield & Celinska, 2011, p. 39). Such order control mechanisms can generally be characterized by a one-size-fits-all approach, as school discipline takes remarkably similar forms in widely divergent school contexts, regardless of whether or not schools have high levels of student misbehavior (Kupchik, 2010; Muschert & Madfis, 2013).

Though scholars have been describing the changing features of school discipline and security for decades, theoretical insight into the causes of this process has been slower to emerge. Prominent social theorists tackling diverse topics ranging from the sociology of punishment and education to public policy and legal studies have addressed the origins and intensification of school criminalization, yet the investigation of this emergent phenomenon has rarely been their sole focus. That said, prominent theoretical insight on larger issues of neoliberalism, punitiveness, and risk has a great deal to contribute to the understanding of the contemporary state of school criminalization and thus warrants extensive discussion.

As the prominent political and legal scholar Bernard Harcourt (2010, p. 77) has stated, neoliberal penality is "today in full fruition." He (ibid., p. 77) defines this term as:

> a form of rationality in which the penal sphere is pushed outside political economy and serves the function of a boundary: the penal sanction is marked off from the dominant logic of classical economics as the only space where order is legitimately enforced by the State. On this view, the bulk of human interaction—which consists of economic exchange—is viewed as voluntary, compensated, orderly, and tending toward the common good; the penal sphere is the outer bound, where the government can legitimately interfere, there and there alone.

In many ways, this parallels and augments prior theoretical work on the contemporary culture of control (Garland, 2001) and governance through crime (Simon, 2006), which emphasize the manner in which anxieties and insecurities regarding all manner of larger structural concerns (about job security, economic prosperity, income inequality, family stability, etc.) are addressed via hardline crime fighting measures. Bell (2011) suggests that a neoliberal form of government, no longer able to attain legitimacy through public services or a social safety net, attempts legitimation through a tough law and order mentality that appeals across class lines (see also Wacquant 2009). This may be aligned with what many have described as the more general penal turn toward a "new punitiveness" which encourages longer sentences and harsher treatment for adult offenders (Pratt, Brown, Brown, Hallsworth, & Morrison, 2005).

American public schools have a lengthy tradition of punitive focus upon obedience and discipline (which Brint, 1998 attributes to Puritan asceticism and the needs of industrial labor), and the extent to which a new punitiveness has bled into juvenile justice remains a contested topic (Goldson, 2002; Muncie, 2008; Wald & Losen, 2003). However, the criminalized lens through which student discipline is viewed (wherein school misbehavior is transferred to the juvenile and adult justice systems and even childish threats are redefined as terrorist acts) and the securitized lens through which school safety is viewed (wherein schools are made to resemble airports if not prisons) do represent fairly new developments.

Additionally, there is another key aspect of the wider change in penal philosophy that has undoubtedly altered the face of school discipline and security. In his discussion of the transition to a late modern culture of control, Garland (2001, p. 128) stated that:

> In the past, official criminology has usually viewed crime retrospectively and individually, in order to itemize individual wrongdoing and allocate punishment or treatment. The new criminologies tend to view crime prospectively and in aggregate terms, for the purpose of calculating risk and shaping preventative measures.

Thus, both Garland's (2001, p. 129) notion of new criminologies and Harcourt's (2010) neoliberal penality are situated within a cultural context wherein society is increasingly concerned with the prediction and alleviation of risk. The modern "risk society" (Beck, 1992; Giddens, 1999) or "actuarial age" (Harcourt, 2007) entails a mindset where there is a preoccupation with the future and the systematic manipulation of risk is achievable, global, and primary.

The administration of justice, in particular, has moved toward an "actuarial justice" mindset that reorients penology toward "techniques for identifying, classifying, and managing groups assorted by levels of dangerousness" (Feeley & Simon, 1994, p. 173). Rather than opting for intervention as a means of retribution or rehabilitation, this so-called "new penology" sees crime as inevitable and seeks instead to manage risk and regulate danger (Feeley & Simon, 1992; Rigakos & Hadden, 2001). Likewise, Steiker (1998, p. 774) argues that our justice system increasingly attempts

> to identify and neutralize dangerous individuals before they commit crimes by restricting their liberty in a variety of ways. In pursuing this goal, the state often will expand the functions of the institutions primarily involved in the criminal justice system – namely, the police and the prison. But other analogous institutions, such as the juvenile justice system and the civil commitment process, are also sometimes tools of, to coin another phrase, the "preventive state."

O'Malley (2008) points out that the focus on risk and predictive measures need not be solely punitive and Garland (2001, p. 138) notes that a neoliberal view would likely understand "high rates of imprisonment [as] an ineffective waste of scarce resources." However, Harcourt (2010), through an insightful reading of Foucault's (2009) later work on governmentality, explains how broad trends in neoliberalism relate directly to the transition in governance away from ameliorative forms of preventative treatment (such as anti-poverty programs and mental health facilities) and toward the assessment and management of large numbers of people as dangerous populations in penal institutions.

This punitive and carceral form of prevention and the actuarial mindset that criminal conduct is an unavoidable but manageable risk have certainly expanded into school disciplinary and security practices (Casella, 2006; Kupchik & Monahan, 2006; Lyons & Drew, 2006; Meloy, 2015; Simon, 2006). Americans by and large greatly exaggerate the prevalence and potential risk of school violence (Aitken, 2001; Burns & Crawford, 1999; Cornell, 2006; Madfis, 2016)—for example, a poll conducted shortly after the 2005 school shooting incident on the Red Lake reservation in Minnesota revealed that nearly three-fourths of Americans believed that a similar attack was "very likely" or "somewhat likely" to happen in their communities (Kiefer, 2005). Despite the extensive media coverage which might suggest otherwise, murders at school remain exceedingly rare and mass murders even more so. Compared to their homes and the streets, schools are the safest places for young people, and the risk of homicide for school-age youth is roughly 226 times greater outside of school than at school (National Center for School Safety, 2006). More generally in terms of probability, "only about 1 in 2,000,000 school-age youth will die from homicide or suicide at school each year" (Muschert, 2007, p. 61) and "any given school can expect to experience a student homicide about once every 6000 years" (Borum et al., 2010, p. 27). In the risk society, however, even unfounded and exaggerated perceptions of risk take priority, thus every locale must be wary and implement extensive measures to control risk by preparing for an onslaught of mass violence.

The actuarial justice frame of mind also entails the belief that it is inevitable for certain school students to possess the desire to fatally harm their peers, but the risk of rampage killing may be mitigated through the application of police and prison practices to school settings (i.e., the systematic prediction and surveillance of prospective school shooters and the monitoring and securing of the physical space of school buildings). Therefore, it makes sense that, by and large, the response to school rampage as a social problem has been attempts to predict them with risk assessments, punish anything resembling them (such as weapons violations and threatening comments) with harsh zero-tolerance policies and transfers to the justice system, deter their occurrence with police officers and cameras, and make them more difficult to accomplish through target hardening procedures like locked doors and metal detectors. This stands in stark contrast to less punitive but more ameliorative and restorative forms of school violence prevention, such as broad-based mental health services, systematic mentoring and support structures, as well as conflict resolution, group conferencing, peer mediation, and anti-bullying school programs (Karp & Breslin, 2001; Meyer & Evans, 2012; Schiff, 2013; Sumner, Silverman, & Frampton, 2010; Van Ness & Strong, 2010). While the actuarial justice mindset directly informs contemporary school safety, risk assessment, and disciplinary policies, the chapters to follow will illustrate how many of the practices associated with this approach lack empirical evidence indicating their genuine capability to prevent, deter, or predict school rampage violence. This problematic approach far too frequently presupposes both the inevitability of violence and the flawless nature of deterrence and prediction as currently practiced in American public schools.

Questions for Discussion

1. What is meant by the term "school rampage" and what criteria are included in this definition?
2. How are school rampages different than school shootings—and why do we tend to think of school shootings as mass casualty events with multiple victims?
3. Which of the causes of school rampage attacks mentioned above do you think are the most important?
4. What are some differences between the threat assessment approach and other forms of violence risk assessment like profiling and warning signs?

References

Addington, L. (2013). Surveillance and security approaches across public school levels. In G. W. Muschert, S. Henry, N. L. Bracy, & A. A. Peguero (Eds.), *Responding to school violence: Confronting the Columbine effect* (pp. 71–88). Boulder, CO: Lynne Rienner.

Agnich, L. E. (2015). A comparative analysis of attempted and completed school-based mass murder attacks. *American Journal of Criminal Justice, 40*(1), 1–22.

Aitken, S. C. (2001). Schoolyard shootings: Racism, sexism and moral panics over teen violence. *Antipode, 33*(4), 594–600.

Altheide, D. L. (2009). The Columbine shootings and the discourse of fear. *American Behavioral Scientist, 52*(10), 1354–1370.

American Bar Association. (2001). *Zero tolerance policy report.* Retrieved September 25, 2012, from www.abanet.org/crimjust/juvjus/zerotolreport.html.

American Psychological Association. (1999). *Warning signs: A violence prevention guide for youth.* Retrieved September 30, 2010, from http://helping.apa.org/warningsigns/index.html.

American Psychological Association Zero Tolerance Task Force. (2008). Are zero tolerance policies effective in the schools?: An evidentiary review and recommendations. *American Psychologist, 63*(9), 852–862.

Andrade, J. T. (Ed.). (2009). *Handbook of violence risk assessment and treatment: New approaches for mental health professionals.* New York, NY: Springer.

Andrade, J. T., O'Neill, K., & Diener, R. B. (2009). Violence risk assessment and risk management: A historical overview and clinical application. In J. T. Andrade (Ed.), *Handbook of violence risk assessment and treatment: New approaches for mental health professionals* (pp. 3–40). New York, NY: Springer.

Arluke, A., Lankford, A., & Madfis, E. (2018). Harming animals and massacring humans: Characteristics of active and mass shooters who abused animals. *Behavioral Sciences & the Law, 36*(6), 739–751.

Arluke, A., & Madfis, E. (2014). Animal abuse as a warning sign of school massacres: A critique and refinement. *Homicide Studies, 18*(1), 7–22.

Aronson, E. (2004). How the Columbine high school tragedy could have been prevented. *Journal of Individual Psychology, 60,* 355–360.

Ayers, W., Ayers, R., & Dohrn, B. (2001). *Zero tolerance: Resisting the drive for punishment in our schools.* New York: The Free Press.

Band, S. R., & Harpold, J. A. (1999). School violence: Lessons learned. *FBI Law Enforcement Bulletin, 68,* 9–16.

Beck, U. (1992). *The risk society: Towards a new modernity.* London: Sage.

Bell, E. (2011). *Criminal justice and neoliberalism.* Basingstoke: Palgrave Macmillan.

Best, J. (2002). Monster hype. *Education Next, 2,* 51–55.

Blair, J. P., & Schweit, K. W. (2014). *A study of active shooter incidents, 2000–2013.* Washington, DC: Texas State University and Federal Bureau of Investigation, U.S. Department of Justice.

Borum, R. (2000). Assessing violence risk among youth. *Journal of Clinical Psychology, 56,* 1263–1288.

Borum, R., Cornell, D., Modzeleski, W., & Jimerson, S. (2010). What can be done about school shootings?: A review of the evidence. *Educational Researcher, 39*(1), 27–37.

Brady, K. P., Balmer, S., & Phenix, D. (2007). School-police partnership effectiveness in urban schools. *Education and Urban Society, 39,* 455–478.

Brint, S. (1998). *Schools and societies.* Thousand Oaks: Pine Forge Press.

Burgess, A., Garbarino, C., & Carlson, M. (2006). Pathological teasing and bullying turned deadly: Shooters and suicide. *Victims & Offenders, 1,* 1–13.

Burns, R., & Crawford, C. (1999). School shootings, the media, and public fear: Ingredients for a moral panic. *Crime, Law & Social Change, 32,* 147–168.

Canter, D., & Youngs, D. (2009). *Investigative psychology: Offender profiling and the analysis of criminal action.* New York: Wiley.

Casella, R. (2003). The false allure of security technologies. *Social Justice, 30*(3), 82–93.

Casella, R. (2006). *Selling us the fortress: The promotion of techno-security equipment for schools.* New York: Routledge.

Cohen, S. (2011). *Folk devils and moral panics: The creation of the mods and rockers.* New York: Routledge.

Cornell, D. G. (2003). Guidelines for responding to student threats of violence. *Journal of Educational Administration, 41,* 705–719.

Cornell, D. G. (2006). *School violence: Fear versus facts.* Mahwah, NJ: Lawrence Erlbaum.

Cornell, D. G. (2013). The Virginia student threat assessment guidelines: An empirically supported violence prevention strategy. In N. Böckler, W. Heitmeyer, P. Sitzer, & T. Seeger (Eds.), *School shootings: International research, case studies, and concepts for prevention* (pp. 379–400). New York, NY: Springer.

Cornell, D. G., & Sheras, P. L. (2006). *Guidelines for responding to student threats of violence.* Longmont, CO: Sopris West.

Cornell, D. G., Sheras, P. L., Kaplan, S., McConville, D., Douglass, J., Elkon, A., ... Cole, J. (2004). Guidelines for student threat assessment: Field-test findings. *School Psychology Review, 33*(4), 527–546.

Curran, C. F. (2017). The law, policy, and portrayal of zero tolerance school discipline: Examining prevalence and characteristics across levels of governance and school districts. *Educational Policy, 33*(2), 319–349.

Daniels, J. A. (2019). *A preliminary report on the Police Foundations averted school violence database.* Washington, DC: Office of Community Oriented Policing Services.

Daniels, J. A., & Bradley, M. C. (2011). *Preventing lethal school violence.* New York, NY: Springer.

Daniels, J. A., Buck, I., Croxall, S., Gruber, J., Kime, P., & Govert, H. (2007). A content analysis of news reports of averted school rampages. *Journal of School Violence, 6,* 83–99.

Daniels, J. A., Volungis, A., Pshenishny, E., Gandhi, P., Winkler, A., Cramer, D., & Bradley, M. C. (2010). A qualitative investigation of averted school shooting rampages. *The Counseling Psychologist, 38*(1), 69–95.

Deisinger, G., Randazzo, M., O'Neill, D., & Savage, J. (2008). *The handbook for campus threat assessment and management teams.* Stoneham, MA: Applied Risk Management LLC.

DeVos, B., Nielsen, K., Azar, A., & Whitaker, M. (2018). *Final report of the Federal Commission on School Safety.* US Department of Education. Retrieved June 12, 2019, from https://files.eric.ed.gov/fulltext/ED590823.pdf.

Dinkes, R., Kemp, J., Baum, K., & Snyder, T. D. (2009). *Indicators of school crime and safety: 2009 (NCES 2010–012/NCJ 228478).* Washington, DC: National Center for Education Statistics, Institute of Education Sciences, U.S. Department of Education, and Bureau of Justice Statistics, Office of Justice Programs, U.S. Department of Justice.

Douglas, J. E., Ressler, R. K., Burgess, A. W., & Hartman, C. R. (1986). Criminal profiling from crime scene analysis. *Behavioral Sciences and the Law, 4,* 401–421.

Dwyer, K. P., Osher, D., & Warger, C. (1998). *Early warning, timely response: A guide to safe schools.* Washington, DC: U.S. Department of Education.

Everytown for Gun Safety. (2014, December 9). *Analysis of school shootings.* Retrieved April 26, 2016, from http://everytownresearch.org/reports/analysis-of-school-shootings/.

Farr, K. (2019). Trouble with the other: The role of romantic rejection in rampage school shootings by adolescent males. *Violence and Gender, 6*(3), 147–153.

Feeley, M., & Simon, J. (1992). The new penology: Notes on the emerging strategy of corrections and its implications. *Criminology, 30*(4), 449–470.

Feeley, M., & Simon, J. (1994). Actuarial justice: The emerging new criminal law. In D. Nelken (Ed.), *The futures of criminology* (pp. 173–201). London: Sage.

Fein, R. A., Vossekuil, B., & Holden, G. (1995). Threat assessment: An approach to prevent targeted violence. In *National Institute of Justice: Research in Action* (pp. 1–7). Washington, DC: U.S. Department of Justice, Office of Justice Programs.

Fein, R. A., Vossekuil, B., Pollack, W., Borum, R., Modzeleski, W., & Reddy, M. (2002). *Threat assessment in schools: A guide to managing threatening situations and to creating safe school climates.* Washington, DC: U.S. Department of Education, Office of Elementary and Secondary Education, Safe and Drug-Free Schools Program and U.S. Secret Service, National Threat Assessment Center.

Felson, M. (1994). *Crime and everyday life: Insight and implications for society.* Thousand Oaks, CA: Pine Forge.

Follman, M., Aronsen, G., & Pan, D. (2019). A guide to mass shootings in America. *Mother Jones.* Retrieved May 19, 2019, from https://www.motherjones.com/politics/2012/12/mass-shootings-mother-jones-full-data/.

Foucault, M. (2009). *Security, territory, population: Lectures at the Collège de France 1977—1978.* New York: Palgrave Macmillan.

Fox, J. A., & Burstein, H. (2010). *Violence and security on campus: From preschool through college.* Santa Barbara, CA: Praeger.

Fox, J. A., & DeLateur, M. J. (2014). Mass shootings in America: Moving beyond Newtown. *Homicide Studies, 18*(1), 125–145.

Fox, J. A., Levin, J., & Fridel, E. E. (2018). *Extreme killing: Understanding serial and mass murder.* Thousand Oaks, CA: Sage.

Fox, J. A., Levin, J., & Quinet, K. (2019). *The will to kill* (5th ed.). Thousand Oaks, CA: Sage.

Fox, J. A., & Savage, J. (2009). Mass murder goes to college: An examination of changes on college campuses following Virginia Tech. *American Behavioral Scientist, 52*(10), 1286–1308.

Garland, D. (2001). *The culture of control: Crime and social order in contemporary society.* Chicago: University of Chicago Press.

Giddens, A. (1999). Risk and responsibility. *The Modern Law Review, 62*(1), 1–10.

Glassner, B. (2010). *The culture of fear: Why Americans are afraid of the wrong things* (10th anniversary ed.). New York: Basic Books.

Goldson, B. (2002). New punitiveness: The politics of child incarceration. In J. Muncie, G. Hughes, & E. McLaughlin (Eds.), *Youth justice: Critical readings* (pp. 386–400). London: Sage.

Grisso, T. (2009). Foreword. In J. T. Andrade (Ed.), *Handbook of violence risk assessment and treatment: New approaches for mental health professionals* (pp. xv–xvii). New York, NY: Springer.

Grubin, D., & Wingate, S. (1996). Sexual offence recidivism: Prediction versus understanding. *Criminal Behaviour and Mental Health, 6,* 349–359.

Haider-Markel, D. P., & Joslyn, M. R. (2001). Gun policy, opinion, tragedy, and blame attribution: The conditional influence of issue frames. *Journal of Politics, 63,* 520–543.

Harcourt, B. (2007). *Against prediction: Profiling, policing, and punishing in an actuarial age.* Chicago, IL: University of Chicago Press.

Harcourt, B. (2010). Neoliberal penality: A brief genealogy. *Theoretical Criminology, 14*(1), 74–92.

Harding, D., Fox, C., & Mehta, J. D. (2002). Studying rare events through qualitative case studies: Lessons from a study of rampage school shootings. *Sociological Methods and Research, 31*(2), 174–217.

Henry, S. (2009). School violence beyond Columbine: A complex problem in need of an interdisciplinary analysis. *American Behavioral Scientist, 52*(9), 1246–1265.

Hirschfield, P. J. (2008). Preparing for prison? The criminalization of school discipline in the USA. *Theoretical Criminology, 12*(1), 79–101.

Hirschfield, P. J. (2010). School surveillance in America: Disparate and unequal. In T. Monahan & R. D. Torress (Eds.), *Schools under surveillance: Cultures of control in public education* (pp. 38–54). New Brunswick, NJ: Rutgers University Press.

Hirschfield, P. J. (2018). Trends in school social control in the United States: Explaining patterns of decriminalization. In J. Deakin, E. Taylor, & A. Kupchik (Eds.), *The Palgrave international handbook of school discipline, surveillance, and social control* (pp. 43–64). New York, NY: Palgrave Macmillan.

Hirschfield, P. J., & Celinska, K. (2011). Beyond fear: Sociological perspectives on the criminalization of school discipline. *Sociology Compass, 5*(1), 1–12.

Homant, R. J., & Kennedy, D. B. (1998). Psychological Aspects of crime scene profiling: Validity research. *Criminal Justice and Behavior, 25,* 319–343.

Hong, J. S., Hyunkag, C., Allen-Meares, P., & Espelage, D. L. (2011). The social ecology of the Columbine high school shootings. *Children and Youth Services Review, 33*, 861–868.

International Association of Chiefs of Police. (1999). *Guidelines for preventing and responding to school violence.* VA: Alexandria.

James, S. D. (2009, April 13). *Columbine shootings 10 years later: Students, teacher still haunted by post-traumatic stress.* ABC News. Retrieved May 23, 2019, from https://web.archive.org/web/20130427102132/http://abcnews.go.com/Health/story?id=7300782&page=1.

Jenkins, M. (2019, February 20). *All California public schools may need to have school resource officers.* Retrieved June 12, 2019, from https://sacramento.cbslocal.com/2019/02/20/california-school-resource-officers/.

Jimerson, S. R., Brock, S. E., & Cowan, K. (2005). Threat assessment: An essential component of a comprehensive safe school program. *Principal Leadership, 6*(2), 11–15.

Johnson, E. S. (2019). Contemporary society and the phenomenon of school rampage shootings in the United States: A theoretical approach to understanding. In R. Papa (Ed.), *School violence in international contexts* (pp. 133–146). Thousand Oaks, CA: Sage.

Karp, D. R., & Breslin, B. (2001). Restorative justice in school communities. *Youth & Society, 33*(2), 249–272.

Keppel, R. D. (2006). *Offender profiling.* Mason, OH: Thomson Custom Publishing.

Kiefer, H. M. (2005). *Public: Society powerless to stop school shootings.* Retrieved May 20, 2019, from http://www.gallup.com/poll/15511/Public-Society-Powerless-Stop-School-Shootings.aspx.

Killingbeck, D. (2001). The role of television news in the construction of school violence as a "moral panic". *Journal of Criminal Justice and Popular Culture, 8*(3), 186–202.

Kimmel, M. S., & Mahler, M. (2003). Adolescent masculinity, homophobia, and violence. *American Behavioral Scientist, 46,* 1439–1458.

King, S., & Bracy, N. (2019). School security in the post-Columbine era: Trends, consequences, and future directions. *Journal of Contemporary Criminal Justice, 35*(3), 274–295.

Kinnally, K. (2018, April 12). *Maryland safe to learn act of 2018: What you need to know.* Retrieved June 12, 2019, from https://conduitstreet.mdcounties.org/2018/04/12/maryland-safe-to-learn-act-of-2018-what-you-need-to-know/.

Klein, J. (2012). *The Bully Society: School shootings and the crisis of bullying in American schools.* New York: New York University Press.

Kocsis, R. N. (2007). *Criminal profiling: International theory, research, and practice.* Totowa, NJ: Humana Press.

Kocsis, R. N., Irwin, H. J., Hayes, A. F., & Nunn, R. (2000). Expertise in psychological profiling: A comparative assessment. *Journal of Interpersonal Violence, 15*(3), 311–331.

Kupchik, A. (2010). *Homeroom security: School discipline in an age of fear.* New York: New York University Press.

Kupchik, A., & Monahan, T. (2006). The new American school: Preparation for post-industrial discipline. *British Journal of Sociology of Education, 27*(5), 617–631.

Langman, P. (2005). Can school shootings be prevented? *Healing Magazine, 10*(2), 24–27.

Langman, P. (2009a). *Why kids kill: Inside the minds of school shooters.* New York, NY: Palgrave Macmillan.

Langman, P. (2009b). Rampage school shooters: A typology. *Aggression and Violent Behavior, 14*(1), 79–86.

Langman, P., & Straub, F. (2019). *A comparison of averted and completed school attacks from the Police Foundation's averted school violence database.* Washington, DC: Office of Community Oriented Policing Services.

Lankford, A. (2016). Fame-seeking rampage shooters: Initial findings and empirical predictions. *Aggression and Violent Behavior, 27*(1), 122–129.

Lankford, A., & Madfis, E. (2018). Don't name them, don't show them, but report everything else: A pragmatic proposal for denying mass killers the attention they seek and deterring future offenders. *American Behavioral Scientist, 62*(2), 260–279.

Larkin, R. W. (2007). *Comprehending Columbine.* Philadelphia, PA: Temple University Press.

Larkin, R. W. (2009). The Columbine legacy: Rampage shootings as political acts. *American Behavioral Scientist, 52*(9), 1309–1326.

Lawrence, R. (2007). *School crime and juvenile justice.* New York, NY: Oxford University Press.

Lawrence, R. G., & Birkland, T. A. (2004). Guns, Hollywood, and school safety: Defining the school-shooting problem across the public arenas. *Social Science Quarterly, 85,* 1193–1207.

Leary, M. R., Kowalski, R. M., Smith, L., & Phillips, S. (2003). Teasing, rejection, and violence: Case studies of the school shootings. *Aggressive Behavior, 29,* 202–214.

Levin, J., Fox J. A., & Mazaik, J. (2005). Blurring fame and infamy: A content analysis of cover-story trends in People Magazine. *Internet Journal of Criminology*, 1–17.

Levin, J., & Madfis, E. (2009). Mass murder at school and cumulative strain: A sequential model. *American Behavioral Scientist, 52*(9), 1227–1245.

Lickel, B., Schmader, T., & Hamilton, D. (2003). A case of collective responsibility: Who else was to blame for the Columbine high school shootings? *Personality & Social Psychology Bulletin, 29*, 194–204.

Lott, J. R. (2014, February 17). *Bloomberg's latest stats on school gun violence ignore reality*. Retrieved May 24, 2019, from https://www.foxnews.com/opinion/bloombergs-latest-stats-on-school-gun-violence-ignore-reality.

Lyons, W., & Drew, J. (2006). *Punishing schools: Fear and citizenship in American public education*. Ann Arbor, MI: University of Michigan Press.

Madfis, E. (2014a). Averting school rampage: Student intervention amid a persistent code of silence. *Youth Violence and Juvenile Justice, 12*(3), 229–249.

Madfis, E. (2014b). Triple entitlement and homicidal anger: An exploration of the intersectional identities of American mass murderers. *Men and Masculinities, 17*(1), 67–86.

Madfis, E. (2016). "It's better to overreact": School officials' fear and perceived risk of rampage attacks and the criminalization of American public schools. *Critical Criminology, 24*(1), 39–55.

Madfis, E. (2018). Insight from averted mass shootings. In J. Schildkraut (Ed.), *Mass shootings in America: Understanding the debates, causes, and responses* (pp. 79–84). Santa Barbara, CA: Praeger Books.

Madfis, E., & Cohen, J. W. (2018). Female involvement in school rampage plots. *Violence and Gender, 5*(2), 81–86.

Madfis, E., & Levin, J. (2013). School rampage in international perspective: The salience of cumulative strain theory. In N. Böckler, W. Heitmeyer, P. Sitzer, & T. Seeger (Eds.), *School shootings: International research, case studies, and concepts for prevention* (pp. 79–104). New York, NY: Springer.

Mai, R., & Alpert, J. (2000). Separation and socialization: A feminist analysis of the school shootings at Columbine. *Journal for the Psychoanalysis of Culture and Society, 5*, 264–275.

Martins, L. (2019, March 13). *Inspired by Columbine, Brazil pair kill eight and themselves in school shooting*. Retrieved June 20, 2019, from https://www.reuters.com/article/us-brazil-violence-school/inspired-by-columbine-brazil-pair-kill-eight-and-themselves-in-school-shooting-idUSKBN1QU1TT.

McGee, J. P., & DeBernardo, C. R. (1999). The classroom avenger: A behavioral profile of school based shootings. *The Forensic Examiner, 8*, 16–18.

Meloy, J. R. (2015). Threat assessment: Scholars, operators, our past, our future. *Journal of Threat Assessment and Management, 2*(3–4), 231–242.

Meloy, J. R., Hempel, A. G., Mohandie, K., Shiva, A. A., & Gray, B. T. (2001). Offender and offense characteristics of a nonrandom sample of adolescent mass murders. *Journal of the American Academy of Child and Adolescent Psychiatry, 40*(6), 719–728.

Meyer, L. H., & Evans, I. M. (2012). *The teacher's guide to restorative classroom discipline.* Thousand Oaks, CA: Sage.

Monahan, T., & Torres, R. D. (Eds.). (2010). *Schools under surveillance: Cultures of control in public education.* New Brunswick, NJ: Rutgers University Press.

Morris, M. W. (2016). *Pushout: The criminalization of Black girls in schools.* New York, NY: The New Press.

Mossman, D. (1994). Assessing predictions of violence: Being accurate about accuracy. *Journal of Consulting and Clinical Psychology, 62,* 783–792.

Mullen, P. E. (2004). The autogenic (self-generated) massacre. *Behavioral Sciences and the Law, 22,* 311–323.

Muncie, J. (2008). The "punitive turn" in juvenile justice: Cultures of control and rights compliance in Western Europe and the USA. *Youth Justice, 8*(2), 107–121.

Muschert, G. W. (2007). Research in school shootings. *Sociology Compass, 1*(1), 60–80.

Muschert, G. W., Henry, S., Bracy, N. L., & Peguero, A. A. (Eds.). (2013). *Responding to school violence: Confronting the Columbine effect.* Boulder, CO: Lynne Rienner.

Muschert, G. W., & Madfis, E. (2013). Fear of school violence in the post-Columbine era. In G. W. Muschert, S. Henry, N. L. Bracy, & A. A. Peguero (Eds.), *Responding to school violence: Confronting the Columbine effect* (pp. 13–34). Boulder, CO: Lynne Rienner.

Muschert, G. W., & Peguero, A. A. (2010). The Columbine effect and school anti-violence policy. *Research in Social Problems and Public Policy, 17,* 117–148.

National Association of School Resource Officers. (n.d.). *Frequently asked questions.* Retrieved June 12, 2019, from https://nasro.org/frequentlyaskedquestions/.

National Center for School Safety. (2006). *Serious violent crimes in schools.* Youth Violence Project.

Newman, K. S., Fox, C., Roth, W., Mehta, J., & Harding, D. (2004). *Rampage: The social roots of school shooters.* New York: Perseus Books.

Nolan, K. (2011). *Police in the hallways: Discipline in an urban school.* Minneapolis: University of Minnesota Press.
O'Malley, P. (2008). Neoliberalism and risk in criminology. In T. Anthony & C. Cunneen (Eds.), *The critical criminology companion* (pp. 55–67). Sydney, Australia: Federation Press.
O'Toole, M. E. (2000). *The school shooter: A threat assessment perspective.* Critical Incident Response Group, National Center for the Analysis of Violent Crime, FBI Academy, Quantico, VA. Retrieved July 3, 2019, from https://www.fbi.gov/file-repository/stats-services-publications-school-shooter-school-shooter.
Otto, R. K. (2000). Assessing and managing violence risk in outpatient settings. *Journal of Clinical Psychology, 56,* 1239–1262.
Palermo, G. B., & Kocsis, R. N. (2005). *Offender profiling: An introduction to the sociopsychological analysis of violent crime.* Springfield, IL: Charles C. Thomas Publisher.
Petherick, W. (2006). *Serial crime: Theoretical and practical issues in behavioral profiling.* Burlington, MA: Academic Press.
Pinizzotto, A., & Finkel, N. J. (1990). Criminal personality profiling: An outcome and process study. *Law & Human Behavior, 14,* 215–233.
Pollack, W. S., Modzeleski, W., & Rooney, G. (2008). *Prior knowledge of potential school-based violence: Information students learn may prevent a targeted attack.* Washington, DC: United States Secret Service and United States Department of Education.
Pratt, J., Brown, D., Brown, M., Hallsworth, S., & Morrison, W. (2005). *The new punitiveness: Trends, theories, perspectives.* Portland: Willan Publishing.
Public Agenda. (2004). *Teaching interrupted: Do discipline policies in today's public schools foster the common good?* New York: Public Agenda. Retrieved June 12, 2019, from https://files.eric.ed.gov/fulltext/ED485312.pdf.
Rafa, A. (2019). *The status of school discipline in state policy.* Education Commission of the States. Retrieved May 22, 2019, from https://www.ecs.org/wp-content/uploads/The-Status-of-School-Discipline-in-State-Policy.pdf.
Randazzo, M. R., Borum, R., Vossekuil, B., Fein, R., Modzeleski, W., & Pollack, W. (2006). Threat assessment in schools: Empirical support and comparison with other approaches. In S. R. Jimerson & M. J. Furlong (Eds.), *The handbook of school violence and school safety: From research to practice* (pp. 147–156). Mahwah, NJ: Lawrence J. Erlbaum Associates.
Rappaport, N., & Barrett, J. G. (2009). Under the gun: Threat assessment in schools. *American Medical Association Journal of Ethics, 11*(2), 149–154.

Reddy, M., Borum, R., Berglund, J., Vossekuil, B., Fein, R., & Modzeleski, W. (2001). Evaluating risk for targeted violence in schools: Comparing risk assessment, threat assessment, and other approaches. *Psychology in the Schools, 38*(2), 157–172.

Rigakos, G. S., & Hadden, R. W. (2001). Crime, capitalism and the "risk society": Towards the same olde modernity? *Theoretical Criminology, 5*(1), 61–84.

Ruddy, S. A., Neiman, S., Hryczaniuk, C., Thomas, T. L., Parmer, R. J., & Hill, M. R. (2010). *2007–08 School Survey on Crime and Safety (SSOCS): Survey documentation for public-use data file users.* Washington, DC: National Center for Education Statistics, Institute of Education Sciences, U.S. Department of Education. Retrieved April 13, 2019, from http://nces.ed.gov/pubs2010/2010307.pdf.

Sachsman, S. (1997, September 8). Prof stalkers beware: MOSAIC is here. *Yale Daily News.*

Schiff, M. (2013). Dignity, disparity, and desistance: Effective restorative justice strategies to plus the school-to-prison pipeline. In *Center for Civil Rights Remedies National Conference. Closing the School to Research Gap: Research to Remedies Conference.* Washington, DC.

Schwarz, E., & Kowalski, J. (1991). Malignant memories: Posttraumatic stress disorder in children and adults following a school shooting. *Journal of the American Academy of Child and Adolescent Psychiatry, 30,* 937–944.

Sewell, K. W., & Mendelsohn, M. (2000). Profiling potentially violent youth: Statistical and conceptual problems. *Children's Services: Social Policy, Research, and Practice, 3*(3), 147–169.

Simon, J. (2006). *Governing through crime: How the war on crime transformed American democracy and created a culture of fear.* Oxford: Oxford University Press.

Skiba, R. (2000). *Zero tolerance, zero evidence: An analysis of school disciplinary practice.* Policy Research Report. Indiana Education Policy Center.

Skiba, R., & Peterson, R. L. (1999). The dark side of zero tolerance: Can punishment lead to safe schools? *Phi Delta Kappan, 80*(5), 372–382.

Steiker, C. S. (1998). Forward: The limits of the preventive state. *Journal of Criminal Law & Criminology, 88*(3), 771–808.

Strong, K., & Cornell, D. (2008). Student threat assessment in Memphis City schools: A descriptive report. *Behavioral Disorders, 34,* 42–54.

Student Suspended After Finger Gun Incident. (2010, April 18). Abclocal.go.com. Retrieved October 3, 2010, from http://abclocal.go.com/ktrk/story?section=news/local&id=7392273.

Sumner, M. D., Silverman, C. J., & Frampton, M. L. (2010). *School-based restorative justice as an alternative to zero-tolerance policies: Lessons from West Oakland.* Henderson Center for Social Justice, University of California, Berkeley, School of Law.

Thurau, L. H., & Wald, J. (2010). Controlling partners: When law enforcement meets discipline in public schools. *New York Law School Law Review, 54,* 977–1020.

Times Wire Reports. (2001, February 1). *Child suspended for brandishing chicken.* Retrieved June 20, 2019, from http://articles.latimes.com/2001/feb/01/news/mn-19819.

Turvey, B. E. (2008). *Criminal profiling: An introduction to behavioral evidence analysis* (3rd ed.). Burlington, MA: Academic Press.

Twemlow, S. W., Fonagy, P., Sacco, F. C., O'Toole, M. E., & Vernberg, E. (2002). premeditated mass shootings in schools: Threat assessment. *Journal of the American Academy of Child and Adolescent Psychiatry, 41*(4), 475–477.

Urbina, I. (2009, October 11). It's a fork, it's a spoon, it's a…weapon. *New York Times.* Retrieved May 3, 2019, from http://www.nytimes.com/2009/10/12/education/12discipline.html?_r=2.

Van Ness, D. W., & Strong, K. H. (2010). *Restoring justice: An introduction to restorative justice.* New Providence, NJ: Anderson.

Verlinden, S., Hersen, M., & Thomas, J. (2000). Risk factors in school shootings. *Clinical Psychology Review, 20*(1), 3–56.

Vincent, G. M., Terry, A. M., & Maney, S. M. (2009). Risk/needs tools for antisocial behavior and violence among youthful populations. In J. T. Andrade (Ed.), *Handbook of violence risk assessment and treatment: New approaches for mental health professionals* (pp. 377–424). New York, NY: Springer.

Vossekuil, B., Fein, R., Reddy, M., Borum, R., & Modzeleski, W. (2002). *The final report and findings of the safe school initiative: Implications for the prevention of school attacks in the United States.* Washington, DC: U.S. Secret Service and U.S. Department of Education.

Wacquant, L. (2009). *Punishing the poor: The neoliberal government of social insecurity.* Durham, NC: Duke University Press.

Wald, J., & Losen, D. J. (2003). Editors' notes. In J. Wald & D. J. Losen (Eds.), *New directions for youth development: Deconstructing the school-to-prison pipeline* (pp. 1–2). San Francisco, CA: Jossey-Bass.

Wamsley, L. (2019, May 2). *Florida approves bill allowing classroom teachers to be armed.* Retrieved June 17, 2019 from https://www.npr.org/2019/05/02/719585295/florida-approves-bill-allowing-classroom-teachers-to-be-armed.

Webber, J. A. (2003). *Failure to hold: The politics of school violence*. New York: Rowman & Littlefield.
Welch, K., & Payne, A. A. (2018). Zero tolerance school policies. In J. Deakin, E. Taylor, & A. Kupchik (Eds.), *The Palgrave international handbook of school discipline, surveillance, and social control* (pp. 215–234). New York, NY: Palgrave Macmillan.
Winn, Z. (2018, March 13). *Explaining Florida's new school safety law*. Retrieved June 12, 2019 from https://www.campussafetymagazine.com/safety/explaining-floridas-new-school-safety-law/.

2

Assessing the Substance and Risk of Student Rampage Threats

In the wake of numerous highly publicized multiple-victim shooting sprees which have occurred in mostly rural and suburban American public schools, academics, politicians, and media figures weighed in on what should be done to prevent similar events from occurring in the future. One such commentator, Kay Hymowitz, a fellow at the Manhattan Institute, wrote an impassioned essay in favor of emergent zero-tolerance policies which automatically mandate strict penalties for student misbehavior such as making threats or bringing weapons to school, regardless of individual or situational circumstances. Hymowitz (2005, p. 24) stated that such policies:

> have been criticized for resulting in severe penalties for seemingly minor offenses, such as offhand comments about violence, violent drawings, or playful simulations of violent acts. However, the policies have headed off potentially catastrophic shootings and bombings nationwide. Because it is impossible to discern a teenager's true intentions, any hint of potential violence must be taken seriously in order to protect the safety of other students.

Though formed to argue in favor of a zero-tolerance policy which has been widely condemned in recent years by various academics (Ayers, Ayers, & Dohrn, 2001; Casella, 2001; Skiba, 2000) and political commentators on both the left (Davis, 2014; Holcomb & Allen, 2009) and right (Schlafly, 2003; Whitehead, 2001) as well as by the American Bar Association (2001), and the American Psychological Association (APA Zero Tolerance Task Force, 2008), her assertion nevertheless directly addresses the difficulty of predicting and responding appropriately to student threats to commit school violence on a massive scale.

Ultimately, zero-tolerance approaches evoke an artificial simplicity and certainty to the imminently complicated issue of appraising the violent potentiality of students. Hymowitz (2005, p. 24) alerts us to just this complexity by acknowledging that "it is impossible to discern a teenager's true intentions," yet her insistence that this troubling fact need necessarily lead to serious investigations and consequences for violent drawings or rowdy play neglects the impact that such an overzealous school disciplinary environment can have upon the quality, not to mention cost, of American education. Moreover, though she briefly acknowledges the depth of complexity inherent in discerning the true intentions of young people, she ultimately retreats to punitive ideology in the pursuit of the simplicity that zero-tolerance claims to provide. While Hymowitz is correct that many school rampage attacks have been averted over the last twenty years in the United States (Daniels, 2019; Daniels et al., 2007; Madfis, 2014a; O'Toole, 2000), there is absolutely no empirical evidence of any kind attributing zero-tolerance policies to these positive outcomes. In fact, as evidence from Chapter 4 of this volume will demonstrate, a zero-tolerance climate actually makes school rampage attacks more likely to occur, for students in schools that emphasize one-size-fits-all punishment over supportive environments where kids feel as if they can trust and confide in school staff are far less likely to report serious threats.

As Cornell and Sheras (2006; Cornell, 2013) have pointed out, simply excluding students from school via suspensions or expulsions does nothing to resolve the original causes of problems or to prevent conflicts from escalating. In fact, a zero-tolerance punishment has the potential to exacerbate the isolation and anger of a student contemplating a

2 Assessing the Substance and Risk of Student Rampage Threats

rampage attack at their school as various disciplinary infractions such as suspensions and expulsions have been vital precipitating factors in numerous previous school rampages around the world (Langman & Straub, 2019; Levin & Madfis, 2009; Madfis & Levin, 2013). For example, the fourteen-year-old boy who shot two students and two teachers before committing suicide at the SuccessTech alternative high school in Cleveland, Ohio on October 10, 2007, had been placed on a three-day suspension for being involved in a fistfight two days prior to the shooting.[1] He told his uncle that he felt the suspension was unfair and that his teachers wouldn't listen to him or help him deal with the many bullies who tormented him daily at the school. The shooting began after another student at the school punched him in the face for bumping into him. When that student walked away after punching him, the offender shot the boy bullying him in the abdomen before shooting three others and ultimately shooting himself (Langman, 2017). Thus, the suspension did not prevent this shooting from happening and one might argue that it served as a fairly significant contributing factor.

Thus, determining how best to respond to the threatening behavior of students is a controversial but extremely important task. Some commentators have concluded that schools ought to move beyond the punitive simplicity of zero-tolerance discipline, and instead adopt an emergent approach that purports to appraise if not predict violent behavior. While this approach takes numerous names in varied disciplines and specializations that pertain to the academic understanding of aggressive behavior, they are often collectively referred to as "violence risk assessment" (Andrade, 2009; Reddy et al., 2001). Like the other enhancements of school discipline and security described in the previous chapter (and of which zero-tolerance policies constitute one component), the increased value placed upon risk evaluation, control, and management in a post-Columbine actuarial age can similarly explain the major development and popular implementation of risk assessment procedures.

While there have undoubtedly been major advancements in diverse literatures that claim to aid in the contemporary understanding of violent threats and their relationship to violence prediction, the success and underlying consequences of these techniques remain hotly contested

(Harcourt, 2007; Mossman, 2006; Sacco & Larsen, 2003) and lacking in extensive empirical testing in the school context (Reddy et al., 2001; Verlinden, Hersen, & Thomas, 2000). In particular, little is known about the manner in which assessments of violence risk are actually understood and conducted by school and police officials, nor how these authorities feel about the evaluative certainty such techniques are designed to provide. The phenomenon of averted school rampage killing represents a crucial arena for the investigation of violence risk assessment in the school context as these incidents, at least in theory, represent the ultimate institutional goal of successful evaluation and intervention during one of the most potentially devastating hazards that schools may face. In addition, the entirely of scholarship on averted school rampage is surprisingly sparse, and as a result, is often rife with unexplored and problematic assumptions about what the phenomenon entails and how it may be assessed.

Accordingly, the goals of this chapter are to (1) problematize the notion of averted rampage and clarify what have often been haphazard linguistic distinctions between threat, risk, and plot and (2) examine the forms of evidence present when claims are made that a school rampage threat has been averted. The resultant data prove vital as the phenomenon of averted rampage killing has yet to be subjected to careful conceptual scrutiny or extensive empirical study. Likewise, it is hoped that the findings and discussion to follow may lead to more sophisticated threat assessment language and guidelines and subsequently away from both simplistic zero-tolerance solutions and problematic predictive and characteristic-based forms of violence risk assessment.

Distinguishing Threats, Risks, Plots, and Genuine Aversion

As described in further detail in the Methodological Appendix (Chapter 6), the evidence to follow comes from a range of sources—most centrally through the personal accounts of police and school authorities, but I also consulted news reports, police incident reports, legal briefs, and court transcripts from trials and hearings as a way of assuring accuracy via data triangulation. Data are drawn from the in-depth analysis of eleven incidents in which at least some school administrators, police officers, parents, and/or news reporters believed that an incident of school rampage violence was planned but ultimately prevented. As such, the notion of an averted rampage leaves room for a wide range of severity between cases wherein students' genuine desire to complete a rampage attack is problematically assumed. While numerous comments or actions by students have the potential to be classified as evidence of an averted rampage, the application of this uniform label glosses over major differences between cases in terms of the level of premeditated planning, the substance of the threat, and the actual level of risk present (Reddy et al., 2001). Likewise, as the academic study of averted rampage violence is still new and emergent, it is vital to note what a mistake it would be for future researchers to assume too much similarity among the numerous cases described by the media as averted school rampages, plots, risks, and/or threats. The scholarship on violence risk assessment, and the threat assessment literature in particular, helps to distinguish between these too easily conflated terms and the associated levels of severity that must be recognized if schools are to have an accurate understanding of the extent of the problem of school rampage violence, let alone how to prevent its occurrence or mitigate its risk.

The multifaceted process by which school and police officials implement these techniques and actually discern the severity of threats in practice warrants far more empirical investigation, and my data reveal the actual criteria utilized in these cases as a means to assess the level of risk. However, before these forms of assessment criteria can be described, it is necessary to problematize the concept of averted school rampage. Beyond the initial operationalization of completed school rampage debated in previous works (such as Newman, Fox, Roth, Mehta, & Harding, 2004; Muschert, 2007), my data have helped to elucidate the fact that the phenomenon of averted rampage has its own conceptual concerns which must be addressed. Though the terms "threat," "risk," "plot," and "averted" are often used uncritically if not interchangeably by the media and many academics to address the phenomenon, they represent different components of a rampage event and its assessment. Each one of these features warrants specific discussion.

Examining the Form and Content of Threats in Averted Rampage Violence

First, as the threat assessment literature makes clear, one must not conflate the terms threat and risk (Cornell & Sheras, 2006; O'Toole, 2000). While risks refer broadly to the potential exposure to harm, threats refer more specifically to the declaration of an intention to inflict harm. Thus, threats themselves constitute a major evidentiary factor in the assessment of risk. As some (such as O'Toole, 2000; Reddy et al., 2001) have insightfully noted, not all threats signify serious risk, and some very high-risk incidents may likewise take place in the absence of a direct threat—this latter point is often discussed as a problematic feature of the threat assessment approach which is only useful in the presence of an existent threat.

In ten out of the eleven cases under investigation in this study, however, there was evidence of a threat of violence declared against others in some form. The one possible exception, at Greenvale High, entailed a student's list of several of his current and former teachers where the word "fuck" was inserted into the middle of each of the teachers' last names. There is no indication that this handwritten list, found in a notebook in the student's locker, ever would have been shared with anyone else and therefore represented an actual communication of harmful intent, yet it was interpreted as both a threat and hit list by some (though by no means all) members of the school staff. Aside from this particular incident, threats were clearly expressed in the remaining ten cases, and they took at least three distinct forms—via verbal, written, and electronic media.

Verbal threats were the most common. In one occurrence at Finley High School, there were numerous verbal threats. These included: a male student offering to kill, for his female friend, anyone that she didn't like; the same male student telling another girl who drove him to school that he wanted to blow people up at a large public park in the center of the city of Boston; and the same student threatening to cut out the tongue of any of his co-conspirators or other peers aware of the plot, if they were to reveal anything to authorities. In another instance of verbal threatening at Adams High School, a student offered to kill the girlfriend of one of his friends for him, after the friend discussed some issues he was having in their relationship. In addition, in at least five more cases (at Adams, Blane, Courtside, Everton, and Finley), there is evidence that students verbally made mention to various peers of attacking their school, though these comments were often, but not always, perceived as flippant jokes rather than legitimate threats.

This research also revealed numerous electronic threats. In one electronic threat at Adams High School, a student posted YouTube clips of himself shooting a rifle and blowing up pipe bombs which he communicated were "1/8 of the size were gonna use" and which he sent to at least one other student. In another incident at Hastings Jr./Sr. High School, students made death threats on a social networking site against various members of the football team and other popular students. In a similar but much more elaborate electronic threat at Everton High, several students created detailed profiles on a social networking website where they referred to themselves as ES420, the Everton Shooters April 20th. These online profiles featured a digital countdown clock ticking down to the anniversary of Columbine on April 20th, the Columbine killers listed as heroes, pictures of guns, and publically visible communications discussing how serious each member was about the plot, with one comment explicitly stating plans to "kill everyone." In addition to their social network profiles, the students in this case also posted on YouTube three disturbingly violent and threatening videos, one of which shared the same title as a recording made by the Columbine killers called "Hitmen for Hire." Juxtaposed with a series of violent images from Columbine and elsewhere, the students' video montage stated, "Nine years ago two boys has a vision…but they never got to accomplish it…but nine years later two boys will carry out that vision and restore that lost fear into the hearts of millions…comming [sic] this Thanksgiving." While no individuals were directly threatened by name in this latter incident, the video still qualifies as a direct threat in O'Toole's (2000) classification system, for it was expressed in a straightforward manner and identified a specific date and particular albeit symbolic target—the school as a whole.

Several cases also involved written threats. Two cases (at Iverson and Kranston) included deadly warnings written on the walls of boys' bathroom stalls in high school buildings. One such note declared that "Tomorrow will be worse than Virginia Tech," and another one stated that "Columbine could happen here." The other written form of threat was the presence of physical hit lists. These were believed to be present in four of the eleven instances—at Adams, Donovan, Greenvale, and Jefferson. One such hit list consisted of a sheet of paper that was clearly entitled "people to kill," another was labeled "targets" and "social targets," a third list found on students included only the names of several of their peers known to have bullied them, and the fourth one previously mentioned as less clearly a threat consisted of a student listing and cursing the names of several teachers in his notebook.

Examining the Levels of Risk in Averted Rampage Violence

The actual level of risk for violence present in a given incident of threat is, likewise, not uniform. It is here where the terms risk and threat remain problematically conflated, even in the more nuanced threat assessment literature which first strove to clarify these distinctions. For example, the scholars (Cornell, 2013; Cornell & Sheras, 2006; O'Toole, 2000) who have written what are otherwise arguably the most sophisticated classification schematics for assessing the severity of risk in the presence of existent threats, continue to use the term "threat," as in "high level threats" (O'Toole, 2000, p. 9) and "very serious threats" (Cornell & Sheras, 2006, p. 30), when they are clearly referring to risk, the potential exposure to harm (and thus, the terms "high level risks" and "very serious risks" would be more consistent terminology). This confusing linguistic inconsistency aside, the threat assessment approach of these scholars is very useful in determining the level of risk present in each of the eleven cases.

According to the threat assessment standards laid out by Cornell (2013; Cornell & Sheras, 2006), none of the eleven incidents under investigation in this study could be strictly classified as transient threats, those made carelessly in jest or in moments of anger. Six cases (Adams,

Blane, Courtside, Donovan, Everton, and Finley) should certainly be classified as very serious substantive threats, as they were death threats with much specificity. These same six cases would also qualify as a "high level of threat," using O'Toole's (2000) classification system, because of the direct, detailed and plausible nature of their plans and the fact that concrete steps were taken in these cases toward carrying them out.

In contrast, the remaining five cases are less clearly defined for, while they were not momentary acts of anger, they lacked much specificity or any clear indication that the students had taken any steps toward actually carrying them out. They would qualify as either low- or medium-level threats, according to O'Toole's (2000) system. This is consistent with Cornell's (2013, p. 381) observation that "threats are a frequent but largely unrecognized occurrence in schools," many of which are not particularly serious. In two of these lower risk incidents (at Greenvale and Jefferson), students who had written lists of the names of people they disliked saw these interpreted as hit lists for rampage shootings. In the Hastings case, students threatened their classmates with violence on a social networking website in a manner that some parents, police, and the media interpreted as genuine and fatal. In the final two incidents (Iverson and Kranston), threats referencing previous school rampage shootings were written on bathroom walls. While the eleven incidents varied widely in severity, at least according to how they would be evaluated via the threat assessment approach, if one was to rely on media coverage alone, it would be rather difficult to discern these very significant differences, as all eleven incidents were covered (albeit not to the same extent) as potentially averted rampage plots.

Examining Plots and Planning in Averted Rampage Violence

The term school "plot," which is often used interchangeably with school rampage in the media, implies a certain amount of previous planning and forethought, but this should more properly be understood as an empirical question. Can there be averted rampage without a plot in place? As the findings section on planning will soon reveal, my data indicate that, while extensive planning represents one of the strongest features to convince officials of students' intentions to do harm, students have been accused, both by their schools and in the press, of being engaged in an averted rampage incident without any indication of the presence of detailed planning. Thus, evidence of a rampage plot, while a very common feature of averted rampages (and likely one of the best indicators of genuine intent), is not a necessary component for some school officials or the news media to label a student's action as an averted rampage incident.

Examining the Notion of Aversion in Rampage Violence

Finally, and perhaps most importantly, the term "averted" rampage implies that an attack was inevitably and certainly going to take place before it was prevented. Perhaps, for instance, a student's flippant verbal remarks or written personal grievances could be misinterpreted as genuine threats. Even a carefully planned attack might likewise represent only a hypothetical fantasy for a student who never intended to carry it out. As the findings in this chapter will later indicate, the contentious question of "what would have happened" remains disturbingly unsettled terrain for numerous (though by no means all) school and police officials who have been directly involved in these events. They are often not entirely certain of the genuine intentions of students accused of plotting school rampages, though these officials may increase their certainty through the use of various risk assessment criteria.

The Assessment of Evidence in Averted Rampage Violence

The categories of evidence utilized as a means to assess the seriousness of rampage violence threats are myriad, but they may essentially be divided into two distinct types. The threat assessment approach emphasizes criteria that signify detailed planning for the crime and active preparations undertaken toward carrying it out. As such, plot details entailing specific people, places, or timing and the training in or existent, potential, or desired access to weapons all represent forms of threat assessment criteria. In contrast, risk assessments based on the identification of individual or group characteristics are more in line with a profiling or warning sign approach. As both types of assessment criteria were either implicitly or explicitly discussed by school and police officials as important for making decisions during the course of handling these cases, they both warrant extensive discussion. These findings will begin with an exploration of the forms of evidence utilized that may be classified as threat assessment criteria (i.e., plot details and the role of weaponry) and then turn to those forms that may be understood as relating to profiles and warning signs of likely school rampage offenders (i.e., individual and group characteristics).

Assessing the Plot's Detail

The first major category used by school and police officials to determine risk is the level of detail involved in the planning of violence. This criterion is already a vital feature of the threat assessment approach, and, as O'Toole (2000) pointed out, the planning involved in carrying out a school rampage is often a lengthy process. According to Vossekuil, Fein, Reddy, Borum, & Modzeleski (2002), most school rampage shooters create a plan at least two days before initiating their attack on students and/or teachers. Many of them develop and fantasize about their plots for weeks or even months prior to carrying them out (Fox & Levin, 1994; Madfis & Levin, 2013; Newman et al., 2004; Verlinden et al., 2000; Vossekuil et al., 2002). The Columbine killers spent more than a year extensively preparing their attack (Larkin, 2007). While it is quite popular to depict mass shootings as the result of individuals simply "snapping" and committing violent onslaughts in a spur-of-the moment manner, this does not accurately describe the vast majority of mass murders, whether they occur on school grounds or elsewhere (Levin & Madfis, 2009). In many of the cases under investigation in this study, evidence of planning a school rampage attack was often extensive and constituted a major determinant in the assessment of a threat's severity. For example, Dr. Sable, an adjustment counselor who dealt directly with the students accused of planning a rampage attack at Finley High School noted that, "they spent so much time thinking about the attack that, if it was a fleeting thought, they wouldn't have had maps or this whole list. They also spent so much time coming up with a list of people to harm."

In terms of the physical and digital evidence collected by police and/or school authorities, the existence of detailed plots were determined by the presence of hit lists and even "do not kill" lists, suicide notes, maps of the school with attack plans drawn on them, daily planners and journals describing the desired targets, methods, and outcomes, supply shopping lists, discussions about the plots on social media websites, and internet searches relating to research on how to execute an attack (such as for details about previous rampage shootings, attaining firearms, or building bombs). These various forms of evidence convinced school and police officials that the risk of rampage violence was more significant because of the detailed nature of how the plan was to be strategically implemented. Specifically, plots were comprised of details such as who was to be purposely targeted, what locations were to be attacked in what order, and when the attacks were to take place.

The first subcategory of planning, the extent to which certain individuals or groups were targeted as potential victims, is important not only because school and police officials viewed this as indicative of more serious intent, but because this very issue constitutes a hotly contested debate, both internal and external to academia, about whether or not specific targets are victimized during a rampage attack. Cullen (2010) rather famously argued that prior news accounts misreported the "myth" that the Columbine shooters specifically targeted minorities and jocks (see also Ogle, Eckman, & Leslie, 2003 on the media revisionism of this issue). Likewise, some scholars (Kimmel & Mahler, 2003; Volokh, 2000) have characterized school rampage shootings as "random" events at least in part because of the much-touted (though not empirically tested) notion that school rampage shooters attack peers and teachers in an indiscriminate manner without deliberate targets in mind. In fact, the presence of random victims has often been used as an operational criterion for rampage shootings. For example, Newman et al. (2004) specifically limited her definition of school rampage to include only those cases in which at least some of the victims were chosen randomly or symbolically. Likewise, Muschert (2007) distinguished "targeted" school shootings with multiple specifically intended victims from "rampage" school shootings which necessitate random or symbolic victims. The present study is uniquely suited to tackle this particular question for at least two reasons. First, unlike many of the school rampage killers who have committed suicide (or suicide-by-cop) after completing their deadly plans, my entire sample of would-be school attackers was still alive when they were caught and thus could explain their intentions to police and other officials with whom I was then able to speak. Secondly, in averted incidents, the plots themselves are the criminal offenses and so the extant news media reporting and legal documentation are far more focused on the planning aspects of these cases rather than on other issues more prominently featured in the aftermath of completed rampages, such as offenders' actions on the day of their attacks, the manner in which victims were killed or injured, the victims' identities and extent of their injuries, or the impact of the event upon effected communities, families, and survivors. This wealth of data revealed that most of my sample of cases did in fact desire to target specific individuals or groups of people rather than, or in addition to, random victims and the school as a whole.

In the incident at Adams High School, the people the student planned to kill on the day of his attack were specifically chosen because they were individuals who he felt had slighted him in the past. For example, the sheet of paper found in his bedroom labeled "targets" contained the names of thirty students at the school, as well as the names of four additional students with "NK" (no kill) listed next to their names, and a distinct "Do Not Kill" section listing the names of another sixteen students. The student did tell police that his plan was not to kill strangers and only to kill those students who had been picking on him for years. There was also one girl in particular who he wanted to kill, and he had extensive written notes about her, such as where she lived and worked, what vehicle she drove, as well as exactly how he wanted to kill her by shooting her in the head. He also told a friend about wanting to kill her specifically. Further, he informed police that he added the names one by one, gradually over time. However, he also selected what Newman et al. (2004, p. 50) called "symbolic" targets and what the student, in his notebook, called "social targets." These included various cliques such as "Goths," "Punks," "Commies," "Hippies," "Preps," "Gays," "Ghetto Wiggers," and "Muslims" where asterisks were placed next to the names of certain students to indicate to which groups they belonged. One of his journal entries repeated this theme, as he indicated that he thought many people needed to die, but he singled out "muslims, niggers, spics, towelheads, Goths, punks, and especially faggots."

Many of the other incidents echo this theme. At Courtside High, the would-be rampage killer specifically planned to execute the students he did not like, and even intended to tell his friends at the high school not to attend class on the day of the attack. In fact, this student even convinced one of his friends to hold onto his stolen weapons for him because he promised the friend that he would warn him in advance to assure that he and his girlfriend would not be on the premises. The three Donovan High School students apprehended with an arsenal of weaponry on them also carried a hit list of particular students who had teased them. The Everton High students did target specific people such as the SRO and other administrators, but also discussed attacking people more widely and randomly.

In at least one case, the importance of who was to be targeted was so paramount to the Finley High student plotters that all of the other elements of their planning criteria (such as what locations were to be targeted, when the attacks were to take place, and how the plan was to be strategically implemented) reflected a desire to harm specific people while protecting the safety of others. In this incident, some of the student plotters argued that their group was originally formed to protect kids who were being bullied and only intended to hurt certain individuals. In a binder found at the home of one of the students, police found a hit list with the names of roughly a dozen people on it, including both students and staff. The star football player at the school was a particularly significant target for another member of the group, who felt that this student athlete constantly harassed him. They also intended to kill members of the school administration including the principal and assistant principal, the SRO, and the gym teacher. They harbored special resentment for the gym teacher and desired to torture her by cutting her Achilles tendon, forcing her to run a mile in seven minutes as she had made them do in gym class, and then shooting her in the head if she could not succeed. In addition, they planned to put CO_2 bombs in the lockers of the students that they didn't like. So concerned with seeking revenge upon their targets, they even developed a contingency plan if Plan A, the school rampage attack, didn't work out. Plan B, which they all concluded was far less preferable, was to break into each of their targets' homes to cut their throats. Conversely, they took time to discuss the most strategic way to get all of their friends into the cafeteria in order to protect these certain students from harm. Despite these precautions and the focus on particular targets, the student plotters still desired to kill as many people as possible. They sought to specifically time their attack for 2:02 p.m. when school was dismissed because they concluded that this was when the highest number of students would be in the hallways.

In three additional cases (Greenvale, Hastings, and Jefferson), threats were made against specific people either online or through written documents which were interpreted as hit lists. In the remaining three cases (Blane, Iverson, and Kranston), it is unclear from all available evidence if those threatened as potential victims would have been randomly selected, targeted as individuals or social groups, or some combination of both. Ultimately, this finding suggests that strict dichotomous distinctions between targeted and rampage violence are at least somewhat untenable. Moreover, whenever specific groups of people or individuals were targeted in the planning process of a rampage plot, school and police officials viewed this as substantially magnifying the risk.

The second subcategory of planning that school and police authorities understood to be a vital risk factor was the extent to which certain locations, both external and internal to the school, were targeted with in-depth planning. These plans typically entailed targeting just the school building itself. However, the Donovan High students' goal was to attack the town at large in addition to the school, and, as previously mentioned in the Finely High School case, homicidal home invasions were discussed as a secondary option if a school attack would not be feasible. The Finley

High case is also notable here because, in the plan these students devised, they intended first to blow up a gas station on the opposite side of town from the school in order to divert emergency personnel away during the time of their school attack.

Strategic decision-making regarding location could also be seen in how some students designated certain areas of the school as targets in their attempt to maximize carnage. In the Adams High case, police found a floor plan map of the school building when they searched the student's bedroom. The map had been extensively written on with lines and arrows to indicate his intended travel routes during the attack and where several propane bombs would be placed. When questioned about this map of the school, he informed the school's SRO that his plan was to start the attack by going to this officer's room in the school and incapacitating him by handcuffing and taking his radio. He would then proceed to kill his intended targets by starting in the cafeteria and then moving around the building in a counterclockwise circle which would culminate with him committing suicide in the library. In another incident at Everton High, school administrators also found a detailed map of the school, but in this case it was publically available on the website of one of the student plotters, while an additional physical map was found in a student's backpack. These maps had the names of the three students listed on them in different colors, matching color-coded dots and lines going around the building which identified areas within the school that were to be targeted, including the boys' locker room, and the offices of the principal, building security, and the SRO. As in the previous two cases, the students at Finley High also possessed maps of their high school. One was hand-drawn and the other was a building floor plan stolen from the SRO's desk. The plan these students devised also included a division of labor so that one student would move to one wing of the school to shoot the jocks where they were in class, while another student killed the SRO, and a third student murdered the administration. Another component of their plan was to put one of them on the roof of the school to kill any approaching emergency personnel who tried to intervene.

The third subcategory of planning was decisions detailing when the attacks were to take place, both in terms of the desired date to execute the rampage and the timing of how the rampage was to proceed on that

2 Assessing the Substance and Risk of Student Rampage Threats

day. The desired date was frequently the anniversary of the Columbine massacre, which occurred on April 20, 1999. However, in any given year, when April 20th fell on a weekend or during a school vacation, students made do with a date in close proximity. School officials at Adams High found a daily planner in the high school student's locker in which he had highlighted a particular date in April that was the closest school day to April 20th. Likewise, in the case at Finley High, the attack was originally scheduled to take place on April 20th, specifically because of the fact that this was both Hitler's birthday and the anniversary of Columbine, but the date was later changed to April 15th as classes would not be in session on the 20th due to school vacation. However, an April date was not planned in every case. For example, the Everton High students engaged in a detailed conversation on a social networking site about what day should be chosen for their attack. They debated over whether they should choose a random day, the date that Martin Luther King was assassinated, or the first day of school during the following year.

In addition to choosing a specific date for the attack, some students also designed plans for what was to take place in what order on the day itself. The example of this which occurred at Adams High was so extreme that Detective Brown, the SRO at the scene when the student's planning folder was discovered, had the following to say about it: "He had it written, verbatim, in chronological order…Exact with detail, step by step. It was wicked wicked detailed. Almost like a briefing that a swat team would have." In fact, the crime/incident report on this case included a copy of what was originally a handwritten document titled "April 10, 2007 NBK Plan" that contained a detailed timeline for the day of the attack. It stated the following:

6:00   1. Wake up at 6:00
6:15   2. Take caffeine pills, energy drinks, and xtra energy etc.
6:40   3. Make sure all guns ammo are ready, bombs are prepped, guns clean, all equipment ready, cigs, lighters, slings, ammo holders, alcohol
7:00   4. Have last meal, place all equipment on side of house
7:15   5. Get dropped off/walk to school
9:30   6. Wait until 9:30 then go back home
10:00 7. Prep, bombs, guns explosive in car
10:15 8. Get cell phone numbers

10:20 9. Enjoy life for half an hour
10:50 10. Go to parking lot, call friends
11:00 11. Prep car bomb, ANFO
11:05 12. Go inside have some fun
          13. When done have some vodka, a smoke
          14. Commit suicide

While other students may have made similarly sophisticated schedules for the day of their attacks (such as at Everton and Finley), only the Adams High School student took the time and care to write it down chronologically moment to moment in such an explicit fashion.

Whether the level of detail present in a rampage plot was found to be about who was to be targeted, where the rampage was to take place, or how and when it would be executed, these specifics were interpreted as signs that threats ought to be considered less improvident or transient. Thus, broadly in line with the threat assessment approach, school and police officials felt that the existence of any and all detailed facets of planning dramatically enhanced the potential risk for violence.

Appraising the Role of Weaponry

Clearly, the role that weaponry plays in school rampage cannot be overstated. As Levin and Madfis (2009) and Madfis and Levin (2013) note, the availability of and training in firearms are crucial facilitating factors in carrying out a mass murder. Police and school officials consider various aspects of weaponry when they seek to discern if a student has engaged in a plot to commit school rampage. These aspects include the existent, potential, or desired access to weapons, evidence of weapons training, the glorification and fascination with weapons, and threats mentioning the use of weapons.

The first crucial subcategory is the presence of weapons or evidence that students were attempting to attain or manufacture weapons. This criterion has long been cited as crucial in the threat assessment literature in terms of judging how "actionable" a threat may be (Cornell, 2013; Cornell & Sheras, 2006; O'Toole, 2000) and punishment for students bringing guns to school was the impetus for the initial zero-tolerance policies (Ayers et al., 2001; Skiba & Peterson, 1999). Though weapons were present in some cases, they were not present in every case, nor was there evidence that the accused students sought out or had access to weaponry in all instances. Thus, while weapons possession or access was not viewed as a fundamental necessity in terms of being perceived as a potential rampage incident, it undoubtedly signified increased severity and an enhanced potential for lethal violence to both school and police officials. As Officer Jones, Iverson High's SRO, stated:

> We seriously consider whether he has access to weapons. I always go back and check the in-house computer and see if mom or dad has weapons at home. I've called home and said, "Hi, we're concerned. Are there weapons in the household? Is there access to weapons?" We always find that out. So you take that factor into account, majorly.

Understandably, access to large amounts of lethal weapons represented one of the most significant concerns for school and police authorities.

In the incident at Adams High School, a student amassed a vast arsenal of weaponry including knives, ammunition, two assault rifles, and at least two additional guns all legally registered in his father's name. With his father's permission, the student kept all of these in his bedroom closet. This student had also made numerous pipe bombs in his basement and many other materials used to manufacture a wide variety of bombs were found in his bedroom. There, police also found a written shopping list of desired supplies that included different firearms, bombs, and bomb-making materials. Another incident at Blane High School involved a student bringing tennis balls to his high school that had been filled with explosives. Police later found four additional explosive devices at the student's home. A third event at Courtside High entailed a student stealing three guns and hundreds of rounds of ammunition from his father's safe before giving them to a friend to hold onto until they would be needed to execute the plot. Yet another case at Donovan High School entailed the arrest of three teenagers who were walking down a street while carrying rifles, handguns, swords, knives, and a shotgun along with thousands of rounds of ammunition, after failing in their attempt to steal a car to embark on a killing spree meant to include the local high school.

A fifth incident at Everton High involved numerous students who had taken a large arsenal of weapons, including rifles, shotguns, and handguns, from their parents' collections. On a social networking website, they discussed the need to attain earplugs to protect their hearing while firing the weapons.

Unlike the previous five cases, in the incident at Finley High School, none of the four student plotters were found with firearms or explosives, but they were stockpiling gunpowder and had previously created and tested many homemade explosives including napalm. According to a shopping list found in the bedroom of one of the boys, they were also actively attempting to attain trip wire explosives, cannon fuses, PVC piping, semiautomatic weaponry, propane tanks, as well as chains and bike locks to seal the rear and main doors of the school. One of the accused plotters approached at least two other students on separate occasions to request that firearms be purchased or lent out to him, but he was denied in both attempts. This same student also indicated that he could access guns by stealing them from his father who was a police officer. In each of the aforementioned four cases where juveniles gained access to firearms, these weapons were legally registered in their parents' names. In all of the six cases listed above, a large portion of school and police officials expressed serious concerns about students' intentions which were directly linked to their access to weapons. In contrast, in the remaining five incidents (Greenvale, Hastings, Iverson, Jefferson, and Kranston), there was no evidentiary or even speculative indication of the presence of any weapons of any kind, nor the attempt on the part of the plotters to attain weapons, and confidence that students intended to carry out their threats was far less uniform in these cases.

Another major criterion noted by school and police officials was evidence that students had actively been training with weapons for their attack (no officials indicated the presence or importance of any other form of training such as physical training, though firearms and explosives surely make mass murder easier to accomplish in the absence of physical fitness). Though even the Columbine shooters videotaped footage of themselves engaged in target practice in the foothills near their homes, weapons training has not previously emerged or been addressed in any of the risk assessment literature. Evidence of training with weapons included physical remnants or damages left after the activity took place or any account or documentation that such preparation occurred. In only two of the cases under investigation did officials confirm that students actively trained with weapons for a school rampage assault, but the training evident in both of these cases was abundant. In the averted incident at Adams High, a student admitted to making over 40 pipe bombs over a four year period, including CO_2 bombs, copper pipe bombs, dry ice bombs, and cherry bombs. One of his bomb-making friends put the number closer to one hundred bombs over a two-year period. The student also filmed himself on numerous occasions blowing up his homemade bombs along with footage of himself firing his father's guns at a shooting range to improve his aim. After being informed about his frequent training sessions in the woods near his parent's home, police searching this area found the remnants of numerous explosive devices. The other plot (at Finley High) which involved extensive training for a school attack similarly entailed a great deal of time devoted to weapons preparation. In this instance, the students also admitted that they spent time in a deserted wooded area where they did target practice and blew up homemade explosives. They experimented by blowing up gun powder in various containers, and even made napalm by thickening gasoline with Styrofoam and lighting it on fire. Though these students, despite their best efforts, were never able to attain their own firearms, they did acquire BB guns, knives, and axes, all of which they practiced shooting and throwing at trees which they pretended were their intended victims. Police searching these woods found cans and bottles that had been exploded as well as large gashes in the trees of the surrounding area.

In both of these cases, the intensity of weapon preparation and training was extensive. While an interest in firearms may be a fairly common trait among American adolescent boys (Shapiro, Dorman, & Burkey, 1997), the level of experimentation and fascination present in these two incidents is certainly out of the norm of typical youth behavior, and rightly concerned the school and police officials who learned about these activities (Meloy, Mohandie, Knoll, & Hoffman, 2015). Therefore, the notion of training may be appropriately considered a new addition to the threat assessment literature, and one which certainly qualifies as the sort of concrete steps taken toward carrying out an attack which O'Toole (2000) described as indicative of high-level threats.

In contrast, though school and police officials certainly noted that the student plotters in several of these incidents demonstrated a longstanding fascination with weaponry such as firearms and explosives, the broad interest in weapons more generally did not constitute a vital indicator in their assessments. Despite the fact that a fascination with weapons has been described as a warning sign for school shootings going back to some of the earliest research (Band & Harpold, 1999; Leary, Kowalski, Smith, & Phillips, 2003; McGee & DeBernardo, 1999), the officials seeming lack of concern here might reflect the adoption of the more nuanced threat assessment evaluative mindset over an emphasis on warning signs and profiles which may apply to a broad swath of the population. In other words, a student's interest in weapons (which may be a potential warning sign for school rampage but also applies to many adolescents who would never dream of committing such a crime) didn't represent a significant concern for school and police authorities unless their access to or desire for weapons occurred in the context of an existent threat.

This more nuanced approach to assessing violence risk played out in one incident (at Everton High) where several school administrators and the SRO were monitoring the social networking sites of some of their students about whom they were concerned because the students had posted numerous references praising the Columbine massacre in great detail. The school staff did not collectively make the determination to intervene until they saw a picture of a gun posted as the wallpaper on one of the student's websites along with a conditional threat referencing a firearm that stated, "I swear to god. One more mother fucker says the wrong fucking thing to me and I will pull out a goddamn 45 and kill their sorry asses." Mr. Dougherty, one of the house principals at the school, clarified that at that crucial point in time, "We said, 'All right. Now we've got a mention of a 45. We've got an actual mention.' And Trooper Smith [the SRO] said, 'Okay, now is the time to do something about this.'" Thus, the threat referencing a gun combined with the firearm imagery used as wallpaper represented the decisive criteria in this incident. Similarly, at Adams High, it was a threat to utilize bombs communicated electronically that ultimately initiated serious investigation into the student's activities and already well-known enthrallment with firearms and explosives.

Ultimately, while the existent, potential, or desired access to weapons and evidence of weapons training represented significant assessment criteria for school and police authorities (i.e., a sufficient cause for concern), it was not a necessary condition to be judged an averted rampage attack as several incidents did not involve evidence of weapons in any way. Likewise, though a fascination with weapons amplified concern in the presence of an existent threat alluding to their use, an interest in weapons did not by itself foster great concern among school authorities.

Assessing the Role of Personal and Group Characteristics

In addition to the significance of weaponry and detailed planning, various personal and group characteristics were often considered as a component of the assessment process. Unlike the previous two evaluative categories which are more in line with a threat assessment approach, concern with individual characteristics and personality traits is more closely aligned with the profiling and guided professional judgment (warning sign) approach to violence risk assessment. Within this grouping of criteria, individual characteristics (such as ethnic/racial and gender identity as well as previous behavior and mental health concerns) and social characteristics (such as school social status and an affiliation with the culture of deviant groups) both represented significant evaluative factors for police and school officials as part of stereotypical school shooter profiles or warning signs.

Both of the original school shooter profiles (Band & Harpold, 1999; McGee & DeBernardo, 1999) described typical offenders as white males. In fact, mass murder, of which school rampage violence constitutes a subset, is the only form of homicide that is committed by non-Hispanic whites in numbers disproportionately high relative to their share of the population (Fox & Levin, 1998, p. 435; Madfis, 2014b). While it is certainly not the case that all school rampages have been committed by whites (for example, the Red Lake Senior High School killer was Native American, the Virginia Tech shooter was Korean American, and the shooter at the Tasso da Silveira Municipal School was Brazilian), the vast majority have in fact been white. For example, Langman and Straub (2019, p. 10) recently discovered that 71% of perpetrators who attacked k-12 schools were non-Hispanic Caucasians. Likewise, Daniels (2019) similarly found that among the cases of averted school violence he compiled, most would-be attackers were also non-Hispanic Caucasians—86.4% of the perpetrators for whom racial/ethnic identity was known. As a result, some scholars (Madfis, 2014b; Mingus & Zopf, 2010; Schiele & Stewart, 2001; Wise, 2001) have attempted to theoretically link white racial identity and privilege to rampage. Additionally, many researchers (Collier, 1998; Consalvo, 2003; Kalish & Kimmel, 2010; Kiilakoski & Oksanen, 2011; Kimmel & Mahler, 2003; Klein, 2005; Mai & Alpert, 2000; Myketiak, 2016; Neroni, 2000; Schiele & Stewart, 2001) have observed that the vast majority of rampage school shooters have been male and asserted the role that dominant notions of masculinity play in reinforcing and legitimizing such violence.

Despite these myriad academic studies asserting the significance of demographic variables, none of my respondents would acknowledge that race/ethnicity or sex/gender played any role in how schools or the police assessed risk. This omission may simply reflect social desirability bias on the part of respondents wary that the use of any such criteria would be interpreted as prejudicial. However, as African American youth are vastly overrepresented in school suspensions and expulsions when compared to white students who commit identical infractions (Fenning & Rose, 2007; Robbins, 2005), the adjudication of school discipline is anything but colorblind and profiling based on whiteness would go markedly against the grain.

In contrast, maleness has long been associated with increased rates of offending and arrest for violence and delinquency (Messerschmidt, 1993), and so it would have been less surprising to hear some respondents acknowledge that they might, for example, be more suspicious upon hearing rumors of a rampage plot hatched by male students than by female students. This was not the case, as nearly all of my respondents, regardless of whether they were school administrators, police officers, teachers, or counselors, emphatically stated that gender was not something they take into consideration in making assessments about the risk for student violence. In one of the more frank statements in this regard, the vice principal at Courtside High, Mr. O'Brien, stated, "It doesn't matter if it's a boy or girl, I've seen some girls do serious damage." In fact, most respondents reacted to questions pertaining to gender by dismissing its significance entirely and recounting personal experiences dealing with violent female students. For example, when asked whether he would assess the homicidal threats made by both boys and girls in an identical manner, Dr. Phelps, a school psychologist at Greenvale, responded affirmatively that:

> Oh absolutely, yes. Girls sometimes are significantly violent. We had a situation at the high school…There were two sisters, I think one was grade nine and the other one may have been grade eleven. They took on two security people and four police department people trying to get them off the bus. I mean they could be tough. We're not gender specific. We're more tuned into the degree of threat.

Stories that discounted the role of gender by alluding to female violence were common. Not only do such tales amount to discounting aggregate patterns through idiosyncratic examples, but they blur the distinction between fairly typical assaults, which girls may commit with some frequency, and multiple homicides, which are, by and large, committed almost exclusively by boys and men (Fox, Levin, & Quinet, 2019; Madfis, 2014b; Madfis & Cohen, 2018). According to Fox, Levin, and Fridel (2018, p. 140), 93.4% of mass killers are male. Langman and Straub (2019) recently found that 47 out of the 51 (or 92.2% of) completed acts of school violence they investigated were perpetrated by males, while Daniels (2019) similarly found that nearly all (91.4%) of the would-be attackers in his sample of 51 averted incidents of school violence were male. In fact, if one uses Newman and her colleagues' (2004) specific definition of a "rampage school shooting," which is limited to only those school shootings in which multiple people were killed or injured on school property by a current or former student of the targeted school, then only two instances have ever been perpetrated by females (the first was when a 16-year-old girl shot people at Cleveland Elementary School from her home across the street in 1979 and the second was the case of a woman who killed two of her fellow nursing students before committing suicide at Louisiana Technical College in 2008). Furthermore, if one utilizes the traditional and most common operationalization of mass murder in the homicide literature, where the phenomenon is limited only to those cases wherein at least four victims were killed during a single episode at one or more closely related locations (Duwe, 2007; Fox et al., 2018), there has not been a single case of a female committing a mass murder at a school (in this, the 2010 shooting at the University of Alabama in Huntsville comes the closest, but the perpetrator, a professor who had recently been denied tenure, only managed to kill three of her academic colleagues).

Of the 195 cases discovered for this study, only 10 (5.1%) involved female perpetrators, so 94.9% of incidents involved only male plotters (see Madfis & Cohen, 2018 for more information analyzing the cases of female involvement in averted school rampage plots). Interestingly, of the twenty-three students[2] accused of being involved with planning a rampage attack at the eleven schools under detailed investigation in this study, only one was a female. Notably, this girl was accused in the case at Jefferson Middle School, which was previously discussed as a low to medium level threat without any indication of an existent, potential, or desired access to weapons and little evidence of detailed planning outside of having written a list of people she disliked on a sheet of paper that her teacher discovered. The principal of her middle school, Mr. Anderson, did take this girl's gender into account regarding her ultimate lack of genuine intent as he ascribed the girl's motivation for writing the list in the following manner:

> It was because of all the stuff that we see in middle school, especially with girls. It's the jealousy. It's the cliques, okay…The girl who wrote this list, she just was mad at people. That's all. She was mad at these kids. Maybe somebody stole a boyfriend. Maybe they didn't want to be her friend, and she wanted to be their friend. And so she was frustrated and she wrote it on paper and that was as far as it was ever going to go, in my determination, 99.9 percent, you know.

Thus, while nearly all respondents dismissed the role of male gender as a relevant factor both in theory (i.e., that any connection could be found between masculinity and rampage) and in practice (as gender was not deemed germane in the ten incidents involving male students), gender became a suitable mitigating factor for the girl's behavior in her case. This inconsistency becomes particularly distinct when one considers that the same descriptors which were used to mitigate this girl's actions (frustration with peer cliques and relationship troubles) have been used by many scholars to help explain the actions of male school shooters (for example, see Burgess, Garbarino, & Carlson, 2006; Kimmel & Mahler, 2003; Klein, 2005; Klein, 2006a, b; Larkin, 2007; Leary et al., 2003; Levin & Madfis, 2009; Meloy, Hempel, Mohandie, Shiva, & Gray, 2001; Newman et al., 2004). That said, and notwithstanding the lack of additional evidence in the Jefferson Middle School case which likely suggests that this girl did not genuinely intend to cause harm, Mr. Anderson is entirely correct, in probabilistic terms, to view her gender as indicative of decreased risk for committing a school rampage. What's more, the unwillingness, or at least hesitation, on the part of respondents to consider gender as a relevant factor in cases with accused male students may reflect larger patterns of privilege where male (just like white) operates as the default, thus rendering the discussion of gender only pertinent to females (Irigaray, 1985).

Another element of personal characteristics frequently considered was the previous misbehavior of accused students. One school administrator, Dr. Warner, stated that, "the best predictor of violence is past aggression and violence. That's unequivocal." While this may be the case for violence in general (Campbell, 1991; Campbell, Breaux, Ewing, & Szumowski, 1986; Farrington, 1991; Moeller, 2001; Robins, 1966), the same cannot necessarily be said for perpetrators of school violence. In their study of school shooters, Verlinden et al. (2000) found that nine out of the ten under investigation had some history of aggression and seven out of ten had a history of discipline problems. However, a report commissioned by The U.S. Secret Service and the U.S. Department of Education (Vossekuil et al., 2002, p. 22) on incidents of targeted school violence (a broader category than that of Verlinden et al., 2000) found that just 13% of their sample of "attackers were known to have acted violently toward others at some point prior to the incident." Similarly, Vossekuil et al. (2002, pp. 20–22) found that only 27% had any prior arrest history, another 27% of the offending students had ever been suspended, only 10% had been expelled at some previous point in their lives, and 63% had never been or were rarely in trouble at school. Likewise, Langman and Straub (2019, p. 14) recently found that 37.3% of the perpetrators of completed school attacks and 17.6% of the plotters of averted school attacks were known to the criminal justice system prior to these events.

Prior histories of aggression and school discipline, and the lack thereof, were, however, often brought up as influential factors in the assessment of risk. For example, the principal, adjustment counselor, and SRO all directly involved in the case at Finley High each noted the prior troubling behavior of at least one of the accused students. In addition, the police officer who arrested these students made it clear that he already knew three out of four of them as they "had a history" with the town police department.

In the same way, during the numerous instances when the accused students had no prior behavioral issues, this led school and police officials to express doubt regarding the authenticity of the risk. For example, Mr. Dougherty, a house principal at Everton High, recalled that "none of these kids had a discipline record or anything." Similarly, the assistant principal of Courtside High School, Mr. O'Brien, pointed out that when a parent came to express concern over the deadly intentions of one of his son's friends, he originally discounted the risk because that student had not previously been in trouble. He stated:

> I remember thinking, well, whatever, I've never seen this kid for any type of discipline before that I can remember that was a major problem or issue. Both of these students really were not what you would call major behavior problems. I did not even know who these two students were until this whole incident started to unravel.

Therefore, though having a history of aggression and school misbehavior may not be unequivocally linked empirically to school rampage, school and police authorities certainly valued this criteria, whether that meant

2 Assessing the Substance and Risk of Student Rampage Threats

giving students they had not previously come across in a disciplinary setting the benefit of the doubt, assuming students they did have prior positive relationships with would be less likely to plot a violent act, or deeming past misbehavior indicative of enhanced risk for violence.

The next factor that school and police officials weighed in their assessments of personal characteristics was the mental health issues of accused students which were often perceived to be indicative of a troubled mind and increased likelihood of violence risk. Subsumed under this category were formal mental health diagnoses, but also comments, notes, or drawings revealing suicidal or depressed thoughts. Many of these criteria have already been subjected to extensive empirical testing. In their investigation of sixteen cases, McGee and Bernardo (1999, p. 11) included severe mental illness, such as schizophrenia and bipolar disorder, as "characteristics NOT associated with classroom avengers." Similarly, Vossekuil et al. (2002, pp. 21–22) found that just over a third (34%) of student attackers in their study had received a mental health evaluation during their life, and less than a fifth (17%) had been diagnosed with a mental health or behavior disorder prior to the attack. However, this study also indicated that 78% of attackers exhibited a history of suicide attempts or suicidal thoughts at some point before their attack and 61% had a documented history of feeling extremely depressed or desperate. Likewise, in their sample of ten rampage school shooters, Verlinden et al. (2000, p. 43) found that only two of them had previously experienced mental health treatment, but eight out of ten exhibited signs of depression, six had made suicidal threats, and another six had created violent writings or drawings. More recently, Langman and Straub (2019, p. 14) found "depressed mood" to be the most common characteristic found in the lives of both of their samples of perpetrators associated with completed and averted school attacks.

While mental health concerns such as depression, personality disorders, and psychoses were discussed as a key hypothetical cause of rampage school shootings by a large portion of respondents, evidence of these mental health concerns was rarely abundant in these cases. However, any indication that students were of poor mental health was taken very seriously and seen as a profoundly significant warning sign for violence. For example, only in the case at Finley High was there an accused student with a documented history of being institutionalized for mental illness, which occurred after the student was thought to be a suicide risk—though some school officials incorrectly believed he had been institutionalized for threatening his mother with a knife. This troubled history was discussed by everyone interviewed about the incident and was brought up during legal proceedings, thus it surely played a significant role in how both risk and intent were assessed in this case.

Likewise, school and police officials weighed heavily evidence of depression or suicidal thoughts, though these were existent in the minority of incidents (only in the cases at Adams, Courtside, and Finley). Thus, the school principal at Courtside High, Mr. Fernandez, explicitly noted the vital role that he thought depression, if not suicidal thinking, played in motivating the student's threat which enhanced his concern. Mr. Fernandez said:

> I started talking to around 10-15 students that were in class with the student who had [been accused of stealing his father's gun] and I kind of got the same picture, basically that he doesn't have any friends, maybe one friend, they said. He doesn't talk in class. He doesn't participate in class. They don't really think he has any hobbies or that he's into anything…He just presented as someone who was kind of down in the dumps, anxious and I don't know if you'd say suicidal, but he just looked like he was in pain when I was talking to him. He just didn't look like he was feeling well.

The presence of suicidal thoughts or comments more generally was cause for concern. When Detective Brown, Adams High's SRO, initially questioned the accused student in that case, the student admitted to being suicidal, and this did factor into the officer's ultimate conclusion about intent. Police later discovered in the student's bedroom two typed suicide notes. One of these was a detailed note for his parents and the other was intended for everyone else and addressed to a few of his friends. According to the police incident report, the student stated in the second letter that:

> I want to commit suicide, but I don't want all of you to be heartbroken, so to make it easier for you all by shooting up the school, that way

you all would hate me, and I won't worry about anybody missing me. Except my family…I would save everyone's grief by committing suicide but I figured I would rather have some fun and revenge and then kill myself.

Commenting upon the existence of these notes, Detective Brown stated, "That kind of clinched it."

Similarly, Courtside Assistant Principal O'Brien discussed becoming increasingly distressed about the student under suspicion when he spoke with the student's English teacher who recalled finding a particular assignment strange and disturbing. According to Mr. O'Brien, the drawing was "a picture of a tombstone and it said rest in peace and it had [the student's] name and it had some year in the future." Yet another of the student's drawings depicted a person being shot along with the words, "I wish this was me. I hate my life." Thus, in addition to documented mental health concerns, comments, notes, or drawings that reflected depression or suicidal ideation drew a great deal of attention from school and police officials as they represented stark indicators of concern if not culpability.

In addition to the role of individual identity characteristics, school and police officials also considered group dynamics and membership affiliations. The first criterion deemed relevant was social status at the school. Being marginalized by and socially isolated from the rest of the school community are traits long associated with school shooter profiles and warning signs (Band & Harpold, 1999; Dwyer, Osher, & Warger, 1998; McGee & DeBernardo, 1999), but subsequent empirical scholarship has provided mixed results. Though some scholars (such as Langman, 2009a, 2009b; O'Toole, 2000; Vossekuil et al., 2002) have rejected the characterization of all rampage school shooters as "loners," much case study research has found plentiful evidence of isolation and marginalization (for example, Langman & Straub, 2019; Lieberman, 2008; Madfis & Levin, 2013; Meloy et al., 2004; Newman & Fox, 2009; Newman et al., 2004; Silver, Horgan & Gill, 2018). A careful reading across these studies indicates that the characterization of school rampage offenders as significantly marginalized if not entirely isolated is accurate for a large portion, though by no means all, of previous offenders.

The view that social marginalization and peer group conflict plays a considerable role in causing school rampage violence was common among the vast majority of my respondents who often described accused students as "isolated," "unpopular," "socially different," "unconnected," or "on the periphery." For instance, Finley High School principal Mr. McGowan, explained his general belief in how social marginalization plays a role in leading to extreme violence. He said:

> I think when you look at all of the school violence issues that have happened, usually it's a kid that for some reason hasn't been able to make or create positive relationships in school. And so, they pull back, and they spend more time either introverted in the internet world, or they pull back and they find a small group of people that are all of the same likeness and then they start talking about, "Why are we the outcasts? Why aren't we part, you know?" So I think there's a pretty clear picture as to the understanding of who those kids are.

The significance of social marginalization as a predictor for school rampage was not only alluded to in the abstract by the school officials involved in this incident. Finley High's adjustment counselor, Dr. Sable, recounted witnessing some of the students who would later be accused of planning an attack on the school, being mistreated by their peers at a school-sponsored gathering. She recalled that:

> Those two kids just didn't seem to fit. They fit with each other, and they don't seem to fit anywhere else. Those two kids were trying to dance and be with another group of kids, and the kids just kind of kept turning their back to them and turning their back to them and just leaving them out. Whether the kids truly understood what they were doing, they just kept shutting these two boys out, just shut them down, just kept, you know, with their body language, just kind of kept pushing them out on the periphery…And you know this is a leadership camp where these kids are expected to be leaders and this is how they're treating other kids and it was very telling.

Dr. Sable described witnessing this episode as "a turning point" for both herself and the principal, and she reflected that "as we look back, we were both thinking that it was interesting that we would sit there and take that all in, watch it all unfold, and then have that huge thing happen." Thus, for both Mr. McGowan and Dr. Sable, there was a direct link between how the students were treated by their peers and their creation of a rampage plot, and their witnessing of this event certainly impacted how they later assessed the seriousness of the threat.

Though this view was dominant, it did not amount to universal consensus. For example,

Dr. England, Blane High's school psychologist, diminished the role of school social status and peer group conflict as a cause of rampage. She stated:

> When you think of Columbine, you think, you know, the jocks and then these guys who felt really put down by them, and so forth. But that happens with a lot of cliques who are part of high school culture, so I certainly wouldn't just put the blame on that. I mean I think there are much more deeper issues for those students…really mental illness.

Dr. England makes a valid point that social marginalization and bullying are widespread features of school life, and this cannot, by itself, explain rare instances of rampage. It can be, however, one crucial component in a larger multicausal nexus (Muschert & Ragnedda, 2010; Henry, 2009; Levin & Madfis, 2009; Madfis & Levin, 2013; Newman et al., 2004), and thus it is understandable that so many school and police officials view marginalized social status as an important assessment criterion.

Directly related to the notion of social marginalization, the other important criterion based on group characteristics was an affiliation with the culture of deviant groups. In numerous instances, such affiliations, particularly the music and clothing styles associated with certain subcultures such as neo-Nazi skinheads and Goths, were mentioned as informing perceptions about intent. This may be routed in much of the initial reaction to Columbine when musician Marilyn Manson and the Gothic subculture (through associated attire like black trench coats) were blamed for inspiring the attack (Griffiths, 2010; Merelli, 2018; Muzzatti, 2004; Ogle et al., 2003) and many scholars explored the role played by warning signs such as a "preoccupation with violent media/music"

(Verlinden et al., 2000, p. 43) or "some interest in violence, through movies, video games, books, and other media" (Vossekuil et al., 2002, p. 22).

In the incident at Donovan High, an assistant principal pointed out that all three of the students involved in the incident often wore black trench coats, and were teased by much of the student body for doing so. In two additional cases (at Adams and Finley), school administrators, police officers, and legal documentation about the incidents all made specific mention about the accused students wearing black trench coats. While one must be careful about forming broad causal links between any item of clothing worn by lots of innocent people and rare instances of extreme violence, there may be some level of legitimacy in linking trench coats with school shootings in that this particular item of clothing has become widely associated with the Columbine killers who did wear them. As the vast majority of rampage plotters around the world since the 1999 Columbine massacre have been directly inspired by that attack (Larkin, 2009; Madfis & Levin, 2013), signs that students want to repeat elements of Columbine warrant concern. In particular, there are times when clothing choices may genuinely warrant additional suspicion and scrutiny. For example, one of the students accused of plotting a school rampage at Finley High once wore a t-shirt to school which featured a picture of the Columbine shooters on it above the words "Remember the Heroes." This student also reportedly wore swastika t-shirts and drew Nazi symbols on his body in marker. In a separate incident at Adams High School, whereupon, after having police find a black trench coat, a white Jason (from the *Friday the 13th* horror films) mask, and camouflage cargo pants in his bedroom closet, the student proceeded to inform them of his intent to wear these items on the day he would have attacked the school. Police also found, inside a folder full of other planning materials, a hand-drawn image of the student dressed in this trench coat, pants, and mask, while armed with shotgun shells, pipe bombs, magazines, Molotov cocktails, knives, and a duffel bag with bombs. All of these items were labeled individually in the drawing. According to one of the police officers who arrested him, the student additionally commented that he specifically chose the pants and coat in order to hold the maximum amount of pipe bombs.

2 Assessing the Substance and Risk of Student Rampage Threats

Certainly, Nazi imagery and specific allusions to Columbine or other school rampages should raise red flags for concerned parents and educators, but these were not the only clothing features that emerged in discussions with police and school officials. In numerous incidents, authorities asserted the significance of certain alternative styles, such as black Gothic attire, tattoos, and the shaved heads and suspenders associated with the skinhead subculture. For example, Ms. Grey, a former teacher of a student accused with writing threatening notes on Iverson High School's bathroom walls, shared her view that:

> If you see people walking around in trench coats, hats down over their eyes, drawing weird pictures or covered in, I mean I suppose it's politically incorrect, but covered in tattoos or whatever, pay attention, do something.

Though youth subcultures are perennially blamed for a myriad of social ills, it is vital to reiterate the fact that both the skinhead (in both its anti-racist and neo-Nazi incarnations) and Gothic subcultures have had long histories before the contemporary era of school rampage violence (Haenfler, 2016). Additionally, it is extremely problematic to form broad associations declaring common subcultural stylistic choices such as black clothing and tattoos to be signifiers of delinquency, let alone indicators of the next potential school shooter (Muzzatti, 2004). Not only does the focus on these cultural preferences have the potential to marginalize a large segment of students who have done nothing wrong other than to subscribe to less traditional beliefs, values, and/or aesthetics, but it is a flawed guideline with little empirical basis. Numerous students who have attempted and completed school rampage shootings have dressed in a traditional manner. In fact, the official *Columbine Report* by the Jefferson County Sheriff's Office eventually debunked the notion that even the Columbine killers "regularly cloak[ed] themselves in symbols associated with violence or the Goth culture; rather, they 'appeared outwardly normal, [sharing] their dark side only with each other'" (Ogle et al., 2003, p. 23). What's more, the Adams High School student plotter wanted to deliberately target Goths as victims, and the rampage plot by student athletes at Courtside High was taken less seriously by school officials, at least preliminarily, as a result of their clean-cut appearance.

In contrast, perhaps it should be evidence of an abnormal fascination with rampage violence which should stand out as the disconcerting warning sign. In many cases, evidence indicating just this sort of deep and consuming obsession with the Columbine case and other school rampages did exist (in the form of internet searches, comments to peers, and personal writings) and was noted as a decisive factor for both school and police officials. In this criterion, the presence of the copycat effect, where various features of a highly publicized crime are imitated by others (Coleman, 2004; Langman, 2018; Meindl & Ivy, 2017), was not lost on the officials assessing these cases. For example, a house principal at Everton High, Mr. Dougherty, reflected upon how his concern was exacerbated when he found out from several of the peers of one of the accused students that he "was almost obsessed with Columbine and that he literally…would sit in the cafeteria, and he would ask kids to quiz him on Columbine, like ask him any fact about it." Police and school officials involved in the case at Adams High pointed out computer records revealing that the student had extensively researched Columbine and numerous other mass shooting events. In this student's bedroom, police also found a red folder with a picture of the two Columbine killers on the cover. In multiple journal entries, he referred to his plan to attack the school as "NBK," the same code name (referencing the film *Natural Born Killers*) used by the mass killers at Columbine High School. The Finley High students, like in the case at Adams High, had also been referring to themselves as the Natural Born Killers. Officer Dudley, Finley's SRO, described the accused teenagers as being "fascinated with Columbine" and noted that, when one of the student's computer was seized, it indicated that someone had been extensively researching the details about Columbine, as well as material on firearms and bomb making.

By and large, evidence of the copycat phenomenon and a clear obsession with the minutia of previous school rampages did produce greater concern among the respondents than affiliations with youth subcultures such as violent media or subcultural attire, but the latter more problematic associations were still present in the views of some respondents. As such, it's important to recognize these particular assessment criteria for what they are, bias against students with less traditional beliefs, values, and/or aesthetics, and as such, caution against the practice in future empirical research and risk assessment practices.

Conclusion

The phenomenon of averted school rampage presents several unique dilemmas distinct from those of completed school rampages. In these cases, violent schemes and threats have the potential to be either exaggerated or dismissed. Various forms of violence risk assessment provide guidance to school and police officials in how they evaluate the substance of threats—these range from assessing the detail of plots, appraising the role of weaponry, and numerous criteria based on characteristics like ethnic/racial and gender identity, previous disciplinary and mental health history, school social status, and affiliation with deviant groups.

This chapter explored the myriad forms of evidence utilized to assess the seriousness of student threats and discussed the empirical support, or lack thereof, for these evaluative criteria. Risk assessments based upon the identification of characteristics, regardless of whether they are at the individual or group level, remain a contentious area of debate for scholars. Though research has demonstrated that some descriptive traits (i.e., gender and marginalization) have more reliable empirical backing than others (such as race/ethnicity and histories of behavior problems and mental illness), these distinctions are not widely understood or acknowledged by police officers, teachers, administrators, counselors, or even many scholars of school violence. Consequently, problematic forms of risk assessment are still broadly considered in the decision-making processes of school and police officials.

That said, school and police officials do not understand all forms of risk assessment to be equally valid and do privilege certain types of evidence. The next chapter investigates precisely this distinction and addresses the evidence and specific circumstances which lead officials to express confidence in the methods of risk assessment and to believe that justice was carried out properly.

Questions for Discussion

1. Do you think that school rampage attacks are an example of random violence in any way? For example, what patterns exist among multiple cases of school rampage—and is everyone equally likely to become a victim or an offender of a rampage attack? How is this type of violence random and how is it not random?
2. Which forms of evidence used to assess the seriousness of threats are the most important and the most reliable?
3. Which forms of evidence used to assess the seriousness of threats are problematic and should not be used in this process?

Notes

1. No names of mass killers are included in this text, in line with the "No Notoriety" campaign and Lankford and Madfis' (2018) proposal to deny offenders the fame they desire.
2. One student was accused in the cases at Adams, Blane, Greenvale, Iverson, Jefferson, and Kranston, two students at Courtside, three students at Donovan and Everton, four students at Finley, and five students at Hastings.

References

American Bar Association. (2001). *Zero tolerance policy report.* Retrieved September 25, 2012, from www.abanet.org/crimjust/juvjus/zerotolreport.html.
American Psychological Association Zero Tolerance Task Force. (2008). Are zero tolerance policies effective in the schools? An evidentiary review and recommendations. *American Psychologist, 63*(9), 852–862.
Andrade, J. T. (Ed.). (2009). *Handbook of violence risk assessment and treatment: New approaches for mental health professionals.* New York, NY: Springer.
Ayers, W., Ayers, R., & Dohrn, B. (2001). *Zero tolerance: Resisting the drive for punishment in our schools.* New York: The Free Press.
Band, S. R., & Harpold, J. A. (1999). School violence: Lessons learned. *FBI Law Enforcement Bulletin, 68,* 9–16.

Burgess, A., Garbarino, C., & Carlson, M. (2006). Pathological Teasing and Bullying Turned Deadly: Shooters and Suicide. *Victims & Offenders, 1,* 1–13.

Campbell, S. B. (1991). Longitudinal studies of active and aggressive preschoolers: Individual differences in early behavior and in outcome. In D. Cicchetti & S. L. Toth (Eds.), *Internalizing and externalizing expressions of dysfunction* (Vol. 2, pp. 57–90), *Rochester symposium on developmental psychopathology* Hillsdale, NJ: Lawrence Erlbaum Associates.

Campbell, S. B., Breaux, A. M., Ewing, L. J., & Szumowski, E. K. (1986). Correlates and predictors of hyperactivity and aggression: A longitudinal study of parent-referred problem preschoolers. *Journal of Abnormal Child Psychology, 14,* 217–234.

Casella, R. (2001). *Being down: Challenging violence in urban schools.* New York: Teachers College Press.

Coleman, L. (2004). *The copycat effect: How the media and popular culture trigger the mayhem in tomorrow's headlines.* New York: Simon and Schuster.

Collier, R. (1998). *Masculinities, crime, and criminology: Men, heterosexuality, and the criminal(ised) other.* Thousand Oaks, CA: Sage.

Consalvo, M. (2003). The monsters next door: Media constructions of boys and masculinity. *Feminist Media Studies, 3*(1), 27–45.

Cornell, D. G. (2013). The Virginia student threat assessment guidelines: An empirically supported violence prevention strategy. In N. Böckler, W. Heitmeyer, P. Sitzer, & T. Seeger (Eds.), *School shootings: International research, case studies, and concepts for prevention* (pp. 379–400). New York, NY: Springer.

Cornell, D. G., & Sheras, P. L. (2006). *Guidelines for responding to student threats of violence.* Longmont, CO: Sopris West.

Cullen, D. (2010). *Columbine.* New York, NY: Hachette.

Daniels, J. A. (2019). *A preliminary report on the Police Foundations averted school violence database.* Washington, DC: Office of Community Oriented Policing Services.

Daniels, J. A., Buck, I., Croxall, S., Gruber, J., Kime, P., & Govert, H. (2007). A content analysis of news reports of averted school rampages. *Journal of School Violence, 6,* 83–99.

Davis, O. (2014, October 17). *Punitive schooling.* Retrieved January 30, 2020, from https://www.jacobinmag.com/2014/10/punitive-schooling/.

Duwe, G. (2007). *Mass murder in the United States: A history.* Jefferson, NC: McFarland & Company.

Dwyer, K. P., Osher, D., & Warger, C. (1998). *Early warning, timely response: A guide to safe schools.* Washington, DC: U.S. Department of Education.

Farrington, D. P. (1991). Childhood Aggression and Adult Violence: Early Precursors and Later-life Outcomes. In D. J. Pepler & K. H. Rubin (Eds.), *The Development and Treatment of Childhood Aggression* (pp. 5–29). Hillsdale, NJ: Lawrence Erlbaum Associates Inc.

Fenning, P., & Rose, J. (2007). Overrepresentation of African American students in exclusionary discipline: The role of school policy. *Urban Education, 42*(6), 536–559.

Fox, J. A., & Levin, J. (1994). *Overkill: Mass murder and serial killing exposed.* New York: Plenum Press.

Fox, J. A., & Levin, J. (1998). Multiple homicide: Patterns of serial and mass murder. *Crime and Justice, 23,* 407–455.

Fox, J. A., Levin, J., & Fridel, E. E. (2018). *Extreme killing: Understanding serial and mass murder.* Thousand Oaks, CA: Sage.

Fox, J. A., Levin, J., & Quinet, K. (2019). *The will to kill* (5th ed.). Thousand Oaks, CA: Sage.

Griffiths, R. (2010). The gothic folk devils strike back! Theorizing folk devil reaction in the post-Columbine era. *Journal of Youth Studies, 13*(3), 403–422.

Haenfler, R. (2016). *Goths, gamers, and grrrls: Deviance and youth subcultures.* Oxford: Oxford University Press.

Harcourt, B. (2007). *Against prediction: Profiling, policing, and punishing in an actuarial age.* Chicago, IL: University of Chicago Press.

Henry, S. (2009). School violence beyond Columbine: A complex problem in need of an interdisciplinary analysis. *American Behavioral Scientist, 52*(9), 1246–1265.

Holcomb, A., & Allen, M. J. (2009, December 9). *Moving beyond zero tolerance.* American Civil Liberties Union of Washington. Retrieved May 20, 2019, from http://www.aclu-wa.org/news/moving-beyond-zero-tolerance.

Hymowitz, K. S. (2005, April 18). Zero tolerance policies are necessary to prevent school violence. In S. Barbour (Ed.), *How can school violence be prevented?* (pp. 24–26). New York, NY: Thomson-Gale.

Irigaray, L. [translated by C. Porter and C. Burke]. (1985). *This Sex Which Is Not One.* New York: Cornell University Press.

Kalish, R., & Kimmel, M. (2010). Suicide by mass murder: Masculinity, aggrieved entitlement, and rampage school shootings. *Health Sociology Review, 19*(4), 451–464.

Kiilakoski, T., & Oksanen, A. (2011). Soundtrack of the school shootings: Cultural script, music and male rage. *Young, 19*(3), 247–269.

Kimmel, M. S., & Mahler, M. (2003). Adolescent masculinity, homophobia, and violence. *American Behavioral Scientist, 46,* 1439–1458.

Klein, J. (2005). Teaching her a lesson: Media misses boys' rage relating to girls in school shootings. *Crime, Media, Culture, 1*(1), 90–97.

Klein, J. (2006a). An invisible problem: Everyday violence against girls in schools. *Theoretical Criminology, 10*(2), 147–177.

Klein, J. (2006b). Cultural capital and high school bullies: How social inequality impacts school violence. *Men and Masculinities, 9*(1), 53–75.

Langman, P. (2009a). *Why kids kill: Inside the minds of school shooters.* New York, NY: Palgrave Macmillan.

Langman, P. (2009b). Rampage school shooters: A typology. *Aggression and Violent Behavior, 14*(1), 79–86.

Langman, P. (2017). *School shooters: Understanding high school, college, and adult perpetrators.* Lanham, MD: Rowman & Littlefield.

Langman, P. (2018). Different types of role model influence and fame seeking among mass killers and copycat offenders. *American Behavioral Scientist, 62*(2), 210–228.

Langman, P., & Straub, F. (2019). *A comparison of averted and completed school attacks from the Police Foundation's averted school violence database.* Washington, DC: Office of Community Oriented Policing Services.

Lankford, A., & Madfis, E. (2018). Don't Name Them, Don't Show Them, But Report Everything Else: A Pragmatic Proposal for Denying Mass Killers the Attention They Seek and Deterring Future Offenders. *American Behavioral Scientist, 62*(2), 260–279.

Larkin, R. W. (2007). *Comprehending Columbine.* Philadelphia, PA: Temple University Press.

Larkin, R. W. (2009). The Columbine Legacy: Rampage Shootings as Political Acts. *American Behavioral Scientist, 52*(9), 1309–1326.

Leary, M. R., Kowalski, R. M., Smith, L., & Phillips, S. (2003). Teasing, rejection, and violence: Case studies of the school shootings. *Aggressive Behavior, 29,* 202–214.

Levin, J., & Madfis, E. (2009). Mass murder at school and cumulative strain: A sequential model. *American Behavioral Scientist, 52*(9), 1227–1245.

Lieberman, J. A. (2008). *School shootings: What every parent and educator needs to know to protect our children.* New York: Citadel Press.

Madfis, E. (2014a). Averting school rampage: Student intervention amid a persistent code of silence. *Youth Violence and Juvenile Justice, 12*(3), 229–249.

Madfis, E. (2014b). Triple entitlement and homicidal anger: An exploration of the intersectional identities of American mass murderers. *Men and Masculinities, 17*(1), 67–86.

Madfis, E., & Cohen, J. W. (2018). Female involvement in school rampage plots. *Violence and Gender, 5*(2), 81–86.

Madfis, E., & Levin, J. (2013). School rampage in international perspective: The salience of cumulative strain theory. In N. Böckler, W. Heitmeyer, P. Sitzer, & T. Seeger (Eds.), *School shootings: International research, case studies, and concepts for prevention* (pp. 79–104). New York, NY: Springer.

Mai, R., & Alpert, J. (2000). Separation and socialization: A feminist analysis of the school shootings at Columbine. *Journal for the Psychoanalysis of Culture and Society, 5*, 264–275.

McGee, J. P., & DeBernardo, C. R. (1999). The classroom avenger: A behavioral profile of school based shootings. *The Forensic Examiner, 8*, 16–18.

Meindl, J. N., & Ivy, J. W. (2017). Mass shootings: The role of the media in promoting generalized imitation. *American Journal of Public Health, 107*, 368–370.

Meloy, J. R., Hempel, A. G., Gray, B. T., Mohandie, K., Shiva, A. A., & Richards, T. C. (2004). A comparative analysis of North American adolescent and adult mass murderers. *Behavioral Sciences & the Law, 22*(3), 291–309.

Meloy, J. R., Hempel, A. G., Mohandie, K., Shiva, A. A., & Gray, B. T. (2001). Offender and offense characteristics of a nonrandom sample of adolescent mass murders. *Journal of the American Academy of Child and Adolescent Psychiatry, 40*(6), 719–728.

Meloy, J. R., Mohandie, K., Knoll, J. L., & Hoffman, J. (2015). The concept of identification in threat assessment. *Behavioral Sciences & the Law, 33*(2–3), 213–237.

Merelli, A. (2018, May 22). *What US guns rights advocates would like to ban instead of guns*. Retrieved April 19, 2019, from https://qz.com/1285430/all-the-things-gun-advocates-have-blamed-for-school-shootings/.

Messerschmidt, J. W. (1993). *Masculinities and crime: Critique and reconceptualization of theory*. New York: Rowan & Littlefield.

Mingus, W., & Zopf, B. (2010). White means never having to say you're sorry: The racial project in explaining mass shootings. *Social Thought and Research, 31*, 57–78.

Moeller, T. G. (2001). *Youth Aggression and Violence: A Psychological Approach*. Mahwah, NJ: Lawrence Erlbaum Associates Inc.

Mossman, D. (2006). Critique of pure risk assessment or, Kant meets Tarasoff. *University of Cincinnati Law Review, 75*, 523–609.

Muschert, G. W. (2007). Research in school shootings. *Sociology Compass, 1*(1), 60–80.

Muschert, G. W., & Ragnedda, M. (2010). Media and control of violence: Communication in school shootings. In W. Heitmeyer, H. Haupt, A. Kirschner, & S. Malthaner (Eds.), *Control of violence: Historical and international perspectives on violence in modern societies* (pp. 345–361). New York, NY: Springer.

Muzzatti, S. L. (2004). Criminalising marginality and resistance: Marilyn Manson, Columbine, and cultural criminology. In J. Ferrell, K. Hayward, W. Morrison, & M. Presdee (Eds.), *Cultural criminology unleased* (pp. 143–154). London: Glasshouse Press.

Myketiak, C. (2016). Fragile masculinity: Social inequalities in the narrative frame and discursive construction of a mass shooter's autobiography/manifesto. *Contemporary Social Science, 11*(4), 289–303.

Neroni, H. (2000). The men of Columbine: Violence and masculinity in American culture and film. *Journal for the Psychoanalysis of Culture and Society, 5*, 256–263.

Newman, K. S., & Fox, C. (2009). Repeat tragedy: Rampage shootings in American high school and college settings, 2002–2008. *American Behavioral Scientist, 52*(9), 1286–1308.

Newman, K. S., Fox, C., Roth, W., Mehta, J., & Harding, D. (2004). *Rampage: The social roots of school shooters*. New York: Perseus Books Group.

Ogle, J. P., Eckman, M., & Leslie, C. A. (2003). Appearance cues and the shootings at Columbine High: Construction of a social problem in the print media. *Sociological Inquiry, 73*(1), 1–27.

O'Toole, M. E. (2000). *The school shooter: A threat assessment perspective*. Critical Incident Response Group, National Center for the Analysis of Violent Crime, FBI Academy, Quantico, VA. Retrieved July 3, 2019, from https://www.fbi.gov/file-repository/stats-services-publications-school-shooter-school-shooter.

Reddy, M., Borum, R., Berglund, J., Vossekuil, B., Fein, R., & Modzeleski, W. (2001). Evaluating risk for targeted violence in schools: Comparing risk assessment, threat assessment, and other approaches. *Psychology in the Schools, 38*(2), 157–172.

Robins, L. N. (1966). *Deviant Children Grown Up: A Sociological and Psychiatric Study of Sociopathic Personality*. Baltimore, MD: The Williams & Wilkins Company.

Robbins, C. (2005). Zero tolerance and the politics of racial injustice. *The Journal of Negro Education, 74*(1), 2–17.

Sacco, F. C., & Larsen, R. (2003). Threat assessment in schools: A critique of an ongoing intervention. *Journal of Applied Psychoanalytic Studies, 5*(2), 171–188.

Schiele, J. H., & Stewart, R. (2001). When white boys kill: An Afrocentric analysis. *Journal of Human Behavior in the Social Environment, 4*(4), 253–273.

Schlafly, P. (2003, April 23). Zero tolerance or zero common sense. *Eagle Forum.* Retrieved June 25, 2019, from http://www.eagleforum.org/column/2003/apr03/03-04-23.shtml.

Shapiro, J., Dorman, R. L., & Burkey, W. M. (1997). Development and factor analysis of a measure of youth attitudes toward guns and violence. *Journal of Clinical Child Psychology, 26*(3), 311–320.

Silver, J., Horgan, J., & Gill, P. (2018). Shared struggles? Cumulative strain theory and public mass murderers from 1990 to 2014. *Homicide Studies, 23*(1), 64–84.

Skiba, R. (2000). *Zero tolerance, zero evidence: An analysis of school disciplinary practice.* Policy Research Report. Indiana Education Policy Center.

Skiba, R., & Peterson, R. L. (1999). The dark side of zero tolerance: Can punishment lead to safe schools? *Phi Delta Kappan, 80*(5), 372–382.

Verlinden, S., Hersen, M., & Thomas, J. (2000). Risk factors in school shootings. *Clinical Psychology Review, 20*(1), 3–56.

Volokh, A. (2000). A brief guide to school-violence prevention. *Journal of Law and Family Studies, 2*(2), 99–152.

Vossekuil, B., Fein, R., Reddy, M., Borum, R., & Modzeleski, W. (2002). *The final report and findings of the safe school initiative: Implications for the prevention of school attacks in the United States.* Washington, DC: U.S. Secret Service and U.S. Department of Education.

Whitehead, J. W. (2001, January 23). *Zero common sense school discipline rules cheapen students' humanity.* The Rutherford Institute. Retrieved July 26, 2019, from https://www.rutherford.org/publications_resources/john_whiteheads_commentary/zero_common_sense_school_discipline_rules_cheapen_students_humanity.

Wise, T. (2001). School shootings and white denial. *Multicultural Perspectives, 3*(4), 3–4.

3

Confidence and Doubt in Assessing Averted Rampage Violence

In the study of averted incidents of school rampage, one of the most pertinent questions that must be addressed is whether or not the accused students actually intended to carry out their homicidal plans. No one but the perpetrators themselves can possess complete certainly about this vital question, though various forms of risk and threat assessment may provide insight.

The forms of evidence discussed in the previous chapter that were utilized to assess the seriousness of student threats were significant factors not only for the administration of justice to proceed (i.e., the adjudication of offenders in school and/or court). These criteria were also vital in determining how school and police officials make sense of what is otherwise a rather confusing and uncertain experience with what ultimately amounts to a hypothetical event. This chapter explores how school and police officials interpret the magnitude of evidence in their assessments of the likelihood of a potential rampage. Understanding how school and police officials manage and sometimes fail to come to terms with deciphering whether or not homicidal plots would actually have been carried out may lead to a more realistic expectation of what the practice of violence risk assessment can ultimately strive to achieve—namely, the targeting of at-risk youth for additional preventative measures rather than punitive zero-tolerance punishment across the board, and the punishment of people for the crimes they have committed rather than maintaining unrealistic and unfounded expectations about our abilities to predict students' future violent behavior.

Variations in Confidence and Doubt by Risk Assessment Type

While all types of school and police officials (administrators, security and police officers, teachers, and counselors) interviewed in this study made use of some forms of risk assessment in coming to conclusions about students' intent, there was some variation by job type. Broadly it did appear that police and security officers were most convinced by indications of detailed planning and weapons acquisition, while counselors were the most reliant upon the use of identifying characteristics. Administrators and teachers fell somewhere in the middle, though they often saw the most value in knowing students' personal and behavioral histories. My data, being qualitative in nature with a small sample that was not randomly selected, cannot assert generalizable relationships between occupations and assessment preferences, and so this finding is, at best, preliminary and tentative.

In comparison, the detailed knowledge gleaned from qualitative exploration into these cases with numerous officials tasked with assessing and intervening in them does facilitate important comparisons regarding how officials interpret the varied forms of evidence. The utilization of various forms of risk assessment criteria (such as detailed and developed plans, the existent, potential, or desired access to weapons, and conformity to stereotypical school rampage shooter profile characteristics) certainly did enhance how certain people were about their students' ultimate intentions. The threat assessment criteria are notable for providing people with the greatest amount of certainty, far above and beyond that of identifying characteristics. However, this was not always the case and the recognition of other additional factors, such as different motives and shows of remorse, gave officials doubts about whether students genuinely intended to go through with the attacks they were accused of plotting.

Certainty Based on a Convergence of Risk Assessment Criteria

Ideally, at least from a risk assessment approach, the more of the aforementioned types of detailed planning, weapons acquisition, and conformity to profile characteristics that were evident in particular cases, the more confident officials would be of the students' genuine intentions to execute their deadly thoughts. Broadly, this was the case, as many school and police officials could pull from the above risk assessment criteria in order to assure themselves of the inevitability of students' actions. Thus, the numerous forms of assessment criteria matter not just in terms of understanding how threats are practically assessed in situations of school rampage threats, but provide insight into how school and police officials make sense of what is still an extremely misunderstood crime with an uncertain outcome.

In the very serious substantive incident at Adams High where Detective Brown was largely responsible for intervening during his time as an SRO, he could draw from the myriad evidence against the student plotter he arrested in order to gain the certainly that might otherwise elude him. He stated:

> By the time we caught onto him, he says, "I didn't wanna do it anymore." We never will know if he was gonna do it or not. But he had the drawing [of him wearing the clothes he had picked out to wear on the day of the attack]. He had the hit list. And the map…There was also two suicide notes. Just more and more evidence. What else could this guy have shown us to say he was gonna do it?

In addition to this existent threat assessment criteria, the student in this case also broadly fit many stereotypical school rampage shooter profile characteristics (he was a male described as a being marginalized, suicidal, and fascinated with weapons, though he was half-Asian), and thus both elements of risk assessment converged in this case making it understandable for Detective Brown (and the two other respondents involved in this incident who were also interviewed) to feel a high level of certainty.

Certainty Based on Lack of Threat Assessment Criteria

Just as the presence of myriad risk assessment criteria were valued in forging certainty about intent, certainty about a lack of intent was similarly high in the incidents where the evidence of detailed planning and preparation was scarce. This was true regardless of whether or not students had characteristics in common with school shooter profiles. In other words, if, as was the case in some instances (in which graffiti warnings were written on bathroom walls, students posted vague and unrealistic threats on social media websites, and lists of disliked people were interpreted as hit lists), proof amounted to a solitary piece of undetailed albeit threatening writing, very few officials believed that the threat at their school amounted to a serious and actionable plot. This was the case regardless of whether or not the accused students conformed to standard profiles. Such a finding is perhaps more surprising for cases in which students fit much of the stereotypical profile but which lacked the presence of threat assessment criteria (such as evidence of planning and weapons possession) than those cases in which students neither fit profiles nor indicated an abundance of threat assessment criteria. The analysis to follow will start with the less surprising latter variety where the lack of both forms of risk assessment criteria remained convergent and then move to the more interesting phenomenon present in the former variety of cases where the two types of assessment contradict one another.

As might be expected, school and police officials felt more certain about a lack of intent when there was a dearth of threat assessment criteria such as detailed planning and preparation. They especially doubted that students intended to carry out their plans when that lack of planning and preparation converged with students whose identifying characteristics did not conform to that of their expectations regarding what school rampage shooters are commonly believed to look or act like.

For example, in the incident at Jefferson Middle School, the principal, Mr. Anderson, shared his belief that even the presence of a hit list doesn't necessarily amount to a genuine risk for violence if the student deviates from stereotypical profile characteristics. As previously mentioned, gender played some role in how he determined that the preteen female student at his school was not a significant risk. In addition, Mr. Anderson noted that:

> This girl was not what I would call sick. She did not have a mental illness to the best of my knowledge. I'm not a psychologist, okay, but she was a typical teenage girl…and she made a big mistake. Big mistake. I mean I knew the parent. I had a good working relationship with the parent. This was not a kid that would have taken action on her words.

In addition to the fact that this case lacked much evidence of intent to carry out a rampage attack beyond the existence of the hit list, the principal noted that her mental stability, status as a typical teenage girl, and the principal's prior relationship with the parent all meant that she was not a genuine risk. Thus, he came to his conclusion about the girl's lack of genuine intent not only via threat assessment criteria (such as a lack of detailed planning and preparation), but through the consideration of conventional profiling characteristics regarding personal identity and her previous behavior history.

Notably, even when students fit numerous traditional profile characteristics, but lacked evidence of detailed planning and preparation, they were still given the benefit of the doubt and not viewed as genuine threats. For example, Mr. Cross was the principal of Hastings Jr./Sr. High School where several students who could be understood as having traits in line with profiles (they were marginalized white male students who had been bullied) posted threats on a social networking website. He felt that:

> Our whole incident was totally blown out of proportion. I mean this group that we had, this so-called gang, they were calling themselves the Drive-By Kings. They didn't drive! [*He laughs*] So that can tell you a little something about the whole thing.

He understood the students' threats to not be particularly genuine, at least in part, because of their lack of means to carry them out. Thus, the thought process of Mr. Cross is directly in line with that of

O'Toole's (2000) threat assessment approach, wherein implausible unrealistic threats warrant the least concern and the substance of threats signify more than characteristic based profiles.

What's more, some administrators thought being required to proceed harshly (often as a result of zero-tolerance policies) was inappropriate in the incidents at their schools due to the absence of extensive evidence of planning and preparation. In one case that took place at affluent Greenvale High School, a student voluntarily left the school rather than facing expulsion after being accused and punished when a note cursing out many of his previous teachers was found and interpreted as a hit list. The Greenvale principal at the time, Mr. Sacco, stated:

> We had to go the full gamut. I was never convinced in my head he was ever a danger and never was. And it was one of the things where you had to act quickly and harshly with the risk you're going to alienate this kid more if you crush him too hard…The hit list was not a hit list in the true sense. It was his musings about fuck this and fuck that…He had lost of lists, lists of lots of things. He had a list of every teacher he ever had with the twist being the f-bomb planted in the middle of their name. So Mr. Sacco was Mr. Fucko…But, the so-called hit list really was something we had to act on as a school. I had to go through the whole thing, the expulsion, and, I'll be honest with you, I was never comfortable with that.

Mr. Sacco's reaction was not uncommon as numerous teachers and administrators whose schools experienced low-level threats with little evidence of planning and preparation (even when their students exhibited some profile characteristics) felt that parents and the media went overboard in characterizing them as dire risks or potential rampages. Additionally, cases such as this one indicate the value of, and likely support among some of the school community for, assessing threats in the manner suggested by Cornell (2013). That is, the punitive rubber stamp of zero tolerance needlessly treats all threats the same and thus punishes the majority of students excessively, and, in contrast, direct, detailed, and actionable plots ought to warrant more investigation and punishment than those of less severity.

Certainty Based on Threat Assessment Criteria in Spite of Deviation from Profiles

A convergence of both forms of risk assessment criteria (profiles and threat assessment) led to high degree of certainty among officials that students intended to carry out their attacks. Likewise, when cases failed to indicate evidence of threat assessment criteria, school and police officials generally did not consider threats to be serious whether or not the students fit profile characteristics. As a further testament to the broad acceptance of the threat assessment approach, there was still a high level of certainty present among officials when students who did not fit the profile of stereotypical school rampage shooters planned an attack which threat assessment criteria would deem a very serious substantive threat.

This exact phenomenon played out in the case at Everton High School, as the students accused were far from fitting the profile of stereotypical school rampage shooters. While they were white males, they were popular athletes very involved in school activities. At the same time, there was an abundance of threat assessment criteria to signify detailed planning and preparation. Initially, this contradiction between the two types of assessment criteria posed quite a dilemma for the school administrators and SRO attempting to evaluate the risk. Mr. Harris, one of Everton's house principals, revealed his confusion at the fact that:

> They weren't isolated. That was the scary thing. They did not fit what we thought was the profile for the kind of student that would plan something like this. They were engaged in school. They were involved in a sport. They seemed to have a large base of friends. They even had some popularity amongst the student body which was really bizarre.

When asked if the fact that the students did not necessarily fit the classic profile impacted his thinking in how to proceed and assess the seriousness of the threat, Mr. Harris responded, "Definitely. I mean we definitely noticed and were alarmed that they didn't fit the profile. It just didn't fit what we all believed to be the case about the kind of students that would do this sort of thing."

Another Everton house principal, Mr. Dougherty, confirmed that he also found it particularly difficult to take the threat seriously at first because of the type of students who were involved. He proclaimed:

> This is one of those things where people were saying that these guys were angry loners. They weren't. These guys were on the wrestling team. These guys, when the wrestling team would be out running, they would be talking about Columbine…They looked like normal kids. I mean literally just looked like normal kids. They were on the wrestling team!…Looking at them, I will say this; when I heard it was the one kid who I had met before, I was like no way! What are you kidding? No way!…But as time passed and as things turned out, he was pretty into it.

Mr. Dougherty added that it took the evidence of planning present in the students' social networking websites that ultimately convinced him and the rest of the school community of the threat's seriousness. He said:

> The news broke on Wednesday. During that next week, [the change in perception] was almost palpable in the building. The Thursday of that week, it was a joke. It's a joke, it's a joke, it's a joke. By Friday, the next day, it was kind of like you could sense the mood amongst the students and parents change. Because what ended up happening was obviously pretty much every kid and their grandmother went to the MySpace pages because they were still available…So as kids and parents looked at this stuff, by Friday, it was more like, wait, this wasn't a joke. It was palpable, this shift in the attitude of people here in the building.

Thus, the depth of planning evident from the websites convinced not only Mr. Dougherty and the other school officials to take the threat seriously, but the school as a whole. While they were initially more hesitant to see the threat as genuine because of the lack of stereotypical profiling characteristics, the weight of threat assessment criteria (i.e., the intricacy of the students' detailed plot) eventually changed their minds. Despite his initial skepticism, Mr. Dougherty eventually became the most emphatic of all respondents in his confidence regarding the students' intentions. He declared, "I am convinced to my dying day they were going to do something. There is no doubt in my mind."

Remaining Uncertainty Despite Risk Assessment

All of the aforementioned cases and quotations might give the impression that officials gained immense certainty and clarity by pulling from the threat assessment criteria, even if they could put less faith in the consistent validity of profiling stereotypical characteristics. This was not, however, entirely the case. Some school and police officials expressed significant doubt and uncertainty, even in cases with significant evidence of detailed planning and where students had obtained weapons.

For example, Mr. O'Brien, the vice principal at Courtside High School, initially stated that he and his fellow administrators deserved credit for "taking things seriously and investigating fully that led to us averting what could have been another Columbine, if not worse." However, he also gave considerable weight to the fact that the student plotter desperately wanted to get away from a father whom he deeply despised. After noting that his own personal experience meeting the student's father made it very clear how easy it would be to dislike the man, Mr. O'Brien noted that:

> [The accused student] stated to the police that he and his father did not get along. And that he was angry with him, and that's why he stole his gun. As far as we know, psychologically, we know that he had some issues…He didn't want to go home, that was the bottom line. He wanted to continue being placed somewhere, so it kind of goes back to that question about did he really plan on following through with this or was this his way of getting himself out of his house? Who knows what was happening there. So I don't know if he felt desperate enough to actually follow through and shoot some students, or if he was just going to see how far he could go until he got caught because he knew that would get him out of the school. I don't know. I don't really feel like I can say for certain. I know that this kid wanted help.

Thus, as the vice principal considered this alternative motivation for stealing the gun and calling negative attention to himself, he truly struggled with the student's genuine intent. Upon further reflection about the student in question, the vice principal then recalled an interaction that he had during trial proceedings in which the student appeared very apologetic. Mr. O'Brien discussed becoming increasingly uncertain that the student ever genuinely intended to go through with his plan in the first place. He noted that:

> When I was at the trial and the judge basically placed the student after I testified, and I walked by him, he said "I'm sorry for everything, Mr. O'Brien." So for him to say something like that tells me that, if I had to guess, I'd say he wasn't going to follow through, but he was certainly trying to get attention and he got it.

While Mr. O'Brien was not the only official to express doubts and uncertainty about students' ultimate intentions, he was the only one to thoughtfully address possible additional motivations for making a very serious substantive threat.

He was not, however, alone in his belief that expressions of regret might indicate a lack of genuine intent. In the case at Hastings Jr./Sr. High, a guidance counselor at the school, Ms. Hanson, similarly emphasized the important role that she believed remorse played in her determination that the students never would have acted upon their threats. She pointed out that:

> I think the number one thing I look for is if they're remorseful or if they realize what they did was wrong. If they were in my office saying, "yeah, I did it and I'm going to still do it," that would throw up a red flag for me. But these kids were just shocked that they were getting called in for something they didn't really think was going to happen…It was just a couple of kids, wannabes, you know, trying to sound tough…I knew that it wasn't as serious as all the hype, just by talking to them that morning. I think that they knew that it kind of went overboard….I think they just thought they were being cool, making some threats here and there, but I don't think they realized it would turn into a three day shutdown with State Police helicopters landing here.

While expressions of remorse may potentially indicate a lack of intent, this cannot be considered a reliable criterion as numerous perpetrators of completed school rampages have voluntarily expressed regret and publically apologized to their victims and communities (see, for example, Goodrich, 2012; Perez, 2011; Verhovek, 1999).

Conclusion

Ultimately, the threat assessment perspective gave officials the greatest confidence in their judgments deciphering if students intended to carry out their threats. This was demonstrated by the manner in which the greatest certainty abounded in cases where detailed planning and preparation were evident, regardless as to whether or not accused students fit traditional profile characteristics. That said, some officials still lacked full confidence in the infallibility of threat assessment criteria when they perceived alternative motivations for student actions and/or honest displays of regret on the part of students. These empirical findings are significant in revealing how risk assessment is currently understood and conducted in American public schools. However, it is hoped that the other issue to emerge from this research regarding officials' concerns with and hesitations about the certainty of risk assessment will also suggest the need to better comprehend and critically evaluate the purpose and goals of these practices as means of prediction, prevention, and/or punishment.

Risk assessments based upon individual and group characteristics remain controversial among scholars. This is due as much to the inaccuracies prevalent in early profiles and warning signs as to prior unrealistic expectations that any unifying and singular profile could emerge as a means of predicting future behavior. This study indicates that school and police officials generally share such skepticism about predictive profiles and warning signs, for while they may consider the relevance of said traits as a component of their assessments, such criteria was never deemed sufficiently convincing on its own. While few officials were aware of the empirical studies casting doubt on the reliability of school shooter profiles and warning signs, many were cognizant that these descriptions reflect statistical likelihoods rather than predictive certainties. Officials' additional confidence in threat assessment criteria may likewise reflect an aversion for the lofty and problematic objective of predicting school rampage threats and reveal potential opportunities to be found in the more achievable goals of preventing and punishing them. As recent threat assessment scholarship has explicitly addressed the distinctions between these goals, such promising developments warrant discussion.

The first emergent feature of the threat assessment approach is its newfound focus on prevention. All of the prior incarnations of risk assessment, including much of the early work on threat assessment, may be critiqued as a form of "actuarial justice" (Feeley & Simon, 1992, 1994) or what Young (1994) calls "administrative criminology" for being exclusively and perhaps inordinately concerned with the management and control of risky populations over and above the comprehension and alleviation of underlying forces which lead people to engage in violent and threatening behavior in the first place. In contrast, threat assessment scholars have called for a move away from prediction in favor of prevention in violence risk assessment. The former is seen as the ability to correctly estimate which people have the highest probability of being violent under which circumstances, while the latter shifts its emphasis to the most suitable intervention for the particular situation. Randazzo and her colleagues (2006, p. 153) made their case for this change in focus because "by emphasizing prevention as the outcome, the need to provide necessary services takes precedence over the need to be 'right' about whether a given child will become violent." Likewise, in his most recent scholarship, Cornell (2013; Cornell & Sheras, 2006) has argued for a preventative approach to threat assessment, and even developed specific recommendations as to how to go about implementing such a preventative model for student intervention in schools.

Second, as threat assessment is constrained in its application only to those incidents in which individuals communicate threats in advance (Borum, Cornell, Modzeleski, & Jimerson, 2010), its domain is limited to the consideration of comments and actions that have already occurred. Rather than positing that any group of identifying characteristics may be predictive (or even, on a less problematic scale, linked to a greater statistical likelihood) of future violence among populations who have yet to do any actual harm or broken any laws by their broad resemblance to previous offenders, most threat assessment criteria are notable for also being criminal offenses themselves. As Daniels and his colleagues (2007, p. 92) revealed, students accused in these types of cases were often charged with crimes such as making terrorist threats, conspiracy to commit murder or aggravated assault, possession of firearms on school grounds, and interfering with an educational institution. Aside from these, additional charges (whose terms vary by state and thus are not all entirely distinct from those mentioned by Daniels et al., 2007) in my sample included criminal harassment, criminal intent to commit murder, threatening in the first degree, possession of homemade explosives, promotion of anarchy, and conspiracy to commit mass murder. Thus, threat assessment criteria such as communicating threats, forming detailed conspiracies, and weapons possession are all already criminalized, and the consideration of these factors amounts to a step away from the unrealistic aim of predicting the future via an extreme attempt at actuarial justice and toward the more realistic albeit conventional goal of punishing people for past behavior. As Officer Dudley said about one of the students he dealt with at Finley High:

> None of us will know if it ever would have went down, but it certainly had the potential to be a devastation…He deserves what he got because this wasn't just picking on somebody, this was conspiracy, and they terrified the whole school, the whole town.

Officer Dudley felt that while predicting students' ultimate intentions might be impossible, punishment was warranted in this case because of the actions they had already taken. This is not to say that the punishment/crime control paradigm is not without its own share of inherent flaws (Clear, 1994; Menninger, 1968; Western, 2007), but as the threat assessment approach emphasizes taking context and severity into consideration, its widespread adoption could lead to far more logical, proportionate, and equitable punishments and interventions than that of either statistical profiling or uniformly harsh zero-tolerance policies.

Questions for Discussion

1. What form(s) of risk assessment did school and police officials trust the most when determining whether or not students would actually carry out a school rampage attack?
2. If you were working on a case of a school rampage plot, what form(s) of risk assessment do you think would be most important to you in determining whether or not students would actually carry out the attack?
3. Do you think that we can ever be certain as to whether or not someone actually intended to carry out a school rampage attack? If so, how could we know? If not, why not?

References

Borum, R., Cornell, D., Modzeleski, W., & Jimerson, S. (2010). What can be done about school shootings? A review of the evidence. *Educational Researcher, 39*(1), 27–37.

Clear, T. (1994). *Harm in American penology: Offenders, victims, and their communities.* Albany, NY: SUNY Press.

Cornell, D. G. (2013). The Virginia student threat assessment guidelines: An empirically supported violence prevention strategy. In N. Böckler, W. Heitmeyer, P. Sitzer, & T. Seeger (Eds.), *School shootings: International research, case studies, and concepts for prevention* (pp. 379–400). New York, NY: Springer.

Cornell, D. G., & Sheras, P. L. (2006). *Guidelines for responding to student threats of violence.* Longmont, CO: Sopris West.

Daniels, J. A., Buck, I., Croxall, S., Gruber, J., Kime, P., & Govert, H. (2007). A content analysis of news reports of averted school rampages. *Journal of School Violence, 6,* 83–99.

Feeley, M., & Simon, J. (1992). The new penology: Notes on the emerging strategy of corrections and its implications. *Criminology, 30*(4), 449–470.

Feeley, M., & Simon, J. (1994). Actuarial justice: The emerging new criminal law. In D. Nelken (Ed.), *The futures of criminology* (pp. 173–201). London: Sage.

Goodrich, J. (2012, April 11). *Accused gunman in Oakland massacre tells CBS 5 he's "deeply sorry."* Retrieved April 13, 2019, from http://sanfrancisco.cbslocal.com/2012/04/11/exclusive-jailhouse-interview-accused-gunman-in-oakland-massacre-talks-to-cbs-5/.

Menninger, K. (1968). *The crime of punishment.* New York: Penguin Books.

O'Toole, M. E. (2000). *The school shooter: A threat assessment perspective.* Critical Incident Response Group, National Center for the Analysis of Violent Crime, FBI Academy, Quantico, VA. Retrieved July 3, 2019, from https://www.fbi.gov/file-repository/stats-services-publications-school-shooter-school-shooter.

Perez, S. (2011, March 5). *Where is the Santana shooter now?* Retrieved April 13, 2019, from http://santee.patch.com/articles/where-is-the-santana-shooter-now.

Randazzo, M. R., Borum, R., Vossekuil, B., Fein, R., Modzeleski, W., & Pollack, W. (2006). Threat assessment in schools: Empirical support and comparison with other approaches. In S. R. Jimerson & M. J. Furlong (Eds.), *The handbook of school violence and school safety: From research to practice* (pp. 147–156). Mahwah, NJ: Lawrence J. Erlbaum Associates.

Verhovek, S. H. (1999, November 11). *Teenager to spend life in prison for shootings.* Retrieved April 13, 2019, from http://www.nytimes.com/1999/11/11/us/teenager-to-spend-life-in-prison-for-shootings.html?ref=kiplandfkinkel.

Western, B. (2007). *Punishment and inequality in America.* New York: Russell Sage.

Young, J. (1994). Incessant chatter: Recent paradigms in criminology. In M. Maguire, R. Morgan, & R. Reiner (Eds.), *The Oxford handbook of criminology* (pp. 69–124). Oxford: Oxford University Press.

4

Preventing School Rampage Violence Through Student Bystander Intervention and Positive School Environments

The study of averted rampage has clear practical significance. By learning from the numerous instances where school rampage threats came to the attention of authorities and thus were thwarted, there exists the potential for future policies and interventions to be modeled on prior successes. In addition, empirical knowledge about how school rampage incidents have been averted is especially important because many of the most popular and widespread school disciplinary policies and security practices implemented in recent years not only cannot be reliably linked to preventing rampage but also may actually hinder the few preventative measures with an empirical basis.

The findings to follow[1] reveal that it was people coming forward with knowledge about a prospective school rampage that has preempted these potentially deadly occurrences. However, even in many of these successfully averted incidents, numerous student bystanders exposed to threats still did not come forward; those who did were often not close associates or confidants of the accused students, and some of the people who did ultimately come forward did so as a result of being personally threatened or in order to deflect blame away from themselves rather than out of altruistic concern for others. This suggests that schools have not seen as radical a progression away from the student taboo inhibiting information sharing with authorities as previously asserted by scholars, practitioners, and the press. While numerous scholars and many of the school and police officials interviewed in this study acknowledge the important role that encouraging positive student bystander behavior plays in averting school rampage, few recognize how seriously ingrained the code of silence is among students. As a result, this chapter suggests that practitioners and scholars often overstate the degree to which students, after the extensive coverage that the Columbine massacre received, now take the threats of their peers seriously and report them to the authorities. Furthermore, the findings suggest that the lack of positive bystander behavior on the part of students likely reflects increasingly punitive and criminalized school environments that diminish trusting relationships between students and school staff.

School Rampage Violence Prevention and the Student Code of Silence

Since the infamous Columbine massacre, many short-sighted policies have been proposed and implemented in American public schools. The response has generally been to expand punitive disciplinary measures such as zero-tolerance policies, enhance surveillance via security cameras and SRO's, and increase security through target hardening practices such as limited entrances and metal detectors (Muschert & Madfis, 2013). These solutions, however, lack empirical evidence confirming their preventative purpose and amount to short-sighted efforts to alleviate the anxieties of parents, faculty, and students. For example, schools continue to install security cameras and armed security guards specifically to prevent "another Columbine," yet both of these measures were already in place at Columbine High School and did not deter or prevent the killings there (Kupchik & Monahan, 2006, p. 625). Schools across the country now typically lock all but one of their external doors during school hours as a safety precaution, though the mass shooter at Newtown's Sandy Hook Elementary School easily shot through the glass windows at a locked entrance in order to gain entry to the school (Flegenheimer, 2013). Similarly, a rampage killer walked right through the metal detector at Red Lake Senior High School's front entrance. When a security officer confronted him, the perpetrator promptly shot and killed the man (Meloy & O'Toole, 2011). Zero-tolerance policies were embraced widely across the United States by as early as 1993 (Skiba, 2000). However, they did nothing to curb the increased number of multiple-victim shootings that occurred in middle and high schools across the nation in the late 1990s. As Cornell and Sheras (2006; Cornell, 2013) have indicated, excluding students from school through expulsions and suspensions does nothing to resolve student problems or deescalate conflicts, and such punishments have even exacerbated the existing isolation and anger of prior school shooters (Levin & Madfis, 2009; Madfis & Levin, 2013).

Empirical research on averted and completed school rampages, however, has begun to formulate an entirely distinct preventative approach. In her study of targeted school shootings, O'Toole (2000, p. 14) discussed the importance of a concept she named "leakage" that occurs when "a student intentionally or unintentionally reveals clues to feelings, thoughts, fantasies, attitudes, or intentions that may signal an impending violent act. These clues could take the form of subtle threats, boasts, innuendos, predictions, or ultimatums." Vossekuil, Fein, Reddy, Borum, and Modzeleski (2002, p. 25) discovered that at least one person had some previous knowledge about the plans of offenders in 81% of targeted school shooting incidents, while numerous individuals were aware in 59% of their sample. Of those people who possessed this crucial knowledge, 93% were the peers of student perpetrators, such as siblings, schoolmates, or friends (ibid., p. 25). Meanwhile, Gaughan and colleagues' (2001) national report discovered that only 54% of students said that they would inform an adult if they overheard one of their peers planning to shoot someone. These findings amplified discussions about a student "code of silence" which discourages students from coming forward with vital information about the dangerous intentions of their peers (Culley, Conkling, Emshoff, Blakely, & Gorman, 2006; Epstein, 2002; Halbig, 2000; MacDonald & da Costa, 1996; Merida, 1999;

Morris, 2010; Spitalli, 2003; Stancato, 2001; Syvertsen, Flanagan, & Stout, 2009).

The small number of studies that explore how prior incidents of school rampage have been averted (Daniels et al., 2007, 2010; Larkin, 2009; Newman, Fox, Roth, Mehta, & Harding, 2004; Pollack, Modzeleski, & Rooney, 2008) have generally located one common mechanism by which these potentially horrendous tragedies have been thwarted—students breaking through the code of silence to notify school and/or police officials about the violent intentions that prospective school shooters shared with their peers. Accordingly, schools have implemented anonymous e-mail systems and telephone hotlines to mitigate the problematic code of silence (Teicher, 2006; Wilson-Simmons, Dash, Tehranifar, O'Donnell, & Stueve, 2006; Wylie et al., 2010) and employed various bystander prevention programs to encourage students to be more active about reporting problematic behaviors (Lodge & Frydenberg, 2005; Twemlow, Fonagy, & Sacco, 2004). What's more, Larkin (2009) has argued that, in the wake of Columbine, students have become more likely to report violent threats instead of acquiescing to the code of silence. In a *New York Times* interview about an averted rampage attack in 2001, criminologist James Alan Fox stated that "it shows that more and more students are willing to come forward and inform on classmates" and that, while snitching was unacceptable before the Columbine massacre, it is "now O.K., and is often the only thing to do when you can prevent a tragedy to classmates" (Butterfield, 2001). Similarly, in their study of fifteen student bystanders who had previous knowledge of four completed and four averted rampage attacks, Pollack and his colleagues (2008, p. 12) found that numerous students directly characterized the Columbine attack as a "wake-up call" after which threats were taken more seriously by youths increasingly willing to ignore the code of silence and inform authorities. Sharing this view, sociologist Delbert Elliott similarly stated that, "It's a very good sign that the norm around 'snitching' or being a tattle-tale is changing" (McCrimmon, 2009, p. 5).

In addition to the contention that peer pressure prohibiting "snitching" on other students has potentially decreased due, at least in part, to recent incidents of extreme school violence, Pollack et al. (2008)

found that another facet of school culture was influential in determining whether or not students came forward when they were aware of information about threats. This study concluded that bystanders who alerted authorities "were influenced by positive relations with one or more adults, teachers, or staff, and/or a feeling within the school that the information would be taken seriously and addressed appropriately" (ibid., p. 7). Additionally, students who exhibited a disinclination to come forward indicated that they anticipated negative responses from school officials if they were to share information. One student bystander did not come forward because he lacked a positive connection to anyone in a position of authority in the school and commented that he found them "too judgmental," while another student similarly indicated that he didn't tell anyone about the gun he knew was on school property because he anticipated being interrogated or getting into trouble for coming forward (ibid., p. 12). This finding is congruent with plentiful research confirming the positive correlation between trusting, cohesive, and supportive school climates and student willingness to report threats of violence in both middle and high schools (Brank et al., 2007; Brinkley & Saarnio, 2006; Fein et al., 2002; Syvertsen et al., 2009; Wylie et al., 2010) and college and university settings (Sulkowski, 2011).

That said, it has remained unclear to what extent the student code of silence has actually diminished in the post-Columbine era and what role positive bystander behavior and beneficial school climates have played in thwarting school rampage incidents since Columbine. Scholars also lack a clear understanding about the types of relationships that exist between the students who leak threats and those who come forward (as close friends, acquaintances, or strangers), know little about the processes by which students come forward (anonymously or openly), and know almost nothing about which authority figures (such as teachers, administrators, counselors, police officers, etc.) it is whom students confide in when they do reveal information. This chapter explores these questions through the detailed analysis of eleven instances of averted school rampage.

Unlike prior research that has relied upon content analysis of newspapers (Daniels et al., 2007; Larkin, 2009) or interviews with student bystanders (Pollack et al., 2008) or school officials (Daniels et al., 2010), this study entailed triangulating data from legal documents, media accounts, and interviews with school and police officials. Accordingly, I am able to contrast how interested parties explain their perspectives on what led to successfully averted incidents with official documentation from the justice system and news media accounts. Such triangulation was essential as officials' perceptions of events did not always form a consensus with one another, nor with legal documentation or news reporting. While many details described by respondents about the cases can be tested against their colleagues as well as via legal documentation and media reporting, assertions about what occurrences and factors were most crucial in averting potential rampages are inherently subjective and open to interpretation. Thus, while by and large, most respondents involved in the same incident agreed upon the basic elements of their case and how it was prevented generally, several emphasized distinct components as playing the most crucial role in the successful outcome. For example, each of the respondents involved in the averted incident at Finley High School credited their own connection to the case as being a vital factor, if not the crucial determining one. The police officer who arrested these students, Captain Dante, believed that they came forward at least in part as a result of the active shooter drill he conducted a few months before. He noted that "there was a lot of talk of the perpetrators of this crime saying, 'Jeez, the police are prepared for it now. Look what they did'." Finley's Principal, Mr. McGowan, believed the incident was prevented largely because of the trust built between students and staff at a leadership summit he organized, while both an SRO and adjustment counselor at the school discussed the role that rapport with the students played in making them more comfortable coming forward. This is not to say that any of these accounts are necessarily inaccurate, and they may in fact all reflect different elements of the same story. It is, however, important to recognize that all respondents experience events through their own lenses. Therefore, this study's multiple data sources enable a more detailed and nuanced understanding of the role of bystander involvement in preventing school rampage.

Perceiving a Diminished Student Code of Silence Since Columbine

Numerous respondents discussed the student code of silence as a vital factor in rampage violence prevention. Consistent with several scholars (Elliott in McCrimmon, 2009; Fox in Butterfield, 2001; Larkin, 2009; Pollack et al., 2008), this was generally framed in the context of a new post-Columbine era wherein the code had been significantly diminished in response to extreme cases of school violence. For example, the head of school security at Adams High, Mr. Pullman, indicated that:

> I think one of the things that Columbine has done is it has broken in the old adage you know don't rat out your brother kind of a concept. And I think the kids are learning that there is some point when you should be saying something. Obviously, you're never going to get them to say everything, but I think the point has been made about the more important things.

Echoing this idea, Mr. Sacco, Greenvale High's principal, revealed how he believed things had changed since Columbine. He stated that:

> It absolutely made kids much more vigilant about things going on around them…I think it made kids less afraid to speak up if something wasn't sitting right with them. And since that era, I've often had a kid come by, and they're pained and they're tortured because they're thinking about that. They're thinking about could I have been carrying this around for an hour or two hours or three hours, and they'll say, "I've got to tell you this," and so I think that's the real good thing that's happened.

The principal of Blane High School, Mr. Cooper, felt that school lockdown drills, where students practice preparedness for a potential attacker, served to mitigate the code of silence as a reminder of the ever-present risk of school rampage. He asserted that:

> Lockdown drills serve as a reminder to students and staff, and students especially, that, unfortunately, in this day and age, we do need to be ready to try to go into a lockdown. If that helps students to be more aware,

if they see something that doesn't sit right with them, then they might report that to somebody.

Thus, school and police officials repeatedly stated that, in the wake of Columbine, students were far more likely to come forward when they gained knowledge about their peers' intentions to do something harmful or dangerous.

Weakening the Code of Silence Through Positive School Climate

In addition to declaring the significance of Columbine as a watershed event easing the stigma against students coming forward, there was near unanimity about the best methods to weaken the student code of silence; nearly all of the police and school officials articulated a strong belief in fostering supportive, cohesive, and trusting school climates—views very much in line with existing research (Brank et al., 2007; Brinkley & Saarnio, 2006; Fein et al., 2002; Sulkowski, 2011; Syvertsen et al., 2009; Wylie et al., 2010). Nearly without exception, respondents emphasized the significance of creating an atmosphere where "students care about their school" because they "feel involved and part of the community," and "students feel supported" and "know they can trust the adults in the building" because of "predictable and consistent" "close relationships" of "dignity and mutual respect."

This pattern materialized in the abstract, as officials felt confident that a trusting school environment where kids feel safe confiding in the adults in their school building would ultimately mitigate future threats. For example, Kranston High's principal, Mr. Flaherty, said that:

> The best mechanism we have as a deterrent for these sorts of violent acts is good relationships between kids and adults, because kids will tell you. Kids will tell you when something happens. And if they saw a kid with a knife or they heard about it in the locker room… they'll tell you and that's the best security you can have, better than any policeman with a

gun, better than metal detectors, better than locks and cameras. That's the best security…That is the best insurance you could ever buy.

On a more experiential level, this manner of thinking also emerged when officials explained why the specific incidents at their schools were averted. They frequently credited their schools' positive environment with making it easier for student bystanders to come forward with information.

In one instance that demonstrates this typical explanation, the vice principal of Courtside High School, Mr. O'Brien, stated that his current school exhibits a particularly trusting relationship, in contrast to another school he worked at previously, which had "a less respectful and collaborative environment, where what the principal said, goes." Courtside's principal, Mr. Fernandez, similarly emphasized the critical role of school culture when he described why their incident was prevented. He stated that:

> It was the result of a combination of relationships and taking things seriously and investigating fully that led to us averting what could have been another Columbine, if not worse…So the prevention factors were investigating fully and also having…a positive student culture where kids can talk to us and we can talk to them.

Blane High School's school psychologist, Dr. England, shared Mr. Fernandez's belief about the importance of positive relationships between students and school staff. When discussing the incident she dealt with at her school, she shared that:

> What happened was that students came forward and told us about [the threat], so I think the fact that there are connections, such close connections, between administrators and students here that you're much more likely to have students share that kind of information with you.

In addition to generally emphasizing the value of a positive school climate, some officials identified particular key aspects of their schools that helped diminish the code of silence. One Everton High house principal, Mr. Harris, emphasized the positive impact that lower student/faculty ratios and smaller class sizes played in building the sort of trusting environment which ultimately encouraged a student to alert school officials. Mr. Harris pointed out that, "We feel that smaller feel created better relationships for kids at their school and more of a connection and more care for their school. And that led to one student coming forward." Numerous other officials highlighted the rapport that specific individuals, such as certain teachers, SRO's, and counselors, had with students. For example, when Courtside High's Principal Fernandez described the student who revealed information about his friend's plot to his teacher, he discussed the teacher in the following manner:

> The teacher was a favorite among the students. He's a young teacher…And students report that they like this teacher. They know that he works hard for them and that he cares about the school…I mean this is a guy who will volunteer for anything and go anywhere. He's a can-do kind of guy, and I've been able to depend on him for a number of different things. So he gets relationships with the students, and that's why he [the student who came forward] knew that he could trust him to do the right thing or genuinely help him when he shared the information.

Many of the authority figures initially entrusted with crucial information about potential attacks were similarly praised for demonstrating exemplary rapport. A counselor was said to possess a "supportive and caring personality." One SRO was described as follows:

> She was not someone you would think of as a police officer. She handed out lollipops. She was very, very easy to talk to. Not scary in the least bit, not strict and formal as you would assume a police officer to be. So she was very caring and kind and very, very different than what you would assume a school resource officer to be.

Thus, according to the accounts of nearly all of the police and school officials interviewed in this study, the rampage attacks upon their schools were averted principally because of students coming forward due to trusting and supportive school climates where staff had created an inclusive sense of community. Closer scrutiny of the cases themselves, however, reveals a more complex situation and challenges claims about a greatly diminished student code of silence since Columbine.

Breaking the Code of Silence—Interventions Through Leakage

Intervention as a result of leakage took four distinct forms in terms of the ways in which informants came to be aware of crucial information about threats and the types of relationships that existed between informants and the rampage plotters about whom they divulged informed. These categories included bystanders who indirectly gained information from students accused of school rampage schemes, trusted confidants who were informed directly of plans by accused students themselves, targets who were threatened directly by accused students, and co-conspirators who were directly involved, at least at some point and at some level, in the plots themselves. The discourse surrounding student leakage and the code of silence has heretofore only recognized the first two categories of intervention by student bystanders and confidants (though these have not been previously distinguished), and so the characteristics differentiating these groups warrant further clarification.

Indirectly Informed Bystanders

The most common form of intervention, which occurred in five instances (at Everton, Greenvale, Iverson, Jefferson, and Kranston), was through innocent bystanders who were not intentionally entrusted with secretive information by the accused students themselves, but who came to know details about a rampage threat indirectly by inadvertently coming across hit lists, threatening web pages, or intimidating graffiti written on school property. For example, a student and casual acquaintance of the students accused of plotting a rampage attack against Everton High reported the disturbing posts and images on their social network website profiles to the SRO and an assistant principal. The Greenvale case came to light in a fairly analogous way, when numerous students informed school administrators that they observed one of their peers writing what they perceived to be a hit list of names in his notebook. Similarly, at Jefferson Middle School, a teacher notified the school principal after seeing one of her students writing a hit list on a piece of paper at the girl's desk. At Iverson High, a teacher and several students noticed a threatening message scribbled onto a wall in a boys' bathroom stall and informed the school principal. Likewise, Kranston High students noticed a threatening message written on a wall in one of their boys' bathroom stalls, and they informed teachers who in turn told the school principal and SRO.

Directly Informed Confidants

The second most common category of intervention occurred when those coming forward had gained direct information about threats as a result of being confided in by the students accused of plotting attacks. In the averted incident at Adams High, a student who had been sent threatening messages and video clips through the internet informing her of her friend's desire to attack his school led her to tell her mother who then called the local police department. When questioned by police, the accused student confessed his plans to commit a rampage attack and an arsenal of weaponry was discovered in his bedroom. In another case, several Blane High School students came forward to tell administrators that one of their peers had brought explosives to school with him. When school officials later searched this student's backpack, they discovered numerous explosives. Additionally, John, a Courtside High School student, stole guns from his father and gave them to his friend Tim to hold onto until they were needed to carry out the attack. John promised Tim that if he held onto the guns for him, he would not harm Tim or Tim's girlfriend. Tim did ultimately reveal John's plans to his parents. Tim's mother helped Tim get rid of John's weapons by throwing them into a local stream (an act for which she would later be prosecuted herself), and Tim's father later informed the school's principal and vice-principal about John's plans to commit a rampage attack at the school. Shortly after being questioned by the school administrators and denying knowledge about the plot, Tim took it upon himself to tell one of his teachers about his complicity in John's plot. This teacher then immediately informed the school administration. In the case at Finley High, the girlfriend of one of the accused students alerted school officials about the numerous detailed threats made by one of her boyfriend's friends, though she did not come forward until after her boyfriend had already been accused of planning the attack by several of his co-conspirators.

Threatened Targets

A third form of intervention to occur was when people who had been threatened by students came forward to disclose this ominous behavior. Numerous scholars (Pollack et al., 2008; Reddy et al., 2001; Vossekuil et al., 2002) have found that targeted attackers who pose serious risks rarely threaten their victims in advance, but Meloy and his colleagues (2001) found that the majority of the adolescent mass murderers studied in their sample did, in fact, directly threaten their targets before committing crimes. The data in this study revealed two incidents (Donovan and Hastings) in which people who felt directly threatened by interactions with students accused of plotting school attacks alerted authorities to this threatening behavior, though only in the Hastings case did the threatening occur in advance and entail a student coming forward. The Donovan High School students tried and failed to carjack a vehicle, and police later arrested them while they were walking down a street with an arsenal of weapons. It was their potential carjacking victim, an adult stranger with no connection to the students or school, who alerted police. Perhaps as a result of the student code of silence, it is well established that juvenile victims in general are far less likely to report crimes committed against them to police than are adult victims (Watkins, 2005). However, it was one of the numerous students at Hastings Jr./Sr. High School who had been threatened by name on a social networking website by several other students who informed one of his parents of the troubling website exchange. This parent, in turn, called the President of the School Board to express concern.

Involved Co-conspirators

Academic and public discourse has generally neglected to consider the role of co-conspirators who participate in developing a school rampage plot at some point and at some level, but who later come forward to prevent the attack from coming to fruition. The one exception is that of Larkin (2009), who noted that one of the participants in a rampage plot that was averted in New Bedford, Massachusetts in 2001 came forward because she feared for the safety of her favorite teacher. While incidents such as this, where co-conspirators come forward, may be more uncommon than any of the prior categories of intervention through leakage, the incident at Finley High School also followed this pattern. The sequence of events in this case is rather complicated, but as this particular incident seriously complicates and extends existing narratives about student bystander behavior and the code of silence, it warrants extensive elaboration.

The facts of this case begin when Tommy, a Finley student who would later be charged and convicted of conspiracy to commit murder and threatening to use deadly weapons, is discovered hiding a knife from his father during the course of an emotional outburst. Fearing that Tommy is suicidal, his father subsequently has him hospitalized at a psychiatric facility. Matthew, the other student later convicted on conspiracy charges, visits Tommy in the hospital. While there, Matthew becomes convinced that Tommy is being "brainwashed" and has abandoned their joint plan to attack the school along with two other students, Sean and Justin. Matthew makes an angry scene at the hospital in front of Tommy's family and girlfriend. After Tommy is released from the hospital, other students observe a positive change in his behavior. Eventually, Tommy and Matthew get into a fight with one another at a party, and Tommy tells Matthew never to speak to him again. According to Tommy, Tommy also tells Matthew at this time that he hopes someone finds out about Mathew's plot.

Matthew then takes Sean and Justin, the other two student co-conspirators, with him to go speak to the adjustment counselor and later one of the SRO's. Matthew tells both Sean and Justin not to speak during these meetings because he should do the talking, since he knows how to handle cops due to the fact that his father is a police officer. Matthew then tells these school officials that they are all afraid of Tommy, who has been threatening them, mentioning how he wanted to attain weapons and commit a rampage attack against the school. Both Sean and Justin go along with this plan out of fear of Matthew, who had assaulted Sean shortly before this at a party, and also because Matthew had threatened to cut out their tongues if they told anyone. Matthew subsequently blames everything on Tommy, while Sean and Justin concur in relative silence. During this time, Matthew assures Sean and Justin that they will get away with concealing their own involvement, and Matthew destroys evidence linking them to the plot. Police search Tommy's home and find maps of Finley High and lists of weaponry in his bedroom.

Much later, in front of the grand jury, Justin finally has a conversation with police away from Matthew and informs them of Matthew's actual deep involvement in the conspiracy. Sean and Justin are granted immunity in exchange for their testimony in the trial of Tommy. The prosecuting attorneys, arresting officers, SRO's, and adjustment counselor all felt that Matthew went to the police because he believed he might get caught after his relationship with Tommy had deteriorated and he no longer trusted that Tommy would keep silent about their plan. In contrast, Matthew's defense attorneys argued that he abandoned his initial participation in the plot and actually stopped the attack from taking place (though they also denied that any of the accused students ever intended to carry out the attack in the first place). The defense's argument was ultimately unsuccessful in court, and was also not believed by any of the school or police officials interviewed in this study because of the fact that, when Matthew initially came forward, he had clearly lied to everyone in order to hide his true involvement in the plot.

The manner in which this case came to light in order to be averted does not fit in line with the typical rhetoric of an emergent willingness to break the code of silence as a result of Columbine or perhaps a positive school climate. Interestingly, several school officials who handled this case still credited their healthy school environment with how the incident was averted. Mr. McGowan, Finley High's principal, noted that:

The bottom line is, it's about relationships. And when your kids feel comfortable being able to come and talk to you about stuff. We knew about it [the rampage plot] because of what happened in that Leadership Summit, and the fact that that kid trusted [the SRO] because she was with him for those two or three days, and he felt comfortable being able to come and say "I don't know if this is good."

One of the arresting officers in this case, Captain Dante, shared this sentiment. He stated that the school counselor and SRO's:

were close enough with the kids and built a relationship with the kids that they felt like they could sit down and tell them what was going on…when they thought twice, they went to somebody they felt comfortable talking to because they had built a relationship with them. And then I think that's the biggest thing.

However, it was not the case that students ultimately decided to turn to adults whom they trusted and reveal hidden plans to them. In fact, the plotters lied to the school officials they approached when they came forward and denied their own involvement. This was not an example of a trusting environment encouraging innocent bystanders to come forward, but one in which three members of a school rampage conspiracy came forward to inform on the fourth member of their group in order to divert attention and blame away from themselves.

How Interventions Occurred and Who Was Trusted

All available information about these incidents indicates that when people came forward, they did so openly rather than anonymously. To some extent, this may reflect the fact that the incidents under investigation in this study ranged from the years 2000 to 2009 and anonymous reporting systems had only recently been implemented—for example, one of the more prominent anonymous tip lines began serving the state of Colorado in September of 2004 (McMillin, 2009; Payne & Elliott, 2011).

When people did come forward to reveal information to authorities, they were typically students (as in the cases at Adams, Blane, Courtside,

Everton, Finley, Greenvale, Hastings, Iverson, and Kranston), though it was an adult who notified the police at Donovan High and teachers alerted school administration at Iverson and Jefferson. This speaks to Stueve and her colleagues' (2006) call for scholars to expand the definition of bystanders beyond students to include parents, teachers, and school staff members, because they may also possess information about potential violence. In this vein, parents also deserve credit for approaching the authorities in three cases (Adams, Courtside, and Hastings), as students in these cases revealed information to their parents before or instead of school or police officials.

More generally, beyond the three instances where parents were alerted, students informed SRO's in two cases (Everton and Finley), administrators in four cases (Blane, Everton, Greenvale, and Iverson), counselors in one case (Finley), and teachers in two cases (Courtside and Kranston). It is only the instances in which students came forward to school or police officials that technically qualify as breaks in the code of silence. While these criteria apply in seven out of the eleven cases (Blane, Courtside, Everton, Finley, Greenvale, Iverson, and Kranston), the adult victim and teacher involved, respectively, in the cases at Donovan and Jefferson do not qualify, nor do the two instances (Adams and Hastings) in which students informed only their parents rather than school or police officials. This suggests that, in addition to the expanded notion of bystanders proposed by Stueve et al. (2006), perhaps scholars should similarly contemplate whether or not students who reveal information to their parents technically qualify as breaching the code of silence.

Following the Code of Silence—The Persistence of Bystander Inaction

Even in the cases in which some students came forward—and that could subsequently be deemed successes in terms of illustrating positive examples of a broken code of silence—such an unequivocally rosy interpretation oversimplifies the truth. While student bystanders, trusted confidants, and targets deserve credit for individually coming forward and valuing school safety over student norms and concerns about status, positive bystander behavior on the part of a few students often occurred in the larger context of many more students keeping silent about their own knowledge of threats.

The occurrence at Adams High perhaps best illustrates this pattern, for while it is true that a female student is responsible for revealing the threatening behavior of one of her friends by informing her parents and then the police, many more friends and acquaintances of this accused student had been exposed by varying degrees to his disturbing comments and actions. In fact, the accused student in this case, Jessie, leaked various elements of his school rampage plot to a great number of his peers. When later questioned by the police, many of his fellow students acknowledged being aware of his deep fascination with the Columbine attack, as well as guns and explosives more generally. He had posted numerous references to Columbine on his social networking profile page, which many of his friends and school acquaintances read.

Further, several students indicated that he had showed them guns, maps, and/or bombs that he had constructed or detonated at some point prior. Jake, a close friend of the student plotter, said that, after fights with his parents, Jessie made comments about shooting up and using bombs in the high school. Jake added that when Jessie was angry, he would take out all of his knives and guns and lay them out from the smallest to the biggest on his bed. Jake also stated that he saw a map of the high school that Jessie had drawn in his bedroom. Jake said that Jessie discussed an attack once every couple of months, but indicated that he hadn't mentioned it for some time before he was arrested. Tim, another friend of Jessie's, reported that when Jessie got mad, he would sometimes say that he wanted to shoot the kids whose names he had listed on a sheet of paper, but Tim thought Jessie was only joking. Another student, Anthony, said that throughout the previous fall and spring, Jessie sometime talked about how cool it would be if something like Columbine would happen at their high school, and he said that, if it happened there, he hoped that Black and gay people would die. Jessie indicated to Anthony that he would shoot these people if he could, and then he told him that he wanted to shoot up the high school, Columbine style, at the end of their sophomore year. Anthony thought Jessie was joking when he said these things because he would always laugh during or after he said them. Yet another student, Jennifer, said that in the previous spring, Jessie joked that he wanted to bring a gun to school and kill all the kids he hated at lunchtime. She indicated that he brought up this idea of a school shooting many times but always said he was joking. Roughly a month before he got arrested, Jessie said to Jennifer, "Don't go to school tomorrow." When she asked him why, he repeated, "Don't go to school tomorrow. I like you." Jennifer stated that after this exchange, Jessie said that he was only joking, though she later admitted that she understood this to mean that he was talking about committing a Columbine shooting in the future.

As Detective Brown, the SRO directly involved in this incident, commented, "These are all different people, interviewed separately, that are saying the same thing…which makes you wonder why no one said anything." Thus, at least four students entrusted with intimate knowledge about Jesse's intentions as his confidants did not come forward to reveal what they knew until after Jessie had been arrested. When only one in five students (and these four were merely those that the police had extensive knowledge about because they were willing to provide testimony) came forward to the authorities, this is perhaps more of an indication of the continued resilience and power of the student code of silence, rather than a success story of a school somehow breaking through the code via a positive school atmosphere.

Adams High was not alone in illustrating this problematic trend, as many other instances which could potentially be praised for illustrating positive bystander behavior or broken codes of silence actually revealed, upon closer inspection, many more examples of leakage that had gone unnoticed, dismissed, or ignored. One Everton High student came forward to the school's SRO and then to a house principal in order to inform them of his friend's nefarious plans. However, several other students had been asked to join in on the murderous plot; they declined not only to participate in it, but also to inform any adults about its existence.

The four student plotters at Finley High attempted to recruit at least two other students to participate in their conspiracy to attack the school. While these students rejected the offer to join the group of student plotters, none of the reticent would-be recruits ever came forward to reveal what they knew to school or police authorities. One of the SRO's involved in this case, Officer Dudley, stated that:

> We had at least fifteen witnesses that did statements in this case...This evolved from nothing and all of a sudden you've got fifteen kids that knew about this for the last year and a half. And it turned out that a couple of the kids that were key to the verdicts failed to be recruited...and some of those kids turned out to be our best witnesses...But nobody came forward until these boys came forth [to blame their conspiracy on one of their accomplices].

In addition to the students they tried and failed to recruit, one member of the conspiracy also told a female student that if anything were to happen, she would be safe because he considered her a friend, and several other female students were explicitly informed about their plans to shoot up the school without expressly being invited as participants. As previously mentioned, only one of these female students came forward to school officials, and this only took place after initial accusations had already been made.

The Courtside High student plotter intended to tell several of his friends not to go to school on the date he planned to carry out his attack, though it is uncertain how many others knew but did not come forward. Likewise, in the cases at Blane, Greenvale, Hastings, Iverson, and Kranston, some students came forward, but it is uncertain from all available information how many other students knew about these threats or plans in advance who did not do so. At Donovan High and Jefferson Middle School, it was adults rather than students who came forward to alert authorities, and it is also unclear if any student bystanders, confidants, or targets were aware of or subjected to their peers' threats.

Implications of Findings

Ultimately, the findings above confirm previous research and reporting about the manner in which it is people coming forward with important information gained via leakage that leads to rampage attacks being averted. They also reveal that the dominant approach to school violence deterrence via punitive disciplinary policies and enhanced security did not play a prominent preventative role. These events were not deterred due to the presence of metal detectors, locked doors, security cameras, or SRO's. In fact, many of the student plotters considered these developments to be minor stumbling blocks easily resolved through additional preparations among already detailed plans. For example, some plots entailed killing or disarming officers and bringing weapons into the school buildings before entrance doors would be locked for the day. Additionally, though the logic of zero tolerance is similarly deterrence based, wherein strict punishments for threatening behavior or weapons possession in school would dissuade students from these activities, most of the schools where rampages were averted displayed some elements of zero tolerance (though support for the approach varied widely), and all of them were subject to the mandate of the 1994 Gun Free Schools Act wherein bringing a firearm to school warrants a mandatory year long expulsion. Thus, these myriad and copious deterrence-based strategies cannot be credited with thwarting these homicidal threats. However, the data do indicate that SRO's can play a preventative if not deterrent role in averting rampage, as it was SRO's whom students trusted enough to approach in two cases (Everton and Finley, though the latter incident is less indicative of a genuine display of trust), and they did help garner vital confessions from accused students at Adams, Courtside, and Everton.

In addition, the findings suggest that numerous potentially lethal rampage attacks were in fact prevented, at least in part, as a result of school cultures sufficiently positive for students to feel comfortable telling school authorities about threatening behaviors that concerned them. However, school officials at Finley High credited a positive school culture for averting the attack, even though this was undoubtedly not how the incident played out. The same could be said for Adams High, where the head of school security praised his own school's positive school culture, when it was actually a student from another town and school district who actually came forward to the authorities, while none of the students at his school who were exposed to leakage did so. Thus, there may be some tendency on the part of officials to attribute undue credit for averting these incidents to positive school climates.

Certainly, students breaking through the code of silence still constituted the major manner by which most events have been thwarted. That said, close inspection of the details of these cases indicates a murkier and less optimistic picture than the one painted by scholars (Elliott in McCrimmon, 2009; Fox in Butterfield, 2001; Larkin, 2009; Pollack et al., 2008) and generally recognized by the school and police officials interviewed in this study, many of whom agreed that the student code of silence drastically diminished in the wake of numerous highly publicized rampage shooting attacks such as the one at Columbine High School. It seems that both scholars and practitioners came to this conclusion through media reporting (such as Bower, 2001; Butterfield, 2001; Robertson, 2001) upon numerous recent incidents where rampage plots were averted as a result of students coming forward with information gained through leakage. However, by carefully investigating incidents of averted rampage in detail, two distinct elements of the findings of this study suggest previous conclusions based upon superficial accounts in the media are at best premature.

First, those who came forward were not uniformly close friends and confidants of student plotters, as they were also mere acquaintances, the victims of threats, and even the conspirators themselves. MacDonald and da Costa (1996) found that students were more willing to report victimization if the perpetrator was not a friend of theirs, and Pollack and his colleagues (2008, p. 13) noted that one of their student respondents came forward in part because of the fact that "he was not close friends with the potential attackers so that allowed him to be more objective when he learned of a possible attack plan." Thus, it should perhaps not be entirely surprising that authorities are often alerted to the presence of rampage threats by people less close to the accused perpetrators. This does suggest, however, that a student code of silence among close friends remains a significant challenge. Second, this concern about students maintaining secrecy in their most personal friendships is exacerbated by the fact that many of the adolescents exposed to leakage who were the closest to the students accused of plotting attacks did not in fact come forward to authorities. More generally, several cases entailed more students exposed to the leakage of their peers who did not ultimately come forward than the number of students who did in fact do so. Thus, while some scholars and media coverage have depicted even one student who comes forward and has any type of relationship to an accused plotter as evidence that the code of silence has diminished, this narrative is complicated when one considers the actual relationships between student bystanders and plotters as well as the rarely reported on but numerous students who have not come forward even in these averted incidents.

Therefore, if scholars want to interpret these averted incidents as an indication that the student code of silence has diminished, it is worth considering more specific measures or levels of both leakage and, for lack of a better term, code breaking (i.e., positive bystander intervention by students). Meloy and O'Toole (2011, p. 525) suggested that researchers need more sophisticated studies of leakage that explore the various forms it takes in order to ultimately discern which, if any, are the most "predictive of actual targeted violence." In the same way, breaks in the code of silence are not uniform and should not be depicted as such by scholars proclaiming their significance and increased occurrence. It may be the case that students who come to be directly informed of threatening information by their closest friends are exposed to the most profoundly significant form of leakage. It is almost certainly the case, however, that these close confidants who then share that knowledge with authorities engage in a far more substantial breach in the code of silence than students who come forward after being targeted themselves or who only know the students they are accusing as distant acquaintances. Thus, instances in line with the former type (such as at Adams, Blane, and Courtside) constitute a far better indicator of a broken student code of silence than instances of the latter types (such as at Everton, Greenvale, Hastings, Iverson, and Kranston),[2] though all of these latter cases do demonstrate some indication of a willingness to break through the code. At the same time, when only one student comes forward though many more possess information about a threat of violence (as was documented in the Adams and Everton cases), this should not be counted as equivalent evidence of a broken code of silence as would an incident in which multiple or even all students with relevant information came forward. Thus, future scholarship on both leakage and the code of silence must consider these nuanced distinctions in order to properly measure and understand the role that both phenomena play in averting school rampage and other forms of targeted school violence.

Conclusion

The findings of this chapter suggest that, while students' coming forward with important information about threats constitutes the key manner by which rampage attacks are thwarted, a student code of silence persists beyond the previous expectations of academics, police officers, and school officials. This aligns with Wylie and colleagues (2010, p. 351) contention that "[a]lthough policies aimed at improving school climate may increase a student's willingness to report and are important in their own right, improving a school's climate may be a daunting task." Syvertsen and her colleagues (2009, p. 230) point out that decades of bystander research suggests potentially "scores of reasons," aside from strict adherence to a code of silence, which help explain why students do not intervene when confronted with dangerous situations. Bystander scholarship highlights the importance of diffused responsibility, the disinclination to intercede while part of a group because individuals anticipate that others will respond instead (Mathes & Kahn, 1975). As numerous students were aware of the threats made in several of these cases, it is feasible that some students neglected to come forward because they expected their peers to do so. The bystander literature also stresses the role of ambiguity about the situation (Latané & Darley, 1969). Students may not approach adults if they lack certainty about their peers' intentions and interpret legitimate threats as flippant comments or jokes. Though student inaction related to leakage likely results from a combination of these forces (Pollack et al., 2008), and much work remains to be done in the realm of student bystander awareness and education generally, the findings of this chapter reveal an important misunderstanding in how both many practitioners and academics discuss healthy and successful school environments.

Copious empirical evidence (such as Brank et al., 2007; Brinkley & Saarnio, 2006; Eliot, Cornell, Gregory, & Fan, 2010; Fein et al., 2002; Sulkowski, 2011; Syvertsen et al., 2009; Wylie et al., 2010) indicates the relationship between supportive, trusting, and cohesive school climates and positive student bystander behavior. Thus, the problem is not so much that educators and scholars mistake the significance of a beneficial school climate. The problem is that they are largely mischaracterizing the atmosphere of contemporary American public schools. Despite institutional objectives of inclusiveness and the beneficial role of certain especially kind and empathetic school and police officials, any candid examination of recent developments in American schooling reveals a substantial trend away from empathy, inclusivity, and supportiveness, and toward the enhanced security and punitive discipline that Hirschfield and Celinska (2011) call "school criminalization" (see also Hirschfield, 2008; Kupchik, 2010; Kupchik & Monahan, 2006; Lyons & Drew, 2006; Madfis, 2016; Monahan & Torres, 2010; Morris, 2016; Muschert & Peguero, 2010; Nolan, 2011). The increased use of law enforcement personnel, mindsets, and technologies in schools, as well as the increasing transfer of school discipline to the juvenile and criminal justice systems (Advancement Project, 2005; Heitzeg, 2016; Kim, Losen, & Hewitt, 2010; Wald & Losen, 2003), have direct consequences upon the overall school climate. As Casella (2001, p. 35) fittingly described, such "policies…bolster punishment in favor of pedagogy, control in favor of understanding." The result is that many of these features diminish trusting relationships between students and school staff (Lintott, 2004; Noguera, 1995; Watts & Erevelles, 2004).

This lack of trust has direct consequences for the prevention of school rampage. Syvertsen and her colleagues (2009, p. 229) describe the dilemma eloquently when they conclude that:

> In this post-Columbine era, public education has seen an increase in zero tolerance policies…It is possible that these policies create an environment that actually discourages students from revealing their concerns to teachers because of the increased "costs" of revelation…For most adolescents, divulging a peer's confidence is a difficult decision that may be intensified by a zero tolerance climate. As was reflected in our findings,

the more students believed that going to a teacher or principal would result in trouble, the more likely they were to ignore a peer's dangerous plan or to simply tell a friend (but not an adult).

Similarly, Cornell (2013, p. 393) recently explained that, "Students may be more willing to report threats when they see that school authorities are not taking a punitive, zero tolerance approach, but are instead concerned with solving problems and preventing conflicts from escalating into violence."

School criminalization diminishes positive bystander behavior not only as a result of lost trust due to excessive punitiveness, but the perception that such discipline is prejudicial may similarly result in fewer students coming forward. Morris (2010, p. 270) proposed that "if students perceive strict or invasive school discipline as biased, they might resist school authority more vehemently, increasing the social distance between students and the school." It has been widely documented that African American youth are vastly overrepresented in school suspensions and expulsions (Casella, 2001, 2003; Civil Rights Data Collection, 2012; Skiba, Arredondo, Gray, & Rausch, 2018), even when socioeconomic indicators are held constant (Skiba, Michael, Nardo, & Peterson, 2002), and when their punishments are compared directly to white students who committed identical infractions (Fenning & Rose, 2007). Even zero-tolerance policies, formed at least in part with the goal of objectivity in mind, have resulted in disproportionate application toward minority students (Kupchik, 2010; Robbins, 2005). To the extent that students perceive school discipline as fundamentally unjust due to racial prejudice, they will be far less likely to entrust school and police officials with vital but potentially incriminating information.

Consequently, even though many of the recent measures focusing upon punitive discipline and enhanced security were designed specifically to improve school safety in the event of a rampage attack (Madfis, 2016; Muschert & Madfis, 2013), these very practices significantly hinder the one means by which nearly all rampage attacks are actually thwarted—positive bystander behavior on the part of students aware of leakage. Kohn (2004, p. 26) deftly clarifies the most significant point here when he states that such punitive policy "isn't merely ineffective—it's actively counterproductive." Therefore, doing nothing in response to fear of school rampage would have been preferable to many of the authoritarian practices schools have put in place.

In order to prevent future attacks from occurring, schools must abandon these punitive measures and improve upon the means by which these events are actually averted, by forging genuinely positive school climates that encourage student bystanders to intervene in a responsible manner. In this regard, there are numerous emergent approaches to discipline and punishment which may actually improve school climates in exactly the manner necessary to increase trusting relationships between students and school staff, thus potentially resulting in far more positive bystander behavior and accordingly, far less successful incidents of school rampage. Numerous schools across the United States and internationally serve as positive examples of how to utilize the rapidly expanding knowledge from restorative justice in their everyday applications of school discipline through practices of group conferencing, peacemaking and sentencing circles, and victim/offender mediation. In these practices, the conventional goals of deterrence and punitive retribution are replaced by a focus upon the restorative goals of reconciliation, reparation, and transformation (Deakin & Kupchik, 2018; Van Ness & Strong, 2010). In perhaps the most extensive text on the subject of restorative classroom discipline, Meyer and Evans (2012) describe its key characteristics as inclusive and encouraging learning communities that utilize positive behavior management to resolve conflicts, solve problems, and restore harms with clear definitions of appropriate behavior and a consistent application of consequences.

Sherman and Strang (2007) found that, when directly comparing people who received restorative justice interventions to those who did not, victims faired considerably better on a variety of outcomes and offenders demonstrated lower recidivism rates, especially for violent crimes. In addition to these positive outcomes more generally, schools that have implemented restorative practices have seen attendance increase, suspensions and expulsions decline, and even dramatic decreases in bullying and school violence (Karp & Breslin, 2001; Meyer & Evans, 2012; Sumner, Silverman, & Frampton, 2010). These positive outcomes notwithstanding, the crucial element pertaining to the findings of this chapter is the numerous studies which have consistently found that restorative school practices have the ability to strengthen positive school relationships by fostering inclusive school climates, improving student perceptions about the fairness of punishments (i.e. procedural justice), and increasing student trust in school authority figures (McCluskey, 2018; McCluskey et al., 2008; Mirsky, 2003; Morrison, 2007; Sherman & Strang, 2007; Sumner et al., 2010; Youth Justice Board, 2004). These are precisely the sort of outcomes needed in order to minimize the likelihood that marginalized students will feel the sort of extreme exclusion often necessary to build up the desire to commit a rampage attack against their school (Levin & Madfis, 2009). However, even if this improved school climate fails to prevent students from engaging in the planning of homicidal plots, the student peers in these school communities will be far more likely to report any and all information revealed to them through leakage. In fact, one of the very schools investigated for this study, Courtside High School, has recently received a great deal of praise and attention as a leading exemplar of restorative school practices and has experienced both substantial improvements in the school's climate and reductions in disciplinary problems including violence. It is perhaps notable then, that Courtside was highlighted above as an example of the most noteworthy and substantial variety of breaking through the code of silence (i.e., directly informed confidants) when a student divulged his close friend's plot to school authorities.

Thus, as it is crucial to adopt school policies and procedures that encourage positive bystander behavior on the part of students, it is vital for schools to adopt restorative and ameliorative practices in place of the punitive forms of discipline and security that remain currently dominant in American educational institutions. This is essential as the prevailing approach not only fails to prevent and deter school rampage, but the school climates of exclusion, retribution, fear, and mistrust that such policies breed actively discourage positive bystander behavior and permit the student code of silence to persist.

Questions for Discussion

1. How were most school rampage attacks averted?
2. How might we encourage more students to come forward when they are aware of their peers plotting school rampage attacks?
3. What policies, practices, or laws do you think could or should be put into place in order to prevent school rampage killings?

Notes

1. Some sections of this chapter have been substantially revised from an article previously published in the journal *Youth Violence and Juvenile Justice*.
2. The Donovan and Jefferson cases involved adults coming forward rather than students so neither represents a breach in the student code of silence. While the particulars of the Finley case may also disqualify it from counting as an example of breaking the code, the averted New Bedford case indicates that co-conspirators coming forward may still constitute code breaking under some circumstances.

References

Advancement Project. (2005). *Education on lockdown: The schoolhouse to jailhouse track*. Retrieved July 26, 2019, from https://b.3cdn.net/advancement/5351180e24cb166d02_mlbrqgxlh.pdf.

Bower, A. (2001). Scorecard of hatred. *Time Magazine*. Retrieved July 25, 2019, from http://www.time.com/time/magazine/article/0,9171,999476,00.html.

Brank, E. M., Woolard, J. L., Brown, V. E., Fondacaro, M., Luescher, J. L., Chinn, R. G., & Miller, S. A. (2007). Will they tell? Weapons reporting by middle-school youth. *Youth Violence and Juvenile Justice, 5*(2), 125–146.

Brinkley, C. J., & Saarnio, D. A. (2006). Involving students in school violence prevention: Are they willing to help? *Journal of School Violence, 5*, 93–116.

Butterfield, F. with McFadden, R. (2001, November 26). *3 teenagers held in plot at Massachusetts school*. Retrieved July 24, 2019, from http://www.nytimes.com/2001/11/26/us/3-teenagers-held-in-plot-at-massachusetts-school.html.

Casella, R. (2001). *Being down: Challenging violence in urban schools*. New York: Teachers College Press.

Casella, R. (2003). The false allure of security technologies. *Social Justice, 30*(3), 82–93.

Civil Rights Data Collection. (2012). *U.S. Dept. of Education Office for Civil Rights*. Retrieved May 26, 2019, from http://www2.ed.gov/about/offices/list/ocr/docs/crdc-2012-data-summary.pdf.

Cornell, D. G. (2013). The Virginia student threat assessment guidelines: An empirically supported violence prevention strategy. In N. Böckler, W. Heitmeyer, P. Sitzer, & T. Seeger (Eds.), *School shootings: International research, case studies, and concepts for prevention* (pp. 379–400). New York, NY: Springer.

Cornell, D. G., & Sheras, P. L. (2006). *Guidelines for responding to student threats of violence*. Longmont, CO: Sopris West.

Culley, M. R., Conkling, M., Emshoff, J., Blakely, C., & Gorman, D. (2006). Environmental and contextual influences on school violence and its prevention. *The Journal of Primary Prevention, 27*(3), 217–227.

Daniels, J. A., Buck, I., Croxall, S., Gruber, J., Kime, P., & Govert, H. (2007). A content analysis of news reports of averted school rampages. *Journal of School Violence, 6*, 83–99.

Daniels, J. A., Volungis, A., Pshenishny, E., Gandhi, P., Winkler, A., Cramer, D., & Bradley, M. C. (2010). A qualitative investigation of averted school shooting rampages. *The Counseling Psychologist, 38*(1), 69–95.

Deakin, J., & Kupchik, A. (2018). Managing behavior: From exclusion to restorative practices. In J. Deakin, E. Taylor, & A. Kupchik (Eds.), *The Palgrave international handbook of school discipline, surveillance, and social control* (pp. 511–527). New York, NY: Palgrave Macmillan.

Eliot, M., Cornell, D., Gregory, A., & Fan, X. (2010). Supportive school climate and student willingness to seek help for bullying and threats of violence. *Journal of School Psychology, 48*(6), 533–553.

Epstein, J. (2002). Breaking the code of silence: Bystanders to campus violence and the law of college and university safety. *Stetson Law Review, 32*, 91–124.

Fein, R. A., Vossekuil, B., Pollack, W., Borum, R., Modzeleski, W., & Reddy, M. (2002). *Threat assessment in schools: A guide to managing threatening situations and to creating safe school climates*. Washington, DC: U.S. Department of Education, Office of Elementary and Secondary Education, Safe and Drug-Free Schools Program and U.S. Secret Service, National Threat Assessment Center.

Fenning, P., & Rose, J. (2007). Overrepresentation of African American students in exclusionary discipline: The role of school policy. *Urban Education, 42*(6), 536–559.

Flegenheimer, M. (2013). Final report on Sandy Hook killings sheds new light on gunman's isolation. *The New York Times*. Retrieved February 1, 2019, from http://www.nytimes.com/2013/12/28/nyregion/with-release-of-final-sandy-hook-shooting-report-investigation-is-said-to-be-over.html?pagewanted=1&_r=1&.

Gaughan, E., Cerio, J. D., & Myers, R. A. (2001). *Lethal violence in schools: A national survey*. Alfred, NY: Alfred University.

Halbig, W. W. (2000). Breaking the code of silence. *American School Board Journal, 187*(3), 34–36.

Heitzeg, N. A. (2016). *The school-to-prison pipeline: Education, discipline, and racialized double standards*. Santa Barbara, CA: Praeger.

Hirschfield, P. J. (2008). Preparing for prison? The criminalization of school discipline in the USA. *Theoretical Criminology, 12*(1), 79–101.

Hirschfield, P. J., & Celinska, K. (2011). Beyond fear: Sociological perspectives on the criminalization of school discipline. *Sociology Compass, 5*(1), 1–12.

Karp, D. R., & Breslin, B. (2001). Restorative justice in school communities. *Youth & Society, 33*(2), 249–272.

Kim, C., Losen, D., & Hewitt, D. (2010). *The school-to-prison pipeline: Structuring legal reform*. New York: New York University Press.

Kohn, A. (2004). Rebuilding school culture to make schools safer. *The Education Digest, 70*(3), 23–30.

Kupchik, A. (2010). *Homeroom security: School discipline in an age of fear*. New York: New York University Press.

Kupchik, A., & Monahan, T. (2006). The new American school: Preparation for post-industrial discipline. *British Journal of Sociology of Education, 27*(5), 617–631.

Larkin, R. W. (2009). The Columbine legacy: Rampage shootings as political acts. *American Behavioral Scientist, 52*(9), 1309–1326.

Latané, B., & Darley, J. M. (1969). Bystander "apathy". *American Scientist, 57*, 244–268.

Levin, J., & Madfis, E. (2009). Mass murder at school and cumulative strain: A sequential model. *American Behavioral Scientist, 52*(9), 1227–1245.

Lintott, J. (2004). Teaching and learning in the face of school violence. *Georgetown Journal on Poverty Law & Policy, 11*(3), 553–580.

Lodge, J., & Frydenberg, E. (2005). The role of peer bystanders in school bullying: Positive steps toward promoting peaceful schools. *Theory into Practice, 44*(4), 329–336.

Lyons, W., & Drew, J. (2006). *Punishing schools: Fear and citizenship in American public education.* Ann Arbor, MI: University of Michigan Press.

MacDonald, I. M., & da Costa, J. L. (1996). *Exploring issues of school violence: The "code of silence."* Paper presented at the conference of the Canadian Association for the Study of Educational Administration, St. Catherines, ON, Canada.

Madfis, E. (2016). "It's better to overreact": School officials' fear and perceived risk of rampage attacks and the criminalization of American public schools. *Critical Criminology, 24*(1), 39–55.

Madfis, E., & Levin, J. (2013). School rampage in international perspective: The salience of cumulative strain theory. In N. Böckler, W. Heitmeyer, P. Sitzer, & T. Seeger (Eds.), *School shootings: International research, case studies, and concepts for prevention* (pp. 79–104). New York, NY: Springer.

Mathes, E. W., & Kahn, A. (1975). Diffusion of responsibility and extreme behavior. *Journal of Personality and Social Psychology, 31*(5), 881–886.

McCluskey, G. (2018). Restorative approaches in schools: Current practices, future directions. In J. Deakin, E. Taylor, & A. Kupchik (Eds.), *The Palgrave international handbook of school discipline, surveillance, and social control* (pp. 573–593). New York, NY: Palgrave Macmillan.

McCluskey, G., Lloyd, G., Kane, J., Riddell, S., Stead, J., & Weedon, E. (2008). Can restorative practices in schools make a difference? *Educational Review, 60*(4), 405–417.

McCrimmon, K. K. (2009). *The story of Safe2Tell.* Denver, CO: The Colorado Trust. Retrieved May 23, 2012, from http://safe2tell.org/wp-content/uploads/2009/03/storys2t.pdf.

McMillin, S. (2009, April 18). *Getting teens to talk may be key to secure schools.* Retrieved May 23, 2019, from https://gazette.com/news/getting-teens-to-talk-may-be-key-to-secure-schools/article_11a0709c-80a6-5391-ab09-50755353d880.html.

Meloy, J. R., Hempel, A. G., Mohandie, K., Shiva, A. A., & Gray, B. T. (2001). Offender and offense characteristics of a nonrandom sample of adolescent mass murders. *Journal of the American Academy of Child and Adolescent Psychiatry, 40*(6), 719–728.

Meloy, J. R., & O'Toole, M. E. (2011). The concept of leakage in threat assessment. *Behavioral Sciences and the Law, 29,* 513–527.

Merida, K. (1999, April 27). Fearful kids maintain code of silence. *Washington Post*. Retrieved May 3, 2019, from http://www.washingtonpost.com/wp-srv/national/daily/april99/snitch042799.htm.

Meyer, L. H., & Evans, I. M. (2012). *The teacher's guide to restorative classroom discipline*. Thousand Oaks, CA: Sage.

Mirsky, L. (2003). *SaferSanerSchools: Transforming school culture with restorative practices*. International Institute for Restorative Practices. Retrieved February 18, 2019, from http://www.iirp.edu/pdf/ssspilots.pdf.

Monahan, T., & Torres, R. D. (Eds.). (2010). *Schools under surveillance: Cultures of control in public education*. New Brunswick, NJ: Rutgers University Press.

Morris, E. W. (2010). "Snitches end up in ditches" and other cautionary tales. *Journal of Contemporary Criminal Justice, 26*(3), 254–272.

Morris, M. W. (2016). *Pushout: The criminalization of Black girls in schools*. New York, NY: The New Press.

Morrison, B. (2007). *Restoring safe school communities: A whole school response to bullying, violence and alienation*. Sidney, Australia: Federation Press.

Muschert, G. W., & Madfis, E. (2013). Fear of school violence in the post-Columbine era. In G. W. Muschert, S. Henry, N. L. Bracy, & A. A. Peguero (Eds.), *Responding to school violence: Confronting the Columbine effect* (pp. 13–34). Boulder, CO: Lynne Rienner.

Muschert, G. W., & Peguero, A. A. (2010). The Columbine effect and school anti-violence policy. *Research in Social Problems and Public Policy, 17*, 117–148.

Newman, K. S., Fox, C., Roth, W., Mehta, J., & Harding, D. (2004). *Rampage: The social roots of school shooters*. New York: Perseus Books.

Noguera, P. A. (1995). Preventing and producing violence: A critical analysis of responses to school violence. *Harvard Education Review, 65*(2), 189–212.

Nolan, K. (2011). *Police in the hallways: Discipline in an urban school*. Minneapolis: University of Minnesota Press.

O'Toole, M. E. (2000). *The school shooter: A threat assessment perspective*. Critical Incident Response Group, National Center for the Analysis of Violent Crime, FBI Academy, Quantico, VA. Retrieved July 3, 2019, from https://www.fbi.gov/file-repository/stats-services-publications-school-shooter-school-shooter.

Payne, S., & Elliott, D. S. (2011). Safe2Tell®: An anonymous, 24/7 reporting system for preventing school violence. *New Directions in Youth Development, 129*, 103–111.

Pollack, W. S., Modzeleski, W., & Rooney, G. (2008). *Prior knowledge of potential school-based violence: Information students learn may prevent a targeted attack.* Washington, DC: United States Secret Service and United States Department of Education.

Reddy, M., Borum, R., Berglund, J., Vossekuil, B., Fein, R., & Modzeleski, W. (2001). Evaluating risk for targeted violence in schools: Comparing risk assessment, threat assessment, and other approaches. *Psychology in the Schools, 38*(2), 157–172.

Robbins, C. (2005). Zero tolerance and the politics of racial injustice. *The Journal of Negro Education, 74*(1), 2–17.

Robertson, T. (2001, December 16). Across the nation, school attack plots pose legal challenge. *Boston Globe*, pp. A1, A26.

Sherman, L. W., & Strang, H. (2007). *Restorative justice: The evidence.* London: The Smith Institute.

Skiba, R. (2000). *Zero tolerance, zero evidence: An analysis of school disciplinary practice.* Policy Research Report. Indiana Education Policy Center.

Skiba, R., Arredondo, M. I., Gray, C., & Rausch, M. K. (2018). Discipline disparities: New and emerging research in the United States. In J. Deakin, E. Taylor, & A. Kupchik (Eds.), *The Palgrave international handbook of school discipline, surveillance, and social control* (pp. 235–252). New York, NY: Palgrave Macmillan.

Skiba, R., Michael, R. S., Nardo, A. C., & Peterson, R. L. (2002). The color of discipline: Source of racial and gender disproportionality in school punishment. *The Urban Review, 34*(4), 317–342.

Spitalli, S. J. (2003). Breaking the code of silence. *American School Board Journal, 190*(9), 56–58.

Stancato, F. A. (2001). The Columbine tragedy: Adolescent identity and future recommendations. *The Clearing House, 77*(1), 19–22.

Stueve, A., Dash, K., O'Donnell, L., Tehranifar, P., Wilson-Simmons, R., Slaby, R. G., & Link, B. G. (2006). Rethinking the bystander role in school violence prevention. *Health Promotion Practice, 7*(1), 117–124.

Sulkowski, M. L. (2011). An investigation of students' willingness to report threats of violence in campus communities. *Psychology of Violence, 1*(1), 53–65.

Sumner, M. D., Silverman, C. J., & Frampton, M. L. (2010). *School-based restorative justice as an alternative to zero-tolerance policies: Lessons from West Oakland.* Henderson Center for Social Justice, University of California, Berkeley, School of Law.

Syvertsen, A. K., Flanagan, C. A., & Stout, M. D. (2009). Code of silence: Students' perceptions of school climate and willingness to intervene in a peer's dangerous plan. *Journal of Educational Psychology, 101*(1), 219–232.

Teicher, S. A. (2006, October 19). How students can break the 'code of silence': A number of resources let students anonymously voice their concerns about troubling issues at school. *The Christian Science Monitor*. Received April 13, 2019, from http://www.csmonitor.com/2006/1019/p15s01-legn.html.

Twemlow, S. W., Fonagy, P., & Sacco, F. C. (2004). The role of the bystander in the social architecture of bullying and violence in schools and communities. *Annals of the New York Academy of Sciences, 1036*, 215–232.

Van Ness, D. W., & Strong, K. H. (2010). *Restoring justice: An introduction to restorative justice*. New Providence, NJ: Anderson.

Vossekuil, B., Fein, R., Reddy, M., Borum, R., & Modzeleski, W. (2002). *The final report and findings of the safe school initiative: Implications for the prevention of school attacks in the United States*. Washington, DC: U.S. Secret Service and U.S. Department of Education.

Wald, J., & Losen, D. J. (2003). Editors' notes. In J. Wald & D. J. Losen (Eds.), *New directions for youth development: Deconstructing the school-to-prison pipeline* (pp. 1–2). San Francisco, CA: Jossey-Bass.

Watkins, A. M. (2005). Examining the disparity between juvenile and adult victims in notifying the police: A study of mediating variables. *Journal of Research in Crime and Delinquency, 42*(3), 333–353.

Watts, I. E., & Erevelles, N. (2004). These deadly times: Reconceptualizing school violence by using critical race theory and disability studies. *American Educational Research Journal, 41*(2), 271–299.

Wilson-Simmons, R., Dash, K., Tehranifar, P., O'Donnell, L., & Stueve, A. (2006). What can student bystanders do to prevent school violence? Perceptions of students and staff. *Journal of School Violence, 5*(1), 43–62.

Wylie, L. E., Gibson, C. L., Brank, E. M., Fondacaro, M. R., Smith, S. W., Brown, V. E., & Miller, S. A. (2010). Assessing school and student predictors of weapons reporting. *Youth Violence and Juvenile Justice, 8*(4), 351–372.

Youth Justice Board. (2004). *National evaluation of the restorative justice in schools programme*. Retrieved July 17, 2019, from http://www.creducation.net/resources/National_Eval_RJ_in_Schools_Full.pdf.

5

Summary of Findings, Policy Implications, and Future Research

Through in-depth interviews with school and police officials (administrators, counselors, security and police officers, and teachers) as well as content analysis of news reporting and legal documentation covering eleven averted incidents of school rampage in the Northeastern United States, this study has explored perceptions of and reactions to threats of multiple-victim school attacks. Given the dearth of empirical scholarship on averted incidents of school rampage killing, this research unearths important data on the process by which threats of rampage violence are assessed and how previous school rampage plots have been averted.

This study furnishes valuable insight into the institutional cultures and policies conducive to the effective obstruction of rampage attacks. Subsequently, this research reveals the significant shortcomings and sometimes harmful consequences of contemporary risk assessment, violence prevention, and punishment practices prominent in American schools. By examining averted incidents, this work addresses problematic gaps in school violence scholarship and advances existing knowledge about mass murder, violence prevention, bystander intervention, risk assessment, and disciplinary policy in school contexts.

Summary and Implications of Findings

The initial data chapter, Chapter 2, contributes to the literature on violence risk assessment in at least two distinct ways. First, the in-depth analysis of eleven incidents reveals great diversity among even this limited sample, and thus indicates the dire need for future scholars to adopt clearer distinctions and stricter operationalizations when using terms such as "threat," "risk," "plot," and especially when characterizing any event as "averted." Secondly, the findings showcase the wide-ranging manner by which school and police officials make discretionary decisions about how to assess the severity of student threats. Assessment criteria entail how detailed a plot was (including who was to be purposely targeted, what locations were to be attacked in what order, and when the attacks were to take place), the role of weaponry (such as the existent, potential, or desired access to weapons, evidence of weapons training or manufacture, and threats specifically mentioning the use of weapons), individual traits (including ethnic/racial and gender identity as well as previous behavior and mental health concerns), and group characteristics (specifically school social status and affiliations with deviant subcultures). The fact that some of these criteria are substantially more supported with empirical evidence than others reveals a clear need for increased education and programming to better inform school and police officials about the best practices of violence risk assessment.

Chapter 3 explores which forms of risk assessment provide school and police officials with the most confidence in their determinations. Though numerous respondents did believe in and utilize some problematic and stereotypical profiling characteristics to help them make decisions, they ultimately placed their greatest confidence in threat assessment criteria, such as evidence of detailed planning and preparation to commit an attack. Many previous studies have revealed the empirical successes that the threat assessment approach has demonstrated in the appraisal of targeted violence threats over other forms of risk assessment (Borum, Cornell, Modzeleski, & Jimerson, 2010; Cornell, 2013; Reddy et al., 2001). This finding suggests that, additionally, threat assessment may also be credited for an intuitive appeal which leaves officials more confident that justice has been properly served than is the case when the

5 Summary of Findings, Policy Implications, and Future Research

same officials rely upon comparatively more nebulous forms of statistical prediction through identifying profiles.

In the fourth chapter, close scrutiny of the eleven averted incidents indicates that both scholars and educational practitioners overestimate the extent to which the student code of silence has actually been diminished post-Columbine. This does nothing, however, to lessen the perhaps more significant emergent finding that it is most frequently students coming forward with knowledge about their peers' violent intentions that has led to rampage attacks being averted. This has considerable implications for the future administration of school safety in that, while some schools have adopted bystander intervention programs and enacted anonymous tip lines, these solutions have largely taken a back seat to more punitive disciplinary policies and enhanced security measures. As zero-tolerance policies, metal detectors, surveillance cameras, and other law enforcement solutions cannot be credited with either deterring or preventing the crimes in these cases from being planned let alone committed, their utility and prevalence warrants serious reconsideration. Additionally, as restorative approaches to school discipline have been shown not only to reduce violence but to improve school climate in a way which encourages students to come forward to authorities when they have been entrusted with crucial information about an impending attack, such alternatives warrant far more consideration, and ideally, widespread adoption.

The data, taken as a whole, result in numerous significant implications. First, when officials in districts with relatively low rates of crime and violence overestimate the occurrence and likelihood of school rampage and base broad policy decisions on these devastating events, their risk calculation is not only statistically inaccurate but rhetorically dishonest. The public, including school and police officials but also students and parents, ought to be engaging in a debate over whether or not the negative aspects of punitive zero-tolerance policies and enhanced security (such as changes to the school atmosphere as an educational institution, potential violations of students' civil liberties, expenditures of limited resources for security personnel and technology, etc.) are worth the benefits of reducing or preventing typical and relatively minor student misbehavior, rather than having to conduct a cost–benefit analysis where one side of the equation is characterized in such a radically skewed manner (i.e., the cost of not adopting law enforcement and other punitive solutions in schools will immanently result in multiple students deaths).

Secondly, the findings of Chapter 4 amplify such concerns over a school safety discourse disconnected from rampage prevention policies that have an empirical basis. Not only did the aforementioned punitive measures not play a decisive preventative role in the eleven incidents under investigation in this study, but multiple prior studies suggest that these measures negatively impact the most common means by which school rampages are actually prevented by making students less trustful of adult authority figures and thus less likely to come forward when they possess knowledge about potentially dangerous situations.

At the same time, the findings of this study also necessitate careful consideration of the potentially negative consequences to occur if the student code of silence were to entirely dissolve. While a broken or at least diminished student code of silence may mean that numerous future plots will be brought to the attention of authorities and preempted, it also may carry with it a problematic effect on the overall school environment. It is vital that genuine substantial threats are taken seriously, but a suspicious and fearful school culture that overestimates the likelihood and normalcy of rampage violence threats, and encourages students and teachers to come forward with even minor concerns about students' dangerous thoughts, questionable actions, and overall violence potential, amounts to a rather unwelcoming learning environment.

The academic conversation on school criminalization, while notable for its critique of expanding forms of directly oppressive surveillance and punishment, neglects, by and large, to consider the ways in which evolving school violence prevention practices also encourage informal and indirect types of coercive control, in particular, the governing of conduct via student surveillance of themselves and their peers. With regard to this development, Foucault's scholarship proves extremely enlightening. Foucault (1977) famously argued that societies would ultimately move away from formal institutions of social control and toward less official but more omnipresent informal varieties of surveillance and coercion. The main thrust of this proposition has yet to prove accurate, as recent decades have seen rapidly expanded levels of incarceration in general

(Alexander, 2010; Beckett, Beach, Knaphus, & Reosti, 2018; Pattillo, Weiman, & Western, 2004) and, in the school setting, the advent of a "school-to-prison pipeline" in which school misbehavior is punished through the juvenile and criminal justice systems rather than in the educational system (Advancement Project, 2005; Heitzeg, 2016; Kim, Losen, & Hewitt, 2010; King, Rusoja, & Peguero, 2018; Wald & Losen, 2003). Despite this, Foucault's later work (1980, 1991) has been utilized in recent discussions of the sociology of risk to explain how individuals come to take the task of surveillance upon themselves in order to regulate and manage their own behavior and that of others (Mythen, 2008). In particular, his argument regarding the ubiquity of more subtle and coercive forms of control and surveillance is extremely relevant in understanding the potential drawbacks should the student code of silence dissipate in the context of exaggerated risk perception regarding school rampage.

For example, a controversy at a Kansas high school revealed the potential problems of a risk discourse which over-anticipates rampage violence and consequently encourages students to inform school and police authorities of any potential knowledge about a hypothetical threat. When a student with a grudge against five of his classmates falsely claimed that they planned to shoot up their school, this student's bogus story was widely believed by school authorities, though not by the majority of the student body, and all five supposed plotters were arrested (Logan, 2002). More recently, in the wake of a school shooting in Chardon, Ohio on February 27, 2012, rumors widely circulated among high school students from another Ohio town that accused one bullied teenager of planning to bring a gun to school on the following day, which would have marked one week after the Chardon shooting. Though this led police to search the boy's home and caused half of the student body to be absent on the day in question, it was ultimately determined that he was entirely innocent (Leitsinger, 2012). Emergent developments such as anonymous tip lines may, one the one hand, more easily side-step concerns with the student code of silence, but they may also lead to many more instances of false accusations.

Encouraging both students to break through the code of silence and school and police officials to take students seriously when they do come forward is certainly a more productive and empirically driven approach than reactionary measures such as zero-tolerance policies, security cameras, and metal detectors. However, even this reaction may present some troubling manifestations where peers are less trusting of one another, false accusations become prevalent, and relatively benign comments on the part of students may be misinterpreted and subjected to overzealous scrutiny. That said, if we collectively reject the pessimistic view of actuarial justice that school rampage violence is an inevitable phenomenon, then perhaps we can broadly implement restorative approaches toward negotiating conflicts and dealing with student misbehavior in order to create inclusive and supportive schools and even begin to envision a larger society which adopts broad-based ameliorative solutions to the original social strains leading to these conflicts and misbehaviors in the first place.

Other Emergent Areas to Help Prevent and Stop School Rampage Killing

The phenomenon of school rampage killing has a longer history than most people realize, as documented cases in the United States date back to at least 1966, when a student killed and injured dozens of people during an attack on the campus of the University of Texas-Austin. However, recent highly-publicized tragedies over the last few decades (such as those at Colorado's Columbine High School in 1999, Connecticut's Sandy Hook Elementary School in 2012, Florida's Marjory Stoneman Douglas High School in 2018, and Texas' Santa Fe High School in 2018) have significantly increased media and public awareness about these types of events. Over the last twenty years, considerable empirical scholarship on school shootings and other rampage attacks has been conducted (see Böckler, Heitmeyer, Sitzer, & Seeger, 2013; Madfis, 2017; Muschert, 2007; Rocque, 2012; Sommer, Leuschner, & Scheithauer, 2014 for reviews of this literature), yet this budding field of research has infrequently guided public conversations and the enhanced awareness and growing fear of school violence has too rarely come alongside accurate systematic information or insightful solutions.

5 Summary of Findings, Policy Implications, and Future Research

One of the student survivors of the massacre at Marjory Stoneman Douglas High School in Parkland, Florida, Emma Gonzalez, recently characterized this very conundrum in perhaps the most concise and eloquent way. Addressing a rally in an impassioned speech days after a gunman entered her Florida school and killed 17 people, she stated the following:

> The people in the government who were voted into power are lying to us. And us kids seem to be the only ones who notice and our parents to call BS. Companies trying to make caricatures of the teenagers these days, saying that all we are self-involved and trend-obsessed and they hush us into submission when our message doesn't reach the ears of the nation, we are prepared to call BS. Politicians who sit in their gilded House and Senate seats funded by the NRA telling us nothing could have been done to prevent this, we call BS. They say tougher guns laws do not decrease gun violence. We call BS. They say a good guy with a gun stops a bad guy with a gun. We call BS. They say guns are just tools like knives and are as dangerous as cars. We call BS. They say no laws could have prevented the hundreds of senseless tragedies that have occurred. We call BS. That us kids don't know what we're talking about, that we're too young to understand how the government works. We call BS.

This is a remarkably insightful and useful frame of reference for discussing contemporary school rampage prevention policies and practices—much of which is largely nothing more than misinformed BS. This is certainly true regarding aspects of the hotly contested debate over gun control and gun rights in the United States, but there is a great deal of public policy, media strategy, and legal reform more broadly which could be implemented to vastly reduce school and other mass shootings. Debates on school safety and violence are often devoid of empirical evidence. Most proposed solutions may temporarily satiate fear and provide the superficial feeling of improved safety, but they are typically more security theater than genuinely preventative. And it is no coincidence that many of the most frequently proposed solutions (such as adding more security to schools, expelling and incarcerating more students, or allowing more faculty to buy and bring more firearms to school grounds) coincide with profit-making opportunities for powerful lobbying interests like surveillance films, private prisons and detention centers, and firearm manufacturers.

The conversations around reducing school violence rarely attempt to address or mitigate more fundamental deep-seeded issues at the root of this social problem. In fact, as the data from this book reveal, much of what schools have done over the course of the last two decades to deal with school attacks (such as amplifying security and increasing harsh discipline) actually make these types of deadly massacres more likely to occur, as they reduce the likelihood of students coming forward due to the punitive school environment that such measures create. In contrast, it is crucial to focus our collective energy toward debunking false and harmful claims about the causes of and solutions to school violence, to understand and disseminate empirically proven solutions that can actually prevent and thwart future attacks, and to build broad political will to enact truly transformative policies and practices in schools, communities, and throughout society.

In the interest of working toward more empirically based solutions, some new and emergent areas of research to help prevent and stop school rampage killing are worth highlighting. The sections to follow will explore key developing policies and scholarship on access to firearms and on media coverage as they relate to rampage attacks in schools.

Access to Firearms in the United States

The United States has the highest gun ownership rate in the world, as Americans are estimated to own roughly 45% of the word's guns. In fact, there are more guns than people currently living in the United States (Lopez, 2018). Guns are deeply ingrained in American culture, and this colors how policy-makers and the public conceive of and respond to mass killings in schools.

Despite the current spate of highly publicized and particularly deadly incidents of mass shootings in the last few years (Lankford, Adkins, & Madfis, 2019), the only recent successful gun control law put into place at the federal level has been a ban on bump stocks, which are devices that attach to the end of a semiautomatic rifle in order to make it fire more rapidly, approaching the speed of a fully automatic weapon. As this device helped facilitate the death of 58 people and injuries to another 422 during the Harvest music festival in Las Vegas on October 1, 2017, the Department of Justice under the Trump Administration reclassified bump stocks as "machineguns," thus making them illegal to possess or transfer as of March 26, 2019 (Owen, 2019; Savage, 2018).

More broadly, however, the debate over gun control and gun rights remains hotly contested in the politically polarized United States. Some gun control adherents have suggested universal background checks of all gun sales (including currently exempted private sales and sales at gun shows), an assault weapons ban like that which was in place between 1994 and 2004, and bans of high-capacity magazines to decrease the number of fatalities mass shooters could inflict by forcing them to reload more frequently (at which point, bystanders count mount a counter-attack upon the reloading shooter) (Cranley, 2019). These approaches are widely and increasingly popular with the American public (Shepard, 2018), though the current political landscape and impact of powerful lobbying groups makes enacting such policies unlikely at the federal level.

In contrast, there has been some recent bipartisan traction on gun violence restraining orders, sometimes referred to as red flag laws. Donald Trump and even various National Rifle Association spokespersons have spoken about the need to keep guns out of the hands of dangerous people, thus implicitly or explicitly making the case for this type of legislation (French, 2018; Horsley, 2018). These laws enable family members, law enforcement personnel, and sometimes employers or school administrators to file Extreme Risk Protection Orders which restrict or temporarily remove someone's access to firearms when their behavior suggests that they pose a violent threat to themselves and/or others (Cranley, 2019; Giffords Law Center, 2018). A recent study (Lankford et al., 2019) examined the fifteen deadliest public mass shootings that occurred in the United States from 1998 to 2018 and assessed which potential warning signs were observed by law enforcement and community members prior to each incident. Overall, the evidence suggests that most incidents were in fact preventable based on information known about offenders in advance and that extreme risk protection orders could have made a significant difference in averting the attack. Further, this study's findings provide further clarity on which warning signs should be considered when making the determination of risk. In particular, if people who engaged in the most extreme form of leakage—admitting their homicidal thoughts or interest in committing a mass killing—were prevented from acquiring firearms, many of the deadliest incidents of the past 20 years may have been avoided.

In the opposite direction, there have been many calls in recent years to respond to the issue of mass shootings in schools with proposals to eliminate gun free school zones and change concealed carry laws by allowing teachers and other faculty members (and sometimes students in college classes) to be armed on school grounds. Many states and school districts across the United States already have various versions of this in place (May, 2018). In fact, Florida recently became the 15th state to permit teachers to carry firearms in schools, and another 16 states give local school boards the ability to determine if school staff can carry guns (May, 2018; Owen, 2018).

While proponents of arming faculty members have often touted particular incidents where armed school personnel were credited with stopping a mass shooting in progress (see, for example, the 1997 Pearl High School shooting case or the 2002 shooting at the Appalachian School of Law), the details of some of these incidents actually dispel that narrative. For example, the assailant who killed two classmates and wounded seven more at his high school in Pearl, Mississippi was apprehended by Assistant Principal Joel Myrick who confronted the shooter with a .45-caliber pistol he had retrieved from his truck. The killer was attempting to flee the scene in his mother's car, but Myrick put a gun to his neck and held him until police arrived. There is no question that Joel Myrick played a heroic and crucial role in the arrest of the Pearl High School shooter, but Myrick didn't deter or prevent this shooting, as the perpetrator had already shot several people, ended his assault, exited the school, and was attempting to drive away when confronted by the armed assistant principal (Mikkelson, 2015). Similarly, in the incident at the Appalachian School of Law in Grundy, Virginia, the attacker "stopped shooting when his gun ran out of bullets, not because some individuals had retrieved their guns and confronted him" (Siebel & Roston, 2007, p. 9). The unarmed student praised as the hero in this case, Ted Besen,

5 Summary of Findings, Policy Implications, and Future Research

disputed the widely publicized claim made by former House Speaker Newt Gingrich that students with guns had saved the day and stated instead that "Their guns had no effect on [the shooter.] I already had [the shooter] on the ground before they got their guns out" (Siebel & Roston, 2007, p. 9).

That said, there certainly have been incidents where armed civilians have intervened to stop a mass shooting in progress, though it is notable that none of these have occurred in school settings (Active Shooter Incidents, 2018; Blair & Schweit, 2014). The reality is that this approach has far more challenges and negative consequences than suggested by simplistic rhetoric that "the only way to stop a bad guy with a gun is a good guy with a gun" (Lee, 2019).

For one thing, the empirical data that examine this trope in the aggregate does not support the proposition that people carrying more concealed weapons reduces mass shootings or violent crime more generally. As Duwe, Kovandzic, and Moody (2002, p. 289) clearly state in their study of the impact of right-to-carry concealed firearm legislation on public mass shootings, "There is no evidence that the presence of a [right-to-carry] law or the number of people with carry permits … reduces the number of people killed and injured during shooting attacks." In fact, the most comprehensive study on the effects of right-to-carry concealed handgun laws (Donahue, Aneja, & Weber, 2018) discovered that rates of violent crime increased with each additional year that a right-to-carry law was in place, as the population carried more firearms. They also found that these laws "are associated with 13-15 percent higher aggregate violent crime rates ten years after adoption" than predicted if such laws had not been adopted (ibid., p. 1).

Further, the idea that armed teachers or other civilians who lack in-depth military or law enforcement training would be able to avoid accidently shooting bystanders in the chaotic environment of a mass casualty situation is far more fantasy than reality. In simulations of active shootings, armed civilians fare far worse than advocates for this policy imagine, often getting killed or killing innocent bystanders (Lopez, 2017). Even police officers, who are required to do target practice and other firearms trainings on a consistent basis, hit their intended target less than 20% of the time, on average (Morrison, 2006). Active shooting situations are inherently disorganized and confusing scenes where there is great potential risk to accidently target the wrong people, as has happened in numerous cases where both law enforcement (Lockhart, 2019) and armed civilians (Seletan, 2011) have nearly or actually killed completely innocent people who were, in the heat of the moment, wrongly believed to be the assailant.

More generally, a recent report (Drane, 2019) discovered dozens of incidents of guns being mishandled in schools in just the last few years, including guns left in places easily accessible to children, guns unintentionally discharged, students managing to take guns from armed adults, and guns pointed at students for relatively minor disciplinary infractions or during the course of personal conflicts. As no empirical data or even anecdotal evidence exist to conclude that arming school faculty will deter or prevent mass shootings in schools, policy-makers should therefore be far more wary of implementing such programs, especially in light of all the unintended consequences of such a practice.

Media Coverage of Mass Killing

One key emergent area where new research has suggested the potential to prevent and reduce incidents of rampage killing is in media coverage. It is no surprise that incidents of school and other mass shootings receive a great deal of media attention. For example, the shooting at Columbine High School in 1999 was one of the most covered events of that entire decade, receiving a larger audience on *CNN* than other major news events such as the 1992 and 1996 presidential elections, the LA riots, or the death of Princess Diana (Muschert, 2002). More recently, Lankford (2018) found that some mass killers received more coverage in terms of dollar value during the months of their attacks than many of the most famous American movie stars, including Brad Pitt, Jennifer Aniston, and Johnny Depp.

While this media coverage is negative in tone and certainly does not condone mass and school killings, there are often inadvertent consequences to the quantity and quality of such media saturation. Such publicity can make mass killings into potential opportunities for fame, make

5 Summary of Findings, Policy Implications, and Future Research

mass killers into de facto celebrities, and even provides an incentive for perpetrators to kill as many victims as possible in order to gain more attention (Lankford & Madfis, 2018a, 2018b). Further, the role of copycat and contagion effects as consequences of media coverage of mass killers has been well documented in recent research literature (Gould & Olivares, 2017; Helfgott, 2015; Kissner, 2016; Langman, 2018; Lankford, 2016; Lankford & Madfis, 2018a, 2018b; Meindl & Ivy, 2017; Murray, 2017; Perrin, 2016; Sidhu, 2017; Towers, Gomez-Lievano, Khan, Mubayi, & Castillo-Chavez, 2015). As Lankford and Madfis (2018b, p. 264) clarify:

> Both contagion and copycat effects refer to the ways that some people who are exposed to a given behavior may become more likely to behave similarly themselves. Copycat effects are more straightforward, and typically refer to peoples' imitation of an original actor's modeled behavior…Contagion, on the other hand, is based on the notion that behaviors can "go viral" and spread through society like diseases, with increased likelihood of their occurrence either in the short term or long term.

Thus, one clear example of the copycat effect would be the 2012 Sandy Hook Elementary School shooter who created an enormous spreadsheet on his computer containing specific details on hundreds of mass murderers and other killers. He was especially fascinated by the Columbine High School attack and hundreds of videos, images, and documents about this incident where found on his computer (Langman, 2018). Another clear copycat example involved the Greenwood, South Carolina man who committed a school shooting at Oakland Elementary School on September 26, 1988. This man was obsessed with the woman who perpetrated an elementary school shooting in Winnetka, Illinois that took place a few months earlier on May 20, 1988. *People Magazine* published an article about her attack, and this young man was obsessed by the magazine story, reading it daily until he committed his own school shooting. To make the copycat nature of his crime as unambiguous as possible, he stated, after being captured, that "I could understand where she was coming from. I think I may have copied her" (Langman, 2018, p. 214). In contrast, one of the more notable recent examples of contagion effects using mathematical models to analyze attacks over time (Towers et al., 2015) is the finding that one mass killing or school shooting significantly increases the chances that others will occur within the next thirteen days.

In order to address this issue, many scholars have crafted alternative media strategies to make news coverage of mass killings safer and more responsible. Meindl and Ivy (2018) draw key lessons from media's suicide prevention efforts and apply them to mass killings. These are not completely distinct subjects, as mass killing contagion may be partially attributable to suicide contagion because a high percentage of mass killers are suicidal as well. To reduce the likelihood of imitation, journalists and other media figures should avoid making the potential role model seem like someone of high social status (e.g., a celebrity), to avoid rewarding that individual in any way (e.g., with sensationalist coverage, fame, or attention), and to avoid portraying that individual as justified or competent (e.g., at accomplishing a mission or sending a message). In addition to providing recommendations for safer news reporting, these authors also outline how proactive media information campaigns could help reduce mass killings by depicting perpetrators in a less flattering light and by emphasizing the negative consequences of these events. Meindl and Ivy (2018, p. 252) state that:

> In crafting an effective media campaign targeting mass killing, one goal would be to disrupt the relation between the behavior and fame by linking the behavior with unpleasant outcomes instead. Rather than depicting the mass killer as aggressive, dangerous, or menacing (all qualities that may be appealing to some individuals), mass killers may be portrayed as weak, cowardly, or ineffectual (qualities most people tend to find undesirable)…Rather than depicting the killer as a vicious loner who took the lives of many people while devastating a community and avoiding justice though suicide, for example, the killer could be portrayed as an impulsive nobody who lacked the strength to handle his own problems and who ultimately engaged in a violent tantrum.

Previous mass media campaigns have successfully changed public perceptions and even behaviors across large populations of people regarding other highly imitative behaviors, such as tobacco and alcohol

5 Summary of Findings, Policy Implications, and Future Research

use (Wakefield, Loken, & Hornik, 2010). A similar opportunity may exist with mass killings, if altered media coverage can begin to degrade the appeal of these attacks and their perpetrators among the audiences who find them most captivating.

Another recent proposal (Lankford & Madfis, 2018b) makes a pragmatic and evidence-based case for the media to simply stop publishing the names and photos of mass killers (except during ongoing searches for escaped suspects), but to continue reporting the other details of these crimes as needed. This approach is influenced by but modifies two prior important popular campaigns that similarly emphasize how problematic it is for media outlets to reward mass killers with lasting fame for their crimes. The first is the "Don't Name Them" campaign, hosted by the ALERRT Center at Texas State University, and the second is "No Notoriety," founded by Tom and Caren Teves, the parents of a victim of the Aurora, Colorado mass shooting. "Don't Name Them" (2019) explains that "The focus of the public campaign is to shift the media focus from the suspects who commit these acts to the victims, survivors and heroes who stop them." Similarly, "No Notoriety" (2019) suggests the media should "Elevate the names and likenesses of all victims killed and/or injured to send the message their lives are more important than the killer's actions." Although stories about victims, survivors, and heroes clearly have an important place in the coverage of these incidents, the details of mass shooters' lives, motivations, and behaviors are also an indispensable component of media reporting. Without this media information on mass shooters themselves, empirical research on mass killers would be significantly inhibited, as most studies rely upon open source data (Huff-Corzine et al., 2014). Thus, we would know even less than we currently do about the behavioral patterns among these perpetrators and the evidence-based solutions for preventing and thwarting them. In addition, details about the life experiences and behaviors of individual mass shooters—including their ideologies, public statements, writings, and struggles—can help inform the public about the key warning signs for those at risk of committing future attacks. Family and friends have been one of the most important lines of defense against mass shootings in schools and other settings, and many thwarted attacks have been prevented because these people saw or heard something concerning and then informed others about this threat (Daniels, 2019; Madfis, 2014; Pollack, Modzeleski, & Rooney, 2008; Vossekuil, Fein, Reddy, Borum, & Modzeleski, 2002). Without media outlets covering the details of offenders' lives, those around them may be less likely to recognize leakage or other warning signs and report them.

In contrast, not publishing the names and images of mass killers could help deny many of these offenders the public attention they crave and disincentivize future attacks. The expectation that one will get credit for what one has done is one of the most powerful behavioral motives (Harsanyi, 1980; Wrangham & Peterson, 1996). Many authors, composers, actors, musicians, journalists, and inventors would be far less motivated—and might even give up—if they thought that no matter what they did, no one would ever know their names. Under comparable constraints, how many prospective mass killers would give up their deadly plans and instead do something else? The exact number may be impossible to determine, but even a small reduction in mass murders would make a huge difference to the victims who might avoid tragic deaths, as well as their families and friends. Further, if media outlets were to refuse to publish the names and images of mass killers, it would be far more difficult for potential copycat offenders to make personal and emotional connections to them. Most people do not select role models based solely on the description of behavior, if they do not even know that person's name and have never seen that person's face (Lankford & Madfis, 2018b).

If this proposal were to be implemented in a widespread manner across various forms of media, mass killers would no longer receive the widespread attention that transforms them into role models for copycats and de facto celebrities with a global online subculture of followers (Raitanen & Oksanen, 2018). Perhaps the impressionable individuals inspired by these killers would look instead toward other types of role models. These benefits could be achieved without giving up much of importance. The particular sequence of letters that comprise the names of offenders and the particular arrangement of flesh, cartilage, and bones that make up the faces of offenders are among the least newsworthy and important details about them. This information by itself tells us nothing and lacks any inherent value. However, by continuing to report everything else about these crimes in as much detail as desired, media outlets can still fulfill their responsibility to the public and concerns from reporters and journalists about censorship should be largely assuaged.

Suggested Areas for Future Research

Through the exploration of the averted school rampage phenomenon undertaken in this study, numerous avenues for future research have come to light. As the topic remains in its infancy with regard to empirical scholarship and even careful conceptual scrutiny, important questions remain.

It is vital that the scholarship on averted school rampage killing be expanded with larger samples in order to gain a more representative picture of the problem and how schools have reacted to it. Distributing surveys to a large random sample of school and police officials would go a long way toward indicating the extent to which the findings in this study are generalizable to the population at large. For example, surveys exploring what violence risk assessment practices are currently utilized by school and police officials and eliciting opinions regarding the perceived efficacy of those assessments would be enlightening and important. Because of the significance of the threat assessment approach indicated in this study, there would perhaps be the greatest utility in nationally representative studies of the threat assessment approach that measure not only its perceived efficacy but also its outcomes when utilized in a preventative manner. What's more, my findings indicated that the forms of risk assessment utilized by school and police officials varied to some extent by their job types. This qualitative conclusion, however, can only be considered preliminary, and so a larger quantitative survey exploring these variations in a representative manner would prove useful. There is much the same need for nationally representative surveys of school disciplinary policies and security measures, both in terms of how prevalent various forms are and how officials perceive their effectiveness.

Additionally, as the detailed qualitative aspects of the present study were limited to averted rampages in the Northeastern United States, future scholars should expand to other regions of the country. This is especially important as both averted and completed school rampages are actually more prevalent elsewhere, with more incidents occurring in Southern, Midwestern, and Western states (Kimmel & Mahler, 2003; Langman & Straub, 2019). It also remains unknown whether or not school rampages are perceived, assessed, and responded to differently by geographical regions with distinct political and cultural traditions. For example, my respondents were nearly unanimous in their condemnation of calls to arm faculty members in schools via the scaling back of concealed carry firearm restrictions, but this may reflect a Northeastern predilection for or comfort with gun control that would be far less dominant in other parts of the country.

Beyond the American context, school rampage killings have also been averted in at least two widely publicized incidents in Manchester, England (Carter, 2009) and Cologne, Germany (Attack on German, 2007). However, international cases of averted rampage have never been systematically studied, even in the superficial manner necessary to provide a basic indication of their prevalence.

In addition to an international comparative study of averted rampage incidents, scholars ought to more fully investigate international variations among responses to school rampage. In the aftermath of many school attacks in the United States, Americans have witnessed calls to arm students, teachers, and faculty members, either as a means of deterring future offenders from making an attempt or with the mindset that an armed populace would be able to more easily stop a rampaging killer. In fact, it is now common to see many states consider or adopt new legislation to permit students and faculty to carry firearms on school grounds in the wake of various massacres (May, 2018; Owen, 2018). While the 2012 massacre at Sandy Hook Elementary School in Newtown, Connecticut did spark debates about background checks and limiting magazine capacities, and the 2018 massacre at Marjory Stoneman Douglas High School in Parkland, Florida gave rise to a broad student-led movement for a varied array of new gun control legislation, American policy discussions in recent years have rarely focused upon reducing the access to or availability of firearms. By contrast, the most

5 Summary of Findings, Policy Implications, and Future Research

common reaction to rampage incidents outside of the United States (for example, in Germany and Australia) has been attempts by gun control advocates to reduce teenagers' access to deadly weapons. Thus, international comparative research has the potential to reveal great insight into the manner in which anti-violence policy is often the result of particular cultural, political, and structural manifestations rather than the uncontested or inevitable solution to particular crises.

While no scholarship has explored averted incidents of school rampage outside of the United States, recent research on completed school rampage incidents beyond the American context (Madfis & Levin, 2013) discovered that none of these international school rampage incidents involved students killing in pairs or in groups (like the killer duos of Westside Middle School in Arkansas and Columbine High School in Colorado), while more than one student was accused in five out of the eleven averted incidents in this study (Courtside, Donovan, Everton, Finley, and Hastings). This suggests that it may be the case that the more student plotters involved in a particular incident, the more leakage there will be, and thus the more likely it will be that the students will be caught. However, further in-depth case study research with a larger sample would need to be conducted in order to confirm the existence of this possible relationship.

Finally, averted school rampage can be situated as one subset of the larger phenomenon of averted acts of violence and crime, and thus these findings would be fruitfully compared to similar studies of other prevented transgressions. Averted incidents of mass murder outside of the school setting warrant far more investigation (Madfis, 2018), as Sarteschi (2016) and White-Hamon (2000) remain the only studies yet to address this topic. Likewise, it would be worthwhile to explore whether or not other forms of attempted mass murder (such as workplace avengers, family annihilators, and disgruntled citizens) were thwarted via similar means as those school rampages investigated in this study. It is unclear how frequently adult mass murders display leakage and inform others about their dangerous intentions. Though adults who have been informed about the homicidal plans of a would-be mass killer may not be subject to a student code of silence, they may still be distrustful of law enforcement and/or perceive of "snitching" as an unacceptable violation of the "code of the street" dominant in low income and minority communities (Anderson, 1999; Morris, 2010; Rosenfeld, Jacobs, & Wright, 2003). Thus, comparing the role that intervention by the confidants of adult rampage killers played in averting multiple homicides to that of school rampages averted by peer confidants coming forward would prove insightful. Likewise, though adults are not systematically assessed and monitored in the way that schools do to their students, adults with developed and actionable plans to harm many people en masse may similarly engage in leakage or otherwise raise concerns among their family members, friends, coworkers, mental health providers, or other acquaintances (see, for example, Lankford et al., 2019). This suggests that there may well be value in exploring the role of leakage in incidents of mass murder outside of the school setting.

More broadly, researchers have neglected the much wider phenomenon of attempted and averted incidents of single-victim homicide, even though it's a far more commonly perpetrated and prosecuted crime than averted rampage. The same may be said for advancing the conceptual and empirical understanding of all attempted crimes, for while this has long been an interesting area of debate in law and philosophy (see, for example, Adams, 1998; Arenson, 2005; Bayles, 1982; Becker, 1973/1974; Christopher, 2004; Davis, 1986; Duff, 1997; Enker, 1977; Feinberg, 1995; Ohana, 2007; Spjut, 1987; Yaffe, 2010), the topic has been broadly overlooked by sociologists and criminologists. Even those explicitly exploring the popular topic of crime prevention (such as Clarke, 1995; Rosenbaum, Lurigio, & Davis, 1998; Sherman, Farrington, Welsh, & MacKenzie, 2002; Trembley & Craig, 1995) have neglected to consider how criminal attempts might inform preventative measures. While the existing foci upon understanding the root causes, risk factors, and situational determinants of crime all surely help prevent future offenses, there may be a wealth of knowledge as yet unearthed about the deterrence and hindrance of crime to be gleaned from the study of averted incidents.

References

Active Shooter Incidents in the United States in 2016 and 2017. (2018). *Federal Bureau of Investigation, United States Department of Justice.* Washington, DC. Retrieved July 18, 2019, from https://www.fbi.gov/file-repository/active-shooter-incidents-us-2016-2017.pdf/view.

Adams, D. M. (1998). The problem of the incomplete attempt. *Social Theory and Practice, 24,* 317–343.

Advancement Project. (2005). *Education on lockdown: The schoolhouse to jailhouse track.* Retrieved July 26, 2019, from https://b.3cdn.net/advancement/5351180e24cb166d02_mlbrqgxlh.pdf.

Alexander, M. (2010). *The new Jim Crow: Mass incarceration in the age of colorblindness.* New York: New Press.

Anderson, E. (1999). *Code of the street: Decency, violence and the moral life of the inner city.* New York: Norton.

Arenson, K. J. (2005). The pitfalls in the law of attempt: A new perspective. *The Journal of Criminal Law, 69*(2), 146–167.

Attack on German High School Prevented, Police Say. (2007, November 18). Retrieved July 26, 2019, from http://www.cnn.com/2007/WORLD/europe/11/18/germany.school.plot/index.html.

Bayles, M. D. (1982). Punishment for attempts. *Social Theory and Practice, 8,* 21–29.

Becker, L. C. (1973/1974). Criminal attempt and the theory of the law of crimes. *Philosophy & Public Affairs, 3,* 262–294.

Beckett, K., Beach, L., Knaphus, E., & Reosti, A. (2018). US criminal justice policy and practice in the twenty-first century: Toward the end of mass incarceration? *Law and Policy, 40*(4), 321–345.

Blair, J. P., & Schweit, K. W. (2014). *A study of active shooter incidents, 2000–2013.* Washington, DC: Texas State University and Federal Bureau of Investigation, U.S. Department of Justice.

Böckler, N., Heitmeyer, W., Sitzer, P., & Seeger, T. (Eds.). (2013). *School shootings: International research, case studies, and concepts for prevention.* New York, NY: Springer.

Borum, R., Cornell, D., Modzeleski, W., & Jimerson, S. (2010). What can be done about school shootings?: A review of the evidence. *Educational Researcher, 39*(1), 27–37.

Carter, H. (2009, September 2). *Manchester teenagers planned Columbine-style attack, jury told.* Retrieved July 17, 2019, from http://www.guardian.co.uk/uk/2009/sep/02/manchester-teenagers-columbine-style-attack.

Christopher, R. (2004). Does attempted murder deserve greater punishment than murder? Moral luck and the duty to prevent harm. *Notre Dame Journal of Law, Ethics, and Public Policy, 18*(2), 419–435.

Clarke, R. V. (1995). Situational crime prevention. *Crime and Justice, 19,* 91–150.

Cornell, D. G. (2013). The Virginia student threat assessment guidelines: An empirically supported violence prevention strategy. In N. Böckler, W. Heitmeyer, P. Sitzer, & T. Seeger (Eds.), *School shootings: International research, case studies, and concepts for prevention* (pp. 379–400). New York, NY: Springer.

Cranley, E. (2019, August 5). *How to stop shootings in America: 10 strategies proposed to stop gun violence, and how likely they are to work.* Retrieved January 28, 2020, from https://www.businessinsider.com/how-to-stop-gun-school-shooting-america-2018-11.

Daniels, J. A. (2019). *A preliminary report on the Police Foundations averted school violence database.* Washington, DC: Office of Community Oriented Policing Services.

Davis, M. (1986). Why attempts deserve less punishment than complete crimes. *Law and Philosophy, 5*(1), 1–32.

Donahue, J. J., Aneja, A., & Weber, K. D. (2018). Right-to-carry laws and violent crime: A comprehensive assessment using panel data and a state-level synthetic control analysis. *Journal of Empirical Legal Studies, 16*(2), 198–247.

Don't Name Them. (2019). Retrieved July 17, 2019, from https://www.facebook.com/pg/DontNameThem/about/.

Drane, K. (2019, June 1). *Every incident of mishandled guns in schools.* Retrieved June 26, 2019, from https://giffords.org/2019/06/every-incident-of-mishandled-guns-in-schools/.

Duff, A. (1997). *Criminal attempts.* Oxford: Oxford University Press.

Duwe, G., Kovandzic, T., & Moody, C. (2002). The impact of right-to-carry concealed firearms laws on mass public shootings. *Homicide Studies, 6*(4), 271–296.

Enker, A. N. (1977). Mens rea and criminal attempt. *Law & Social Inquiry, 2*(4), 845–879.

Feinberg, J. (1995). Equal punishment for failed attempts: Some bad but instructive arguments against it. *Arizona Law Review, 37,* 117–133.

Foucault, M. (1977). *Discipline and punish: The birth of the prison.* Harmondsworth: Penguin.

Foucault, M. (1980). *Power/knowledge.* Brighton, UK: Harvester.

Foucault, M. (1991). Governmentality. In G. Burchell, C. Gordon, & P. Miller (Eds.), *The Foucault effect: Studies in governmentality* (pp. 87–104). London, UK: Harvester Wheatsheaf.

French, D. (2018, March 16). *The NRA makes a wise, principled decision to support gun-violence restraining orders.* Retrieved June 7, 2019, from https://www.nationalreview.com/2018/03/nra-gun-violence-restraining-order-support-good-move/.

Giffords Law Center. (2018). *Extreme risk protection orders.* Retrieved June 7, 2019, from https://lawcenter.giffords.org/gun-laws/policy-areas/who-can-have-a-gun/extreme-risk-protection-orders/.

Gould, M. S., & Olivares, M. (2017). Mass shootings and murder-suicide: Review of empirical evidence for contagion. In S. Stack & T. Niederkrotenthaler (Eds.), *Media and suicide: International perspectives on research, theory, and policy* (pp. 41–66). New York, NY: Routledge.

Harsanyi, J. C. (1980). A bargaining model for social status in informal groups and formal organizations. In J. C. Harsanyi (Ed.), *Essays on ethics, social behavior, and scientific explanation: Theory and decision library* (Vol. 12, pp. 204–226). Dordrecht, Netherlands: Springer.

Heitzeg, N. A. (2016). *The School-to-Prison Pipeline: Education, Discipline, and Racialized Double Standards.* Santa Barbara, CA: Praeger.

Helfgott, J. B. (2015). Criminal behavior and the copycat effect: Literature review and theoretical framework for empirical investigation. *Aggression and Violent Behavior, 22,* 46–64.

Horsley, S. (2018, March 12). *Gun advocates are not happy about Trump advocating for risk protection orders.* Retrieved June 7, 2019, from https://www.npr.org/2018/03/12/592965390/gun-advocates-are-not-happy-about-trump-advocating-for-risk-protection-orders.

Huff-Corzine, L., McCutcheon, J. C., Corzine, J., Jarvis, J. P., Tetzlaff-Bemiller, M., Weller, M., & Landon, M. (2014). Shooting for accuracy: Comparing data sources on mass murder. *Homicide Studies, 18,* 105–124.

Kim, C., Losen, D., & Hewitt, D. (2010). *The school-to-prison pipeline: Structuring legal reform.* New York: New York University Press.

Kimmel, M. S., & Mahler, M. (2003). Adolescent masculinity, homophobia, and violence. *American Behavioral Scientist, 46,* 1439–1458.

King, S., Rusoja, A., & Peguero, A. (2018). The school-to-prison pipeline. In J. Deakin, E. Taylor, & A. Kupchik (Eds.), *The Palgrave international handbook of school discipline, surveillance, and social control* (pp. 269–290). New York, NY: Palgrave Macmillan.

Kissner, J. (2016). Are active shootings temporally contagious? An empirical assessment. *Journal of Police and Criminal Psychology, 31,* 48–58.

Langman, P. (2018). Different types of role model influence and fame seeking among mass killers and copycat offenders. *American Behavioral Scientist, 62*(2), 210–228.

Langman, P., & Straub, F. (2019). *A comparison of averted and completed school attacks from the Police Foundation's averted school violence database.* Washington, DC: Office of Community Oriented Policing Services.

Lankford, A. (2016). Fame-seeking rampage shooters: Initial findings and empirical predictions. *Aggression and Violent Behavior, 27*(1), 122–129.

Lankford, A. (2018). Do the media unintentionally make mass killers into celebrities? An assessment of free advertising and earned media value. *Celebrity Studies, 9*(3), 340–354.

Lankford, A., & Madfis, E. (2018a). Media coverage of mass killers: Content, consequences, and solutions. *American Behavioral Scientist, 62*(2), 151–162.

Lankford, A., & Madfis, E. (2018b). Don't name them, don't show them, but report everything else: A pragmatic proposal for denying mass killers the attention they seek and deterring future offenders. *American Behavioral Scientist, 62*(2), 260–279.

Lankford, A., Adkins, K. G., & Madfis, E. (2019). Are the deadliest mass shootings preventable? An assessment of leakage, information reported to law enforcement, and firearms acquisition prior to attacks in the United States. *Journal of Contemporary Criminal Justice, 35*(3), 315–341.

Lee, S. (2019, June 7). How the good guy with a gun became a deadly American fantasy. *The Conversation.* Retrieved June 8, 2019, from https://theconversation.com/how-the-good-guy-with-a-gun-became-a-deadly-american-fantasy-117367.

Leitsinger, M. (2012, March 8). *When rumor, the Internet and school violence fears collide.* Retrieved May 4, 2012, from http://usnews.msnbc.msn.com/_news/2012/03/08/10604539-when-rumor-the-internet-and-school-violence-fears-collide?lite.

Lockhart, P. R. (2019, February 6). *A black security guard caught a shooting suspect—Only to be shot by police minutes later.* Retrieved June 26, 2019, from https://www.vox.com/identities/2018/11/12/18088874/jemel-roberson-police-shooting-illinois-ian-covey-video.

Logan, C. (2002, May 2). Columbine jitters may cost a Kansas town millions. *The Pitch.* Retrieved July 5, 2010, from http://www.pitch.com/2002-05-02/news/tutu-careful/.

Lopez, G. (2017, November 6). *The Texas shooting shows why "a good guy with a gun" isn't enough.* Retrieved June 26, 2019, from https://www.vox.com/policy-and-politics/2017/11/6/16612014/sutherland-springs-shooting-good-guy-gun.

Lopez, G. (2018, June 21). *America's love for guns, in one chart.* Retrieved June 26, 2019, from https://www.vox.com/2018/6/21/17488024/gun-ownership-violence-shootings-us.

Madfis, E. (2014). Averting school rampage: Student intervention amid a persistent code of silence. *Youth Violence and Juvenile Justice, 12*(3), 229–249.

Madfis, E. (2017). In search of meaning: Are school rampage shootings random and senseless violence? *The Journal of Psychology: Interdisciplinary and Applied, 151*(1), 21–35.

Madfis, E. (2018). Insight from averted mass shootings. In J. Schildkraut (Ed.), *Mass shootings in America: Understanding the debates, causes, and responses* (pp. 79–84). Santa Barbara, CA: Praeger Books.

Madfis, E., & Levin, J. (2013). School rampage in international perspective: The salience of cumulative strain theory. In N. Böckler, W. Heitmeyer, P. Sitzer, & T. Seeger (Eds.), *School shootings: International research, case studies, and concepts for prevention* (pp. 79–104). New York, NY: Springer.

May, A. (2018, March 13). *Guns in school: It's not just an idea. Here's how some states are already doing it.* Retrieved June 8, 2019, from https://www.usatoday.com/story/news/nation-now/2018/03/13/can-guns-schools-save-students-during-shooting-heres-what-states-say/418965002/.

Meindl, J. N., & Ivy, J. W. (2017). Mass shootings: The role of the media in promoting generalized imitation. *American Journal of Public Health, 107,* 368–370.

Meindl, J. N., & Ivy, J. W. (2018). Reducing media-induced mass killings: Lessons from suicide prevention. *American Behavioral Scientist, 62*(2), 242–259.

Mikkelson, D. (2015). *Rumor: A school shooter in Pearl, Mississippi, was stopped from killing additional victims by an assistant principal with a gun.* Retrieved June 24, 2019, from https://www.snopes.com/fact-check/full-stop/.

Morris, E. W. (2010). "Snitches end up in ditches" and other cautionary tales. *Journal of Contemporary Criminal Justice, 26*(3), 254–272.

Morrison, G. (2006). Deadly force programs among larger U.S. police departments. *Police Quarterly, 9*(3), 331–360.

Murray, J. L. (2017). Mass media reporting and enabling of mass shootings. *Cultural Studies, Critical Methodologies, 17,* 114–124.

Muschert, G. W. (2002). *Media and massacre: The social construction of the Columbine story.* Unpublished doctoral dissertation, University of Colorado at Boulder, Boulder, CO.

Muschert, G. W. (2007). Research in school shootings. *Sociology Compass, 1*(1), 60–80.

Mythen, G. (2008). Sociology and the art of risk. *Sociology Compass, 2*(1), 299–316.

No Notoriety. (n.d.). Retrieved June 7, 2019, from https://nonotoriety.com/.

Ohana, D. (2007). Desert and punishment for acts preparatory to the commission of a crime. *Canadian Journal of Law and Jurisprudence, 20,* 113–142.

Owen, T. (2018, March 10). *Here's all the states where teachers already carry guns in the classroom.* Retrieved June 8, 2019, from https://news.vice.com/en_us/article/ywq8b5/teachers-armed-guns-classroom-state-laws.

Owen, T. (2019, March 26). *Owning a bump stock can now get you 10 years in prison.* Retrieved June 7, 2019, from https://news.vice.com/en_us/article/3kg9bv/owning-a-bump-stock-can-now-get-you-10-years-in-prison.

Pattillo, M., Weiman, D., & Western, B. (2004). *Imprisoning America: The social effects of mass incarceration.* New York: Russell Sage Foundation Publications.

Perrin, P. B. (2016). Translating psychological science: Highlighting the media's contribution to contagion in mass shootings: Comment on Kaslow (2015). *American Psychologist, 71,* 71–72.

Pollack, W. S., Modzeleski, W., & Rooney, G. (2008). *Prior knowledge of potential school-based violence: Information students learn may prevent a targeted attack.* Washington, DC: United States Secret Service and United States Department of Education.

Raitanen, J., & Oksanen, A. (2018). Global online subculture surrounding school shootings. *American Behavioral Scientist, 62*(2), 195–209.

Reddy, M., Borum, R., Berglund, J., Vossekuil, B., Fein, R., & Modzeleski, W. (2001). Evaluating risk for targeted violence in schools: Comparing risk assessment, threat assessment, and other approaches. *Psychology in the Schools, 38*(2), 157–172.

Rocque, M. (2012). Exploring school rampage shootings: Research, theory, and policy. *The Social Science Journal, 49*(3), 304–313.

Rosenbaum, D. P., Lurigio, A. J., & Davis, R. C. (Eds.). (1998). *The prevention of crime: Social and situational strategies.* Belmont, CA: Wadsworth.

Rosenfeld, R., Jacobs, B. A., & Wright, R. (2003). Snitching and the code of the street. *British Journal of Criminology, 43,* 291–309.

5 Summary of Findings, Policy Implications, and Future Research

Sarteschi, C. (2016). An examination of thwarted mass homicide plots and threateners. *Aggression and Violent Behavior, 30*(1), 88–93.

Savage, C. (2018, December 18). *Trump administration imposes ban on bump stocks.* Retrieved June 7, 2019, from https://www.nytimes.com/2018/12/18/us/politics/trump-bump-stocks-ban.html.

Seletan, W. (2011, January 11). *Friendly firearms: Gabrielle Giffords and the perils of guns: How an armed hero nearly shot the wrong man.* Retrieved June 24, 2019, from https://slate.com/technology/2011/01/joe-zamudio-and-the-gabrielle-giffords-shooting-how-an-armed-hero-nearly-shot-the-wrong-man.html.

Shepard, S. (2018, February 28). *Gun control support surges in polls.* Retrieved June 26, 2019, from https://www.politico.com/story/2018/02/28/gun-control-polling-parkland-430099.

Sherman, L. W., Farrington, D. P., Welsh, B. C., & MacKenzie, D. L. (Eds.). (2002). *Evidence-based crime prevention.* New York: Routledge.

Sidhu, S. S. (2017). Name no names: The role of the media in reporting mass shootings. *Journal of the American Academy of Child & Adolescent Psychiatry, 56,* 3–4.

Siebel, B., & Roston, A. (2007). *No gun left behind—The gun lobby's campaign to push guns into colleges and schools.* Brady Center to Prevent Gun Violence. Retrieved June 24, 2019, from https://papers.ssrn.com/sol3/papers.cfm?abstract_id-987861.

Sommer, F., Leuschner, V., & Scheithauer, H. (2014). Bullying, romantic rejection, and conflicts with teachers: The crucial role of social dynamics in the development of school shootings—A systematic review. *International Journal of Developmental Science, 8,* 3–24.

Spjut, R. J. (1987). When is an attempt to commit an impossible crime a criminal act. *Arizona Law Review, 29*(2), 247–279.

Towers, S., Gomez-Lievano, A., Khan, M., Mubayi, A., & Castillo-Chavez, C. (2015). Contagion in mass killings and school shootings. *PLoS One, 10*(7), e0117259.

Tremblay, R. E., & Craig, W. M. (1995). Developmental crime prevention. *Crime and Justice, 19,* 151–236.

Vossekuil, B., Fein, R., Reddy, M., Borum, R., & Modzeleski, W. (2002). *The final report and findings of the safe school initiative: Implications for the prevention of school attacks in the United States.* Washington, DC: U.S. Secret Service and U.S. Department of Education.

Wakefield, M. A., Loken, B., & Hornik, R. C. (2010). Use of mass media campaigns to change health behaviour. *The Lancet, 376*(9748), 1261–1271.

Wald, J., & Losen, D. J. (2003). Editors' notes. In J. Wald & D. J. Losen (Eds.), *New directions for youth development: Deconstructing the school-to-prison pipeline* (pp. 1–2). San Francisco, CA: Jossey-Bass.

White-Hamon, L. S. (2000). *Mass murder and attempted mass murder: An examination of the perpetrator with an empirical analysis of typologies.* Unpublished doctoral dissertation, California School of Professional Psychology, Fresno, CA.

Wrangham, R., & Peterson, D. (1996). *Demonic males: Apes and the origins of human violence.* New York, NY: Houghton Mifflin.

Yaffe, G. (2010). *Attempts: In the philosophy of action and the criminal law.* New York: Oxford University Press.

6

Methodological Appendix

This study utilized multiple strategies in the research design. The first stage of research entailed searching the *Lexis-Nexis* newspaper database as well as the internet and various academic and governmental publications in order to gather the population of publically reported school rampage plots that occurred in American public schools from 2000 to 2009 which were discovered before the perpetrators had the opportunity to commit them. These quantitative data provided a background understanding of the extent of the phenomenon and its variation by region. After collecting the population of these events, the next stage of research involved contacting principals at schools around the Northeast to request interviews with them and various other school and police officials (administrators, counselors, security and police officers, and teachers) who were directly involved in preventing the potential violence. This stage was necessary in order to glean data regarding perceptions of and reactions to violent threats, violence prevention, and school security. Employing this research strategy was necessary for the exploratory investigation of a fairly new and understudied phenomenon, and it resulted in a wealth of descriptive data triangulated with news reports, court transcripts, and arrest records to assure accuracy.

Operationalizing School Rampage and Averted Threat

Before going into depth about the mechanics of data collection, the purpose and process of operationalization in this study must be addressed as the definition of a "school shooting," and even the more specific term "school rampage," have varied substantially across numerous publications. First, it is vital to note that the notion of an averted rampage leaves room for a wide range of severity between various cases wherein students' genuine desire to complete a rampage attack is perhaps problematically assumed. For example, scrawling a vague threat referencing Columbine on a school bathroom wall and stockpiling an arsenal of weaponry are both actions that could be classified as evidence of an averted rampage, though the actual level of threat present in these two scenarios varies a great deal (Reddy et al., 2001). Cornell et al. (2004) distinguished between "transient" threats made carelessly in jest or in a moment of anger and the more serious "substantive" threats where genuine harm is intended, and found that only 30% of their sample of school violence threats were of the latter more concerning type and a mere three incidents were deemed genuine threats worthy of expulsion. However, as a main goal of this research is to explore how threats are perceived and assessed by school staff, all cases of potentially violent threats of school rampage were included regardless of the magnitude of evidence present.

Since the highly publicized multiple-homicide attacks of the late 1990s, school shootings have often become thought of as events with multiple victims, though most murders on school grounds are actually single-victim homicides (Hagan, Hirschfield, & Shedd, 2002). Thus, some recent scholarship has moved away from the all-encompassing "school shooting" term to more specifically discuss "rampage" events with multiple victims (Muschert, 2007; Newman, Fox, Roth, Mehta, & Harding, 2004). In the literature on homicide, the traditional definition of a "mass murder" limits the phenomenon to those events wherein at least three victims were killed during a single episode at one or more closely related locations (Duwe, 2007; Fox, Levin, & Fridel, 2018;

Holmes & Holmes, 2001). While viewing multiple-victim school attacks as a subset of the larger mass murder phenomenon has certain conceptual benefits (Levin & Madfis, 2009), such a focused definition permits little analysis of cases that have not resulted in multiple deaths (Madfis, 2014). Individuals with the desire and intent to kill numerous people yet who fail to do so only because their plans come to the attention of authorities before they are to be carried out or those who severely injure many people but fail to do so fatally have been excluded from prior operationalizations (White-Hamon, 2000). These less-successful perpetrators may be distinguishable by their overall incompetence with weaponry and/or their inability to maintain secrecy about their future actions, but not necessarily by their original motivations and goals.

Thus, there is a certain conceptual utility in including all cases which involve an attempt to kill numerous people in the study of mass murder (White-Hamon, 2000). Such cases of attempted school mass murders were included in the sample for this study, though "successful" cases where perpetrators fatally injured multiple victims and those where perpetrators injured multiple victims but failed to kill them were excluded. Numerous prior studies have addressed the nature and extent of completed mass murders generally (Duwe, 2004, 2007; Fox & Levin, 1994, 1998; Fox et al., 2018; Holmes & Holmes, 2001; Levin & Fox, 1999; Meloy et al., 2004; Meloy, Hempel, Mohandie, Shiva, & Gray, 2001; Palermo & Ross, 1999; Petee, Padgett, & York, 1997) and at schools in particular (such as Harding, Fox, & Mehta, 2002; Levin & Madfis, 2009; Moore, Petrie, Braga, & McLaughlin, 2003; Newman & Fox, 2009; Newman et al., 2004; Vossekuil, Fein, Reddy, Borum, & Modzeleski, 2002) and it is hoped that future studies will focus upon failed but not averted school mass murders where numerous victims have been non-fatally injured (see Sullivan & Guerette, 2003 for one case study), but these events fall out of the scope of the current research.

Additionally, Newman et al. (2004) limited her definition of school rampage to those school shootings in which multiple people were killed or injured on school property by a student or recent former student of the targeted school and only those cases in which at least some of the victims were chosen in a random and indiscriminate manner. This definition has numerous assets, but also various problems. As mentioned previously, limiting the scope to multiple victims proves helpful in crystallizing the phenomenon and distinguishing it from other types of school shootings. This study similarly limited the cases under investigation to the actions of those committed by current or former students, rather than utilizing Muschert's (2007) larger net for rampage shootings which also includes the homicidal misdeeds of current and former school employees.

The Newman et al. (2004) definition of rampage becomes somewhat problematic when the subject one desires to study is students' foiled plots to commit multiple homicide at their current or former schools, as these authors limit the phenomenon to school "shootings" where firearms were the predominant weaponry. Numerous deadly plots formed by students over the ten years in question in this study involved bombs, explosives, and even knife attacks. Though not all were detonated, bombs were a vital component of the Columbine High School killer duo's plan (Larkin, 2007), and the most deadly mass murder at a school in American history (the Bath School Disaster which took place in Michigan in 1927) involved dynamite and hundreds of pounds of pyrotol, but no firearms (Bernstein, 2009). Accordingly, all manner of plots to commit multiple murder on school grounds were included, regardless of the perpetrator's intended weaponry.

Newman and her colleagues' (2004) latter qualifying criterion of random or symbolic victims also proves rather nebulous. This distinction has similarly caused Muschert (2007) to distinguish between "targeted" and "rampage" school shootings—the latter of which necessitate random or symbolic victims. While the typological distinction has a great deal of value as it is important to distinguish between symbolic attacks on institutions and targeted attacks on individuals, limiting data collection to include only rampages with random or symbolic victims seems premature for this study of averted mass casualty events at schools. Previous mass murders at schools (and elsewhere, for that matter) have variously included victims who were individually targeted, victims specifically selected due to their group membership or social status, victims chosen randomly for their symbolic significance as representatives of an institution, and random victims harmed merely to increase the overall body count (Larkin, 2007; Vossekuil et al., 2002). Perpetrators have killed across these categories during a single episode (Fox et al., 2018). As the empirical literature is currently too underdeveloped to definitively conclude that distinct victimological categories inevitably correspond to distinct school shooter typologies or motives, cases that seem to lack symbolic or random victims were not operationally eliminated from investigation. This was especially salient during the initial stage of investigation via newspaper and internet accounts where offender–victim relationships were rarely discernible. Thus, cases which qualify as averted school "rampages" (Daniels et al., 2007, 2010; Muschert, 2007; Newman et al., 2004) planned by former or current students with multiple specific and nonspecific victims were included in the operational definition used in this study as well as those which would be deemed attempted "targeted school shootings" (Muschert, 2007) with multiple specifically intended victims.

Prior academic definitions have variously limited school rampages by the type of weaponry, by the offender's connection to the school as former students, current students, staff members, or strangers, by the relationship between offenders and victims as specific or random targets, and by the number of victims killed or injured (Daniels et al., 2007, 2010; Levin & Madfis, 2009; Moore et al., 2003; Muschert, 2007; Newman & Fox, 2009; Newman et al., 2004; Vossekuil et al., 2002). In order to preserve as general a concept of rampage as possible while still maintaining a focus upon the assessment of student threats, this study has defined averted school rampage plots as those cases of any form of fatal violence planned by one or more students targeting multiple specific or nonspecific classmates and/or faculty at their former or current school which was preempted from occurring and causing any death or injury and of which there is any evidence of intent.

Research Design and Sample

I first located cases through the *Lexis-Nexis* newspaper database. Like Daniels et al. (2007), the search terms included "school" and "plot*," "school" and "rampage*," and "school" and "shooting*," though the additional terms "school" and "attack*," and "school" and "threat*" were added. Cases that occurred outside of the United States were excluded as were any incidents which involved adult strangers and former or current school staff as perpetrators, those which focused upon colleges or universities as desired targets, and those events which resulted in any injury or death or where only one victim was intended. In addition to the cases located through the newspaper database, numerous academic and government-sponsored publications (such as Larkin, 2009; Newman et al., 2004; Virginia Tech Review Panel, 2007), popular press sources (Bower, 2001; Lieberman, 2008; Robertson, 2001) and various internet sites which compile lists of school violence incidents (Brady Center, n.d.; "List of School-Related Attacks," n.d.) were consulted to gather as comprehensive a list as possible and to confirm the accuracy of data across multiple sources. By means of this method, one hundred and ninety-five cases of averted school rampage attacks which occurred in the United States from 2000 to 2009 were located. These quantitative population data for the entire nation were collected for descriptive purposes to look at the quantity of school rampage threats and how they vary by geographical region. This information advances knowledge in this area substantially because, while Kimmel and Mahler (2003) found that school rampage attacks occur by and large in politically conservative suburban and rural communities, very little previous data exist regarding the geographic distribution of averted rampages (but see Langman & Straub, 2019 for state-level data).

The next stage of data collection was exploratory qualitative research which involved contacting the middle and high schools that experienced and averted rampage threats in the last ten years. To make the project a manageable size and to facilitate as many face-to-face in person interviews as possible, the sample was limited to schools in the Northeastern United States (a geographical area which includes the New England states, New York, New Jersey, Pennsylvania, and Delaware). Of the 195 cases nationwide, twenty-nine incidents occurred in Northeastern schools. To facilitate access, I mailed a letter to the twenty-nine current head principals at these particular schools, informing them about the intended study and requesting permission to conduct interviews. I then emailed and/or telephoned the principals in order to once again request access and to set up a date to conduct interviews with them and any other staff members who possessed personal knowledge of the averted incident.

At the start of each individual interview, I provided further details about the purpose of the study and the respondents' informed consent. Respondents were notified that they could stop the interview at any time, could skip any question for any reason, and should avoid disclosing any information about criminal activities unknown to the authorities. In addition to my verbal explanation, all of this information was included in a written consent form provided to respondents who were interviewed in person, while respondents interviewed over the telephone were emailed copies of the consent form, if they desired them. Though the interview method could not permit anonymity, I did promise confidentiality to my respondents by assuring them that no publications to arise from this research would contain the names of any individuals or schools who participated, and every effort will be made to conceal identifying information.

Of the twenty-nine head principals contacted, eleven were willing to permit me to conduct research about the incident at their school. Three principals refused participation in the study, and the remaining fifteen principals never responded to my repeated attempts to contact them via telephone and email messages. This may be partially explained by job turnover in that my data went back to the year 2000, and many current principals and staff members were not working at the schools in question when the incidents occurred (an extreme example of this was that one of the principals in charge during the course of an averted incident was later removed for having an illicit relationship with a student). Similarly, for some of the cases that had taken place most recently, school administrators were not permitted to speak with me about incidents where hearings and trials were still ongoing. Other rationales for non-participation might be explained by concerns about school reputation, external scrutiny, or simple time limitations (one high school principal informed me that he only agreed to participate because he was impressed by the dedication I showed in calling and emailing him repeatedly over a period of numerous weeks). In the only available information on averted school rampage that exists to serve as a basis for comparison, Daniels et al. (2010) similarly found that only four out of the thirteen schools they contacted would consent to participation. Pollack, Modzeleski, and Rooney (2008) do not reveal their specific response rate for student bystanders or schools involved in averted incidents, but only 15 out of the 29 students they discovered who were involved in either averted or completed rampages agreed to be interviewed.

Though two of the twenty-nine schools originally contacted were private institutions, all of the eleven schools that granted me permission for interviews were public institutions. As the demographic information to follow (which comes from the 2000 census as well as local community and school websites) indicates, these eleven schools were all located in predominantly white regions of the country, and though one incident occurred at a lower middle-class school in a rural area, the rest of the schools under investigation were located in suburban areas with largely middle class and affluent populations. Thus, the demographics of this sample of schools are quite similar to that of schools that have experienced mass shootings nationwide (Livingston, Rossheim, & Hall, 2019).

Adams High School is located in a middle-class suburban community where 93% of town residents are white, the household median income is roughly $57,000, and 3.5% of the population is below the poverty line. Of the nearly 1500 students at the high school, 16% receive free or reduced lunch.

Blane High School serves students in an affluent suburban community where 93% of the population is white, median household income is upwards of $80,000, and 2.1% of the population falls below the poverty line. Of the more than 1500 students at the high school, 5% receive free or reduced price lunch.

Courtside High School is located in a community with a population that is 72% white, the household median income is just under $36,000, and 11.3% of the population is below the poverty line. The school serves roughly 800 students, 45% of which receive either free or reduced lunch.

Donovan High School is located in a suburban borough where 86% of residents are white, the median income for households was just above $43,000, and 6.1% of the population is impoverished. Of the approximately 800 students at the school, 26% are eligible for the free or reduced price lunch program.

Everton High School is a large suburban school of nearly 3500 students, 4% of whom are eligible for free or reduced price lunch. In the town as a whole, 92% of residents are white, 3.7% are below the poverty line, and the median income for a household is roughly $75,000.

Finley High School, a suburban school with roughly 1300 students, has 6% of its students receive free or reduced price lunch. The town is 93% white with 0.9% of the population below the poverty line, and a median household income of roughly $84,000.

Greenvale High School is located in one of the most affluent suburban communities in the nation. In the town where this school is located, 95% of the population is white, the annual median income for a household is more than $140,000, and about 2.5% of the population falls below the poverty line. Approximately 1300 students attend the school, but no data on how many of them receive free or reduced lunch is available.

Hastings Jr./Sr. High School is a combined middle and high school in a rural town. The school has an enrollment of roughly 600 students, 41% of whom are eligible for free or reduced price lunch. The borough where the school is located is 99% white, the median income for a household is just below $27,000, and 15.6% of the population is below the poverty line.

Iverson High School is an affluent suburban school that enrolls more than 1200 students, 4% of whom are eligible for free or reduced price lunch. The town in which the school is located has a population that is 92% white, 3.9% under the poverty line, and household median income is more than $145,000 per year.

Jefferson Middle School serves nearly 800 students, 20% of whom are eligible for free or reduced price lunch. It is located in a borough that is 87% white, has a median household income of nearly $61,000, and where 3.6% of the population are below the poverty line.

Kranston High School is a large school in a suburban town. The school has an enrollment of more than 2000 students, and 23% of them are eligible for free or reduced price lunch. In the town, 73% of residents are white, median income for a household is more than $54,000, and 16% of the population is impoverished.

Many of the principals who agreed to be interviewed also referred me to other individuals at the local schools or police departments who could provide additional insight into the offenders, their threats, and the reactions of the schools and communities. In all, I spoke to thirty-two people (17 administrators, 4 counselors, 7 security and police officers, and 4 teachers) associated with these eleven incidents at schools across the Northeast. Seventeen of these were conducted in person at respondents' schools or police departments, and the other fifteen interviews took place over the telephone when this was the respondent's preference or when on-site interviews could not be coordinated. To triangulate the data gleaned from these interviews and confirm the accuracy of what my respondents told me, I cross-checked their accounts of an incident against their colleagues' accounts of the same incident, as well as with newspaper reporting, and whenever possible, court transcripts, legal briefs, and police incident reports.

Complications of Relying on the News Media to Build a Sampling Frame

Certain limitations exist by relying on news media accounts to gain a sampling frame of averted school rampage plots. In Duwe's (2000) study of how the print news media report mass murder, he found that the most widely publicized mass murders nationwide were disproportionately likely to include large numbers of casualties, victims unknown to the offender, public locations, assault weapons, interracial offender–victim relationships, older offenders, and workplace violence. Cramer's (1995) study found a similarly biased focus upon gun use in news media accounts of mass murder. Hence, a list compiled from newspaper searches may result in a disproportionate number of cases that fit these descriptions. No similar studies have investigated this bias in the school context and my data are already intentionally limited to plots of multiple-casualty events in public locations. However, if such a finding may be generalized to school rampage plots, this may mean that my data would similarly suffer from an inordinate number of cases where students have targeted victims of different races or ethnicities, as well as from undue attention paid to rampage attacks with random victims rather than targeted attacks and an overrepresentation of school shooting plots, as opposed to schemes involving bombings, knives, or other weaponry.

In addition, Duwe (2007, p. 185) found that only 45% of mass murder incidents were reported in the *New York Times*. Likewise, Cornell et al. (2004) indicated the presence of 188 violent threats during one school year in 35 schools across a single county in central Virginia, so there is no question that numerous threats go unnoticed and unreported by the media. Though only three of these 188 incidents were deemed genuine threats (wherein students were expelled for planning violence against particular students), they did locate another sixteen cases "involving multiple or nonspecific victims" (Cornell et al., 2004, p. 537). Nearly three dozen cases in one county during the course of a single year far outnumbers anything found via previously published articles or newspaper accounts, but this high number can likely be explained by the fact that these sixteen events were not deemed sufficiently serious to necessitate law enforcement intervention and thus gain media attention.

Finally, there is anecdotal evidence (McCabe & Martin, 2005, p. 88) that showcases how school administrators responded "quickly and quietly, as the school system did not want parents or the media notified [to] an emotionally disturbed student [who] had compiled a 'hit list' of students" to shoot and kill. As it is often in the interest of principals and other administrators to maintain good reputations for their schools, it should not necessarily be surprising that they would wish to hide potentially embarrassing stories from the media. Accordingly, there are potentially numerous cases of rampage threats which have been handled internally by school officials and thus never publicized by the media.

On Qualitative Methodology

The research strategy employed in this study enabled not only the descriptive investigation of the extent and placement of rampage attacks, but a diverse and in-depth exploratory inquiry into how school rampages are manifested, perceived, and prevented. This is a necessary first step, as little prior scholarship has focused upon the form and content of averted rampage plots. Qualitative methods are uniquely well suited to the study of new phenomena about which little or no previous research has been conducted, as they allow for the identification of new concepts and concerns via inductive discovery, rather than by forcing respondents to express themselves only within the confines of preexisting terminology with preset questions and hypotheses. Furthermore, while the content analysis of newspaper stories is an informative source with which to explore background data on the substance of these incidents, the interpretation of threat and risk are ultimately subjective endeavors which necessitate qualitative methods better suited to "make sense of or interpret, phenomena in terms of the meanings people bring to them" (Denzin & Lincoln, 2005, p. 3). As such, the best method to conduct research which carefully investigates the complex motivations, risk calculations, symbolic meanings, and thought processes by which school officials determine their attitudes and beliefs about violent threat assessment and prevention is in-depth interviews with the school officials tasked with such responsibilities. The thoughts and perspectives of a small number of people examined closely will prove more fruitful in the understanding of common underlying processes and the formulation of theory than a comparatively superficial, albeit more generalizable, look at a larger sample of the population (Athens, 1992). Additionally, triangulating information on averted rampage threats by cross-checking multiple sources is surely the best way to assure the integrity and accuracy of data.

Violent school threats and the manifold ways in which they are perceived, assessed, and prevented are naturally complex and subjective topics that previous theoretical formulations of crime, violence, and fear in other contexts cannot fully explain. Utilizing an inductive approach, this research did not test specific hypotheses upfront, but rather resulted from the formation of conceptual schemes which were explored and investigated so that patterns naturally emerged (Schutt, 2004). After the data collection stage, I used a grounded theory approach (Charmaz, 2001; Glaser & Strauss, 1967) in order to inductively derive typological categories and themes through the process of coding interview transcripts with the ATLAS.ti software program.

Generalizability in Qualitative Research

A common critique of qualitative methods is that the conclusions drawn from small non-random samples cannot be generalized to the population at large. With regard to this study, in particular, my sample is not strictly representative of, nor are its results generalizable to, all averted rampages in the classic quantitative sense. Though I started with as close to the population of averted rampage incidents as possible, those willing to grant me access to their schools may have been running better environments less complicit in the creation of school cultures where students want to engage in rampage attacks in the first place. Additionally, the fact that my interviews were limited to the Northeast means that we still know little about similar incidents in the rest of the country or the world at large. This is particularly significant because the majority of both attempted and completed school shootings have taken place in the Southern and Midwestern regions of the United States.

However, acknowledging the inability of qualitative work to achieve classical notions of generalizability because of a lack of large random samples, some scholars have attempted to form alternative conceptions more useful for qualitative research (see Schofield, 2002 for a detailed review of some recent developments in meta-ethnography, the case survey method, and the qualitative comparative method). One of the more famous may be found in the work of Guba and Lincoln

(Guba, 1981; Guba & Lincoln, 1982; Lincoln & Guba, 1985), who favor the term "transferability" to replace the goal of context-free laws desired via generalizability. In their conceptualization, analytic leaps across times, people, and places are desirable but permissible only under particular circumstances which may be assessed if sufficient thick description is available "to make a reasoned judgment about the degree of transferability possible" (Guba & Lincoln, 1982, p. 247). Still, other qualitative researchers view generalizability as "unimportant, unachievable, or both" (Schofield, 2002, p. 173) and reject it as a goal because every subject "must be seen as carrying its own logic, sense of order, structure, and meaning" (Denzin, 1983, p. 134). Whether or not this same critique applies to the newer qualitative notion of transferability, qualitative studies still maintain their underlying significance, as whatever they lack in generalizable knowledge of those outside the site of interest, they more than make up for with analytic generalizability (Kleinman, Copp, & Henderson, 1997) as a force to formulate knowledge on "larger generic theoretical concerns" (Sanders, 2004, p. xi). Particular behavioral motives, patterns, and outcomes are best understood in complete context, but theoretical constructs transcend their specific circumstances. For example, the conflict between Cohen's (2011) infamous youth subcultures, the Mods and the Rockers, and a public which was so fearful of and fascinated by them, must be situated in postwar English class relations and the demographic and generational changes present at the time, but his theoretical construct of moral panics need not be. Thus, while qualitative research may be less useful for specifying definitive beliefs or behaviors that apply across peoples and locales, it is vital for the generation of new insights, particularly in areas of research which have been understudied. While the manner in which threat is constructed, manifested, and perceived will surely vary across school districts, between regions of the country, and over time, the analytic categories, discourses, and relationships unearthed by this study's detailed qualitative investigation of violent school threats may prove useful regardless of the time or setting.

References

Athens, L. H. (1992). *The creation of dangerous violent criminals.* Chicago: University of Illinois Press.
Bernstein, A. (2009). *Bath massacre: America's first school bombing.* Ann Arbor, MI: University of Michigan Press.
Bower, A. (2001). Scorecard of hatred. *Time Magazine.* Retrieved July 25, 2019, from http://www.time.com/time/magazine/article/0,9171,999476,00.html.
Brady Center to Prevent Gun Violence. (n.d.). *Major school shootings in the United States since 1997.* Washington, DC. Retrieved July 15, 2010, from http://www.bradycampaign.org/xshare/pdf/school-shootings.pdf.
Charmaz, K. (2001). Qualitative interviewing and grounded theory analysis. In J. Gubrium & J. Holstein (Eds.), *Handbook of interview research: Context and method* (pp. 675–694). Thousand Oaks, CA: Sage.
Cohen, S. (2011). *Folk devils and moral panics: The creation of the mods and rockers.* New York: Routledge.
Cornell, D. G., Sheras, P. L., Kaplan, S., McConville, D., Douglass, J., Elkon, A., ... Cole, J. (2004). Guidelines for student threat assessment: Field-test findings. *School Psychology Review, 33*(4), 527–546.
Cramer, C. (1995). Ethical problems of mass murder coverage in the mass media. *Journal on Firearms and Public Policy, 7,* 113–134.
Daniels, J. A., Buck, I., Croxall, S., Gruber, J., Kime, P., & Govert, H. (2007). A content analysis of news reports of averted school rampages. *Journal of School Violence, 6,* 83–99.
Daniels, J. A., Volungis, A., Pshenishny, E., Gandhi, P., Winkler, A., Cramer, D., & Bradley, M. C. (2010). A qualitative investigation of averted school shooting rampages. *The Counseling Psychologist, 38*(1), 69–95.
Denzin, N. K. (1983). Interpretive interactionism. In G. Morgan (Ed.), *Beyond method: Strategies for social research* (pp. 129–146). Beverly Hills, CA: Sage.
Denzin, N. K., & Lincoln, Y. S. (2005). *The Sage handbook of qualitative research.* Thousand Oaks, CA: Sage.
Duwe, G. (2000). Body-count journalism: The presentation of mass murder in the news media. *Homicide Studies, 4*(4), 364–399.
Duwe, G. (2004). The patterns and prevalence of mass murder in twentieth-century America. *Justice Quarterly, 21*(4), 729–761.

Duwe, G. (2007). *Mass murder in the United States: A history*. Jefferson, NC: McFarland & Company.

Fox, J. A., & Levin, J. (1994). *Overkill: Mass murder and serial killing exposed*. New York: Plenum Press.

Fox, J. A., & Levin, J. (1998). Multiple homicide: Patterns of serial and mass murder. *Crime and Justice, 23*, 407–455.

Fox, J. A., Levin, J., & Fridel, E. E. (2018). *Extreme killing: Understanding serial and mass murder*. Thousand Oaks, CA: Sage.

Glaser, B., & Strauss, A. (1967). *The discovery of grounded theory: Strategies for qualitative research*. Chicago, IL: Aldine.

Guba, E. (1981). Criteria for assessing the trustworthiness of naturalistic inquiry. *Educational Communication and Technology Journal, 29*(2), 75–91.

Guba, E., & Lincoln, Y. (1982). Epistemological and methodological bases of naturalistic inquiry. *Educational Communication and Technology Journal, 30*, 233–252.

Hagan, J., Hirschfeld, P., & Shedd, C. (2002). First and last words: Apprehending the social and legal facts of an urban high school shooting. *Sociological Methods and Research, 31*(2), 218–255.

Harding, D., Fox, C., & Mehta, J. D. (2002). Studying rare events through qualitative case studies: Lessons from a study of rampage school shootings. *Sociological Methods and Research, 31*(2), 174–217.

Holmes, R. M., & Holmes, S. T. (2001). *Mass murder in the United States*. Upper Saddle River, NJ: Prentice Hall.

Kimmel, M. S., & Mahler, M. (2003). Adolescent masculinity, homophobia, and violence. *American Behavioral Scientist, 46*, 1439–1458.

Kleinman, S., Copp, M., & Henderson, K. (1997). Qualitatively different: Teaching fieldwork to graduate students. *Journal of Contemporary Ethnography, 25*, 469–499.

Langman, P., & Straub, F. (2019). *A comparison of averted and completed school attacks from the Police Foundation's averted school violence database*. Washington, DC: Office of Community Oriented Policing Services.

Larkin, R. W. (2007). *Comprehending Columbine*. Philadelphia, PA: Temple University Press.

Larkin, R. W. (2009). The Columbine legacy: Rampage shootings as political acts. *American Behavioral Scientist, 52*(9), 1309–1326.

Levin, J., & Fox, J. A. (1999). Making sense of mass murder. In V. B. Van Hasselt & M. Hersen (Eds.), *Handbook of psychological approaches with violent offenders: Contemporary strategies and issues* (pp. 173–187). Norwell, MA: Kluwer Academic.

Levin, J., & Madfis, E. (2009). Mass murder at school and cumulative strain: A sequential model. *American Behavioral Scientist, 52*(9), 1227–1245.

Lieberman, J. A. (2008). *School shootings: What every parent and educator needs to know to protect our children.* New York: Citadel Press.

Lincoln, Y., & Guba, E. (1985). *Naturalistic inquiry.* Beverly Hills, CA: Sage.

List of School-Related Attacks—Foiled or Exposed Plots. (n.d.). Retrieved July 15, 2010, from http://en.wikipedia.org/wiki/List_of_school-related_attacks#Foiled_or_exposed_plots.

Livingston, M. D., Rossheim, M. E., & Hall, K. S. (2019). A descriptive analysis of school and school shooter characteristics and the severity of school shootings in the United States, 1999–2018. *Journal of Adolescent Health, 64*(6), 797–799.

Madfis, E. (2014). Triple entitlement and homicidal anger: An exploration of the intersectional identities of American mass murderers. *Men and Masculinities, 17*(1), 67–86.

McCabe, K. A., & Martin, G. M. (2005). *School violence, the media, and criminal justice responses.* New York: Lang.

Meloy, J. R., Hempel, A. G., Gray, B. T., Mohandie, K., Shiva, A. A., & Richards, T. C. (2004). A comparative analysis of North American adolescent and adult mass murderers. *Behavioral Sciences & the Law, 22*(3), 291–309.

Meloy, J. R., Hempel, A. G., Mohandie, K., Shiva, A. A., & Gray, B. T. (2001). Offender and offense characteristics of a nonrandom sample of adolescent mass murders. *Journal of the American Academy of Child and Adolescent Psychiatry, 40*(6), 719–728.

Moore, M. H., Petrie, C. V., Braga, A. A., & McLaughlin, B. L. (2003). *Deadly lessons: Understanding lethal school violence.* Washington, DC: National Academies Press.

Muschert, G. W. (2007). Research in school shootings. *Sociology Compass, 1*(1), 60–80.

Newman, K. S., & Fox, C. (2009). Repeat tragedy: Rampage shootings in American high school and college settings, 2002–2008. *American Behavioral Scientist, 52*(9), 1286–1308.

Newman, K. S., Fox, C., Roth, W., Mehta, J., & Harding, D. (2004). *Rampage: The social roots of school shooters.* New York: Perseus Books Group.

Palermo, G. B., & Ross, L. E. (1999). Mass murder, suicide, and moral development: Can we separate the adults from the juveniles? *International Journal of Offender Therapy and Comparative Criminology, 43*(1), 8–20.

Petee, T. A., Padgett, K. G., & York, T. S. (1997). Debunking the stereotype: An examination of mass murder in public places. *Homicide Studies, 1*(4), 317–337.

Pollack, W. S., Modzeleski, W., & Rooney, G. (2008). *Prior knowledge of potential school-based violence: Information students learn may prevent a targeted attack.* Washington, DC: United States Secret Service and United States Department of Education.

Reddy, M., Borum, R., Berglund, J., Vossekuil, B., Fein, R., & Modzeleski, W. (2001). Evaluating risk for targeted violence in schools: Comparing risk assessment, threat assessment, and other approaches. *Psychology in the Schools, 38*(2), 157–172.

Robertson, T. (2001, December 16). Across the nation, school attack plots pose legal challenge. *Boston Globe*, pp. A1, A26.

Sanders, C. (2004). Foreword. In A. Arluke, *Brute force: Animal police and the challenge of cruelty* (pp. vii–xiii). West Lafayette, IN: Purdue University Press.

Schofield, J. W. (2002). Increasing the generalizability of qualitative research. In A. M. Huberman & M. Miles (Eds.), *The qualitative researcher's companion* (pp. 171–203). Thousand Oaks, CA: Sage Publications.

Schutt, R. K. (2004). *Investigating the social world: The process and practice of research.* Thousand Oaks: Pine Forge Press.

Sullivan, M. L., & Guerette, R. T. (2003). The copycat factor: Mental illness, guns, and the shooting incident at Heritage high school, Rockdale County, Georgia. In M. H. Moore (Ed.), *Deadly lessons: Understanding lethal school violence* (pp. 25–69). Washington, DC: National Academies Press.

Virginia Tech Review Panel. (2007). *Mass shootings at Virginia Tech April 16, 2007: Report of the Virginia Tech Review Panel presented to Timothy M. Kaine, Governor, Commonwealth of Virginia.* Retrieved April 11, 2019, from https://scholar.lib.vt.edu/prevail/docs/VTReviewPanelReport.pdf.

Vossekuil, B., Fein, R., Reddy, M., Borum, R., & Modzeleski, W. (2002). *The final report and findings of the safe school initiative: Implications for the prevention of school attacks in the United States.* Washington, DC: U.S. Secret Service and U.S. Department of Education.

White-Hamon, L. S. (2000). *Mass murder and attempted mass murder: An examination of the perpetrator with an empirical analysis of typologies.* Unpublished doctoral dissertation, California School of Professional Psychology, Fresno, CA.

References

Active Shooter Incidents in the United States in 2016 and 2017. (2018). *Federal Bureau of Investigation, United States Department of Justice.* Washington, DC. Retrieved July 18, 2019, from https://www.fbi.gov/file-repository/active-shooter-incidents-us-2016-2017.pdf/view.

Adams, D. M. (1998). The problem of the incomplete attempt. *Social Theory and Practice, 24,* 317–343.

Addington, L. (2013). Surveillance and security approaches across public school levels. In G. W. Muschert, S. Henry, N. L. Bracy, & A. A. Peguero (Eds.), *Responding to school violence: Confronting the Columbine effect* (pp. 71–88). Boulder, CO: Lynne Rienner.

Advancement Project. (2005). *Education on lockdown: The schoolhouse to jailhouse track.* Retrieved July 26, 2019, from https://b.3cdn.net/advancement/5351180e24cb166d02_mlbrqgxlh.pdf.

Agnich, L. E. (2015). A comparative analysis of attempted and completed school-based mass murder attacks. *American Journal of Criminal Justice, 40*(1), 1–22.

Aitken, S. C. (2001). Schoolyard shootings: Racism, sexism and moral panics over teen violence. *Antipode, 33*(4), 594–600.

Alexander, M. (2010). *The new Jim Crow: Mass incarceration in the age of colorblindness.* New York: New Press.

Altheide, D. L. (2009). The Columbine shootings and the discourse of fear. *American Behavioral Scientist, 52*(10), 1354–1370.

American Bar Association. (2001). *Zero tolerance policy report.* Retrieved September 25, 2012, from www.abanet.org/crimjust/juvjus/zerotolreport.html.

American Psychological Association. (1999). *Warning signs: A violence prevention guide for youth.* Retrieved September 30, 2010, from http://helping.apa.org/warningsigns/index.html.

American Psychological Association Zero Tolerance Task Force. (2008). Are zero tolerance policies effective in the schools?: An evidentiary review and recommendations. *American Psychologist, 63*(9), 852–862.

Anderson, E. (1999). *Code of the street: Decency, violence and the moral life of the inner city.* New York: Norton.

Andrade, J. T. (Ed.). (2009). *Handbook of violence risk assessment and treatment: New approaches for mental health professionals.* New York, NY: Springer.

Andrade, J. T., O'Neill, K., & Diener, R. B. (2009). Violence risk assessment and risk management: A historical overview and clinical application. In J. T. Andrade (Ed.), *Handbook of violence risk assessment and treatment: New approaches for mental health professionals* (pp. 3–40). New York, NY: Springer.

Arenson, K. J. (2005). The pitfalls in the law of attempt: A new perspective. *The Journal of Criminal Law, 69*(2), 146–167.

Arluke, A., Lankford, A., & Madfis, E. (2018). Harming animals and massacring humans: Characteristics of active and mass shooters who abused animals. *Behavioral Sciences & the Law, 36*(6), 739–751.

Arluke, A., & Madfis, E. (2014). Animal abuse as a warning sign of school massacres: A critique and refinement. *Homicide Studies, 18*(1), 7–22.

Aronson, E. (2004). How the Columbine high school tragedy could have been prevented. *Journal of Individual Psychology, 60,* 355–360.

Athens, L. H. (1992). *The creation of dangerous violent criminals.* Chicago: University of Illinois Press.

Attack on German High School Prevented, Police Say. (2007, November 18). Retrieved July 26, 2019, from http://www.cnn.com/2007/WORLD/europe/11/18/germany.school.plot/index.html.

Ayers, W., Ayers, R., & Dohrn, B. (2001). *Zero tolerance: Resisting the drive for punishment in our schools.* New York: The Free Press.

Band, S. R., & Harpold, J. A. (1999). School violence: Lessons learned. *FBI Law Enforcement Bulletin, 68,* 9–16.

Bayles, M. D. (1982). Punishment for attempts. *Social Theory and Practice, 8,* 21–29.
Beck, U. (1992). *The risk society: Towards a new modernity.* London: Sage.
Becker, L. C. (1973/1974). Criminal attempt and the theory of the law of crimes. *Philosophy & Public Affairs, 3,* 262–294.
Beckett, K., Beach, L., Knaphus, E., & Reosti, A. (2018). US criminal justice policy and practice in the twenty-first century: Toward the end of mass incarceration? *Law and Policy, 40*(4), 321–345.
Bell, E. (2011). *Criminal justice and neoliberalism.* Basingstoke: Palgrave Macmillan.
Bernstein, A. (2009). *Bath massacre: America's first school bombing.* Ann Arbor, MI: University of Michigan Press.
Best, J. (2002). Monster hype. *Education Next, 2,* 51–55.
Blair, J. P., & Schweit, K. W. (2014). *A study of active shooter incidents, 2000–2013.* Washington, DC: Texas State University and Federal Bureau of Investigation, U.S. Department of Justice.
Böckler, N., Heitmeyer, W., Sitzer, P., & Seeger, T. (Eds.). (2013). *School shootings: International research, case studies, and concepts for prevention.* New York, NY: Springer.
Borum, R. (2000). Assessing violence risk among youth. *Journal of Clinical Psychology, 56,* 1263–1288.
Borum, R., Cornell, D., Modzeleski, W., & Jimerson, S. (2010). What can be done about school shootings?: A review of the evidence. *Educational Researcher, 39*(1), 27–37.
Bower, A. (2001). Scorecard of hatred. *Time Magazine.* Retrieved July 25, 2019, from http://www.time.com/time/magazine/article/0,9171,999476,00.html.
Brady Center to Prevent Gun Violence. (n.d.). *Major school shootings in the United States since 1997.* Washington, DC. Retrieved July 15, 2010, from http://www.bradycampaign.org/xshare/pdf/school-shootings.pdf.
Brady, K. P., Balmer, S., & Phenix, D. (2007). School-police partnership effectiveness in urban schools. *Education and Urban Society, 39,* 455–478.
Brank, E. M., Woolard, J. L., Brown, V. E., Fondacaro, M., Luescher, J. L., Chinn, R. G., & Miller, S. A. (2007). Will they tell? Weapons reporting by middle-school youth. *Youth Violence and Juvenile Justice, 5*(2), 125–146.
Brent, J. J., & Wilson, A. (2018). Student responses to policing in schools. In J. Deakin, E. Taylor, & A. Kupchik (Eds.), *The Palgrave international handbook of school discipline, surveillance, and social control* (pp. 351–367). New York, NY: Palgrave Macmillan.

Brinkley, C. J., & Saarnio, D. A. (2006). Involving students in school violence prevention: Are they willing to help? *Journal of School Violence, 5,* 93–116.

Brint, S. (1998). *Schools and societies.* Thousand Oaks: Pine Forge Press.

Burgess, A., Garbarino, C., & Carlson, M. (2006). Pathological teasing and bullying turned deadly: Shooters and suicide. *Victims & Offenders, 1,* 1–13.

Burns, R., & Crawford, C. (1999). School shootings, the media, and public fear: Ingredients for a moral panic. *Crime, Law & Social Change, 32,* 147–168.

Butterfield, F. with McFadden, R. (2001, November 26). *3 teenagers held in plot at Massachusetts school.* Retrieved July 24, 2019, from http://www.nytimes.com/2001/11/26/us/3-teenagers-held-in-plot-at-massachusetts-school.html.

Campbell, S. B. (1991). Longitudinal studies of active and aggressive preschoolers: Individual differences in early behavior and in outcome. In D. Cicchetti & S. L. Toth (Eds.), *Internalizing and externalizing expressions of dysfunction: Volume 2 (Rochester symposium on developmental psychopathology)* (pp. 57–90). Hillsdale, NJ: Lawrence Erlbaum Associates.

Campbell, S. B., Breaux, A. M., Ewing, L. J., & Szumowski, E. K. (1986). Correlates and predictors of hyperactivity and aggression: A longitudinal study of parent-referred problem preschoolers. *Journal of Abnormal Child Psychology, 14,* 217–234.

Canter, D., & Youngs, D. (2009). *Investigative psychology: Offender profiling and the analysis of criminal action.* New York: Wiley.

Carter, H. (2009, September 2). *Manchester teenagers planned Columbine-style attack, jury told.* Retrieved July 17, 2019, from http://www.guardian.co.uk/uk/2009/sep/02/manchester-teenagers-columbine-style-attack.

Casella, R. (2001). *Being down: Challenging violence in urban schools.* New York: Teachers College Press.

Casella, R. (2003). The false allure of security technologies. *Social Justice, 30*(3), 82–93.

Casella, R. (2006). *Selling us the fortress: The promotion of techno-security equipment for schools.* New York: Routledge.

Charmaz, K. (2001). Qualitative interviewing and grounded theory analysis. In J. Gubrium & J. Holstein (Eds.), *Handbook of interview research: Context and method* (pp. 675–694). Thousand Oaks, CA: Sage.

Christopher, R. (2004). Does attempted murder deserve greater punishment than murder? Moral luck and the duty to prevent harm. *Notre Dame Journal of Law, Ethics, and Public Policy, 18*(2), 419–435.

Civil Rights Data Collection. (2012). *U.S. Dept. of Education Office for Civil Rights*. Retrieved May 26, 2019, from http://www2.ed.gov/about/offices/list/ocr/docs/crdc-2012-data-summary.pdf.

Clarke, R. V. (1995). Situational crime prevention. *Crime and Justice, 19,* 91–150.

Clear, T. (1994). *Harm in American penology: Offenders, victims, and their communities.* Albany, NY: SUNY Press.

Cohen, S. (2011). *Folk devils and moral panics: The creation of the mods and rockers.* New York: Routledge.

Coleman, L. (2004). *The copycat effect: How the media and popular culture trigger the mayhem in tomorrow's headlines.* New York: Simon and Schuster.

Collier, R. (1998). *Masculinities, crime, and criminology: Men, heterosexuality, and the criminal(ised) other.* Thousand Oaks, CA: Sage.

Consalvo, M. (2003). The monsters next door: Media constructions of boys and masculinity. *Feminist Media Studies, 3*(1), 27–45.

Cornell, D. G. (2003). Guidelines for responding to student threats of violence. *Journal of Educational Administration, 41,* 705–719.

Cornell, D. G. (2006). *School violence: Fear versus facts.* Mahwah, NJ: Lawrence Erlbaum.

Cornell, D. G. (2013). The Virginia student threat assessment guidelines: An empirically supported violence prevention strategy. In N. Böckler, W. Heitmeyer, P. Sitzer, & T. Seeger (Eds.), *School shootings: International research, case studies, and concepts for prevention* (pp. 379–400). New York, NY: Springer.

Cornell, D. G., & Sheras, P. L. (2006). *Guidelines for responding to student threats of violence.* Longmont, CO: Sopris West.

Cornell, D. G., Sheras, P. L., Kaplan, S., McConville, D., Douglass, J., Elkon, A., … Cole, J. (2004). Guidelines for student threat assessment: Field-test findings. *School Psychology Review, 33*(4), 527–546.

Cramer, C. (1995). Ethical problems of mass murder coverage in the mass media. *Journal on Firearms and Public Policy, 7,* 113–134.

Cranley, E. (2019, August 5). *How to stop shootings in America: 10 strategies proposed to stop gun violence, and how likely they are to work.* Retrieved January 28, 2020, from https://www.businessinsider.com/how-to-stop-gun-school-shooting-america-2018-11.

Crews, G., Crews, A. D., & Burton, C. (2013). The only thing that stops a guy with a bad policy is a guy with a good policy: An examination of the NRA's "National School Shield" proposal. *American Journal of Criminal Justice, 38*(2), 183–199.

Cullen, D. (2009). *Columbine*. New York: Twelve.
Cullen, D. (2010). *Columbine*. New York, NY: Hachette.
Culley, M. R., Conkling, M., Emshoff, J., Blakely, C., & Gorman, D. (2006). Environmental and contextual influences on school violence and its prevention. *The Journal of Primary Prevention, 27*(3), 217–227.
Curran, C. F. (2017). The law, policy, and portrayal of zero tolerance school discipline: Examining prevalence and characteristics across levels of governance and school districts. *Educational Policy, 33*(2), 319–349.
Daniels, J. A. (2019). *A preliminary report on the Police Foundations averted school violence database*. Washington, DC: Office of Community Oriented Policing Services.
Daniels, J. A., & Bradley, M. C. (2011). *Preventing lethal school violence*. New York, NY: Springer.
Daniels, J. A., Buck, I., Croxall, S., Gruber, J., Kime, P., & Govert, H. (2007). A content analysis of news reports of averted school rampages. *Journal of School Violence, 6,* 83–99.
Daniels, J. A., Volungis, A., Pshenishny, E., Gandhi, P., Winkler, A., Cramer, D., & Bradley, M. C. (2010). A qualitative investigation of averted school shooting rampages. *The Counseling Psychologist, 38*(1), 69–95.
Davis, M. (1986). Why attempts deserve less punishment than complete crimes. *Law and Philosophy, 5*(1), 1–32.
Davis, O. (2014, October 17). *Punitive schooling*. Retrieved January 30, 2020, from https://www.jacobinmag.com/2014/10/punitive-schooling/.
Deakin, J., & Kupchik, A. (2018). Managing behavior: From exclusion to restorative practices. In J. Deakin, E. Taylor, & A. Kupchik (Eds.), *The Palgrave international handbook of school discipline, surveillance, and social control* (pp. 511–527). New York, NY: Palgrave Macmillan.
Deisinger, G., Randazzo, M., O'Neill, D., & Savage, J. (2008). *The handbook for campus threat assessment and management teams*. Stoneham, MA: Applied Risk Management LLC.
Denzin, N. K. (1983). Interpretive interactionism. In G. Morgan (Ed.), *Beyond method: Strategies for social research* (pp. 129–146). Beverly Hills, CA: Sage.
Denzin, N. K., & Lincoln, Y. S. (2005). *The Sage handbook of qualitative research*. Thousand Oaks, CA: Sage.
Devlin, D., & Gottfredson, D. C. (2018). Policing and the school-to-prison pipeline. In J. Deakin, E. Taylor, & A. Kupchik (Eds.), *The Palgrave international handbook of school discipline, surveillance, and social control* (pp. 291–308). New York, NY: Palgrave Macmillan.

DeVos, B., Nielsen, K., Azar, A., & Whitaker, M. (2018). *Final report of the Federal Commission on School Safety.* US Department of Education. Retrieved June 12, 2019, from https://files.eric.ed.gov/fulltext/ED590823.pdf.

Dinkes, R., Kemp, J., Baum, K., & Snyder, T. D. (2009). *Indicators of school crime and safety: 2009 (NCES 2010–012/NCJ 228478).* Washington, DC: National Center for Education Statistics, Institute of Education Sciences, U.S. Department of Education, and Bureau of Justice Statistics, Office of Justice Programs, U.S. Department of Justice.

Donahue, J. J., Aneja, A., & Weber, K. D. (2018). Right-to-carry laws and violent crime: A comprehensive assessment using panel data and a state-level synthetic control analysis. *Journal of Empirical Legal Studies, 16*(2), 198–247.

Don't Name Them. (2019). Retrieved July 17, 2019, from https://www.facebook.com/pg/DontNameThem/about/.

Douglas, J. E., Ressler, R. K., Burgess, A. W., & Hartman, C. R. (1986). Criminal profiling from crime scene analysis. *Behavioral Sciences and the Law, 4,* 401–421.

Drane, K. (2019, June 1). *Every incident of mishandled guns in schools.* Retrieved June 26, 2019, from https://giffords.org/2019/06/every-incident-of-mishandled-guns-in-schools/.

Duff, A. (1997). *Criminal attempts.* Oxford: Oxford University Press.

Duwe, G. (2000). Body-count journalism: The presentation of mass murder in the news media. *Homicide Studies, 4*(4), 364–399.

Duwe, G. (2004). The patterns and prevalence of mass murder in twentieth-century America. *Justice Quarterly, 21*(4), 729–761.

Duwe, G. (2007). *Mass murder in the United States: A history.* Jefferson, NC: McFarland & Company.

Duwe, G., Kovandzic, T., & Moody, C. (2002). The impact of right-to-carry concealed firearms laws on mass public shootings. *Homicide Studies, 6*(4), 271–296.

Dwyer, K. P., Osher, D., & Warger, C. (1998). *Early warning, timely response: A guide to safe schools.* Washington, DC: U.S. Department of Education.

Edwards, H. S. (2018, May 22). School shootings are becoming the new normal. *Time.* Retrieved May 14, 2019, from http://time.com/5286666/school-shootings-new-normal-santa-fe/.

Eliot, M., Cornell, D., Gregory, A., & Fan, X. (2010). Supportive school climate and student willingness to seek help for bullying and threats of violence. *Journal of School Psychology, 48*(6), 533–553.

Enker, A. N. (1977). Mens rea and criminal attempt. *Law & Social Inquiry, 2*(4), 845–879.
Epstein, J. (2002). Breaking the code of silence: Bystanders to campus violence and the law of college and university safety. *Stetson Law Review, 32,* 91–124.
Everytown for Gun Safety. (2014, December 9*). Analysis of school shootings.* Retrieved April 26, 2016, from http://everytownresearch.org/reports/analysis-of-school-shootings/.
Farr, K. (2019). Trouble with the other: The role of romantic rejection in rampage school shootings by adolescent males. *Violence and Gender, 6*(3), 147–153.
Farrington, D. P. (1991). Childhood aggression and adult violence: Early precursors and later-life outcomes. In D. J. Pepler & K. H. Rubin (Eds.), *The development and treatment of childhood aggression* (pp. 5–29). Hillsdale, NJ: Lawrence Erlbaum Associates.
Feeley, M., & Simon, J. (1992). The new penology: Notes on the emerging strategy of corrections and its implications. *Criminology, 30*(4), 449–470.
Feeley, M., & Simon, J. (1994). Actuarial justice: The emerging new criminal law. In D. Nelken (Ed.), *The futures of criminology* (pp. 173–201). London: Sage.
Fein, R. A., Vossekuil, B., & Holden, G. (1995). Threat assessment: An approach to prevent targeted violence. In *National Institute of Justice: Research in Action* (pp. 1–7). Washington, DC: U.S. Department of Justice, Office of Justice Programs.
Fein, R. A., Vossekuil, B., Pollack, W., Borum, R., Modzeleski, W., & Reddy, M. (2002). *Threat assessment in schools: A guide to managing threatening situations and to creating safe school climates.* Washington, DC: U.S. Department of Education, Office of Elementary and Secondary Education, Safe and Drug-Free Schools Program and U.S. Secret Service, National Threat Assessment Center.
Feinberg, J. (1995). Equal punishment for failed attempts: Some bad but instructive arguments against it. *Arizona Law Review, 37,* 117–133.
Felson, M. (1994). *Crime and everyday life: Insight and implications for society.* Thousand Oaks, CA: Pine Forge.
Fenning, P., & Rose, J. (2007). Overrepresentation of African American students in exclusionary discipline: The role of school policy. *Urban Education, 42*(6), 536–559.
Flegenheimer, M. (2013). Final report on Sandy Hook killings sheds new light on gunman's isolation. *The New York Times.* Retrieved February 1,

2019, from http://www.nytimes.com/2013/12/28/nyregion/with-release-of-final-sandy-hook-shooting-report-investigation-is-said-to-be-over.html?pagewanted=1&_r=1&.

Follman, M., Aronsen, G., & Pan, D. (2019). A guide to mass shootings in America. *Mother Jones*. Retrieved May 19, 2019, from https://www.motherjones.com/politics/2012/12/mass-shootings-mother-jones-full-data/.

Foucault, M. (1977). *Discipline and punish: The birth of the prison*. Harmondsworth: Penguin.

Foucault, M. (1980). *Power/knowledge*. Brighton, UK: Harvester.

Foucault, M. (1991). Governmentality. In G. Burchell, C. Gordon, & P. Miller (Eds.), *The Foucault effect: Studies in governmentality* (pp. 87–104). London, UK: Harvester Wheatsheaf.

Foucault, M. (2009). *Security, territory, population: Lectures at the Collège de France 1977—1978*. New York: Palgrave Macmillan.

Fox, J. A., & Burstein, H. (2010). *Violence and security on campus: From preschool through college*. Santa Barbara, CA: Praeger.

Fox, J. A., & DeLateur, M. J. (2014). Mass shootings in America: Moving beyond Newtown. *Homicide Studies, 18*(1), 125–145.

Fox, J. A., & Levin, J. (1994). *Overkill: Mass murder and serial killing exposed*. New York: Plenum Press.

Fox, J. A., & Levin, J. (1998). Multiple homicide: Patterns of serial and mass murder. *Crime and Justice, 23*, 407–455.

Fox, J. A., Levin, J., & Fridel, E. E. (2018). *Extreme killing: Understanding serial and mass murder*. Thousand Oaks, CA: Sage.

Fox, J. A., Levin, J., & Quinet, K. (2019). *The will to kill* (5th ed.). Thousand Oaks, CA: Sage.

Fox, J. A., & Savage, J. (2009). Mass murder goes to college: An examination of changes on college campuses following Virginia Tech. *American Behavioral Scientist, 52*(10), 1286–1308.

French, D. (2018, March 16). *The NRA makes a wise, principled decision to support gun-violence restraining orders*. Retrieved June 7, 2019, from https://www.nationalreview.com/2018/03/nra-gun-violence-restraining-order-support-good-move/.

Gallup, G. (1999). *Many teens report copycat-related problems at school in wake of Littleton shooting: Nearly half say their school has violent or violence-prone groups*. Retrieved June 19, 2019, from http://www.gallup.com/poll/3838/Many-Teens-Report-CopycatRelated-Problems-School-Wake-Little.aspx.

Garland, D. (2001). *The culture of control: Crime and social order in contemporary society*. Chicago: University of Chicago Press.

Gaughan, E., Cerio, J. D., & Myers, R. A. (2001). *Lethal violence in schools: A national survey.* Alfred, NY: Alfred University.

Giddens, A. (1999). Risk and responsibility. *The Modern Law Review, 62*(1), 1–10.

Giffords Law Center. (2018). *Extreme risk protection orders.* Retrieved June 7, 2019, from https://lawcenter.giffords.org/gun-laws/policy-areas/who-can-have-a-gun/extreme-risk-protection-orders/.

Glaser, B., & Strauss, A. (1967). *The discovery of grounded theory: Strategies for qualitative research.* Chicago, IL: Aldine.

Glassner, B. (2010). *The culture of fear: Why Americans are afraid of the wrong things* (10th anniversary ed.). New York: Basic Books.

Goldson, B. (2002). New punitiveness: The politics of child incarceration. In J. Muncie, G. Hughes, & E. McLaughlin (Eds.), *Youth justice: Critical readings* (pp. 386–400). London: Sage.

Goodrich, J. (2012, April 11). *Accused gunman in Oakland massacre tells CBS 5 he's "deeply sorry."* Retrieved April 13, 2019, from http://sanfrancisco.cbslocal.com/2012/04/11/exclusive-jailhouse-interview-accused-gunman-in-oakland-massacre-talks-to-cbs-5/.

Gould, M. S., & Olivares, M. (2017). Mass shootings and murder-suicide: Review of empirical evidence for contagion. In S. Stack & T. Niederkrotenthaler (Eds.), *Media and suicide: International perspectives on research, theory, and policy* (pp. 41–66). New York, NY: Routledge.

Graham, C. (2018, February 15). *"The new normal": With a school shooting every 60 hours, US faces grim reality.* Retrieved May 14, 2019, from https://www.telegraph.co.uk/news/2018/02/15/new-normal-school-shooting-every-60-hours-us-accepts-grim-reality/.

Griffiths, R. (2010). The gothic folk devils strike back! Theorizing folk devil reaction in the post-Columbine era. *Journal of Youth Studies, 13*(3), 403–422.

Grisso, T. (2009). Foreword. In J. T. Andrade (Ed.), *Handbook of violence risk assessment and treatment: New approaches for mental health professionals* (pp. xv–xvii). New York, NY: Springer.

Grubin, D., & Wingate, S. (1996). Sexual offence recidivism: Prediction versus understanding. *Criminal Behaviour and Mental Health, 6,* 349–359.

Guba, E. (1981). Criteria for assessing the trustworthiness of naturalistic inquiry. *Educational Communication and Technology Journal, 29*(2), 75–91.

Guba, E., & Lincoln, Y. (1982). Epistemological and methodological bases of naturalistic inquiry. *Educational Communication and Technology Journal, 30,* 233–252.

Haenfler, R. (2016). *Goths, gamers, and grrrls: Deviance and youth subcultures.* Oxford: Oxford University Press.

Hagan, J., Hirschfeld, P., & Shedd, C. (2002). First and last words: Apprehending the social and legal facts of an urban high school shooting. *Sociological Methods and Research, 31*(2), 218–255.

Haider-Markel, D. P., & Joslyn, M. R. (2001). Gun policy, opinion, tragedy, and blame attribution: The conditional influence of issue frames. *Journal of Politics, 63,* 520–543.

Halbig, W. W. (2000). Breaking the code of silence. *American School Board Journal, 187*(3), 34–36.

Harcourt, B. (2007). *Against prediction: Profiling, policing, and punishing in an actuarial age.* Chicago, IL: University of Chicago Press.

Harcourt, B. (2010). Neoliberal penality: A brief genealogy. *Theoretical Criminology, 14*(1), 74–92.

Harding, D., Fox, C., & Mehta, J. D. (2002). Studying rare events through qualitative case studies: Lessons from a study of rampage school shootings. *Sociological Methods and Research, 31*(2), 174–217.

Harsanyi, J. C. (1980). A bargaining model for social status in informal groups and formal organizations. In J. C. Harsanyi (Ed.), *Essays on ethics, social behavior, and scientific explanation: Theory and decision library* (Vol. 12, pp. 204–226). Dordrecht, Netherlands: Springer.

Heitzeg, N. A. (2016). *The school-to prison pipeline: Education, discipline, and racialized double standards.* Santa Barbara, CA: Praeger.

Helfgott, J. B. (2015). Criminal behavior and the copycat effect: Literature review and theoretical framework for empirical investigation. *Aggression and Violent Behavior, 22,* 46–64.

Henry, S. (2009). School violence beyond Columbine: A complex problem in need of an interdisciplinary analysis. *American Behavioral Scientist, 52*(9), 1246–1265.

Hirschfield, P. J. (2008). Preparing for prison? The criminalization of school discipline in the USA. *Theoretical Criminology, 12*(1), 79–101.

Hirschfield, P. J. (2010). School surveillance in America: Disparate and unequal. In T. Monahan & R. D. Torress (Eds.), *Schools under surveillance: Cultures of control in public education* (pp. 38–54). New Brunswick, NJ: Rutgers University Press.

Hirschfield, P. J. (2018). Trends in school social control in the United States: Explaining patterns of decriminalization. In J. Deakin, E. Taylor, & A. Kupchik (Eds.), *The Palgrave international handbook of school discipline, surveillance, and social control* (pp. 43–64). New York, NY: Palgrave Macmillan.

Hirschfield, P. J., & Celinska, K. (2011). Beyond fear: Sociological perspectives on the criminalization of school discipline. *Sociology Compass, 5*(1), 1–12.

Holcomb, A., & Allen, M. J. (2009, December 9). *Moving beyond zero tolerance.* American Civil Liberties Union of Washington. Retrieved May 20, 2019, from http://www.aclu-wa.org/news/moving-beyond-zero-tolerance.

Holmes, R. M., & Holmes, S. T. (2001). *Mass murder in the United States.* Upper Saddle River, NJ: Prentice Hall.

Homant, R. J., & Kennedy, D. B. (1998). Psychological Aspects of crime scene profiling: Validity research. *Criminal Justice and Behavior, 25,* 319–343.

Hong, J. S., Hyunkag, C., Allen-Meares, P., & Espelage, D. L. (2011). The social ecology of the Columbine high school shootings. *Children and Youth Services Review, 33,* 861–868.

Horsley, S. (2018, March 12). *Gun advocates are not happy about Trump advocating for risk protection orders.* Retrieved June 7, 2019, from https://www.npr.org/2018/03/12/592965390/gun-advocates-are-not-happy-about-trump-advocating-for-risk-protection-orders.

Huff-Corzine, L., McCutcheon, J. C., Corzine, J., Jarvis, J. P., Tetzlaff-Bemiller, M., Weller, M., & Landon, M. (2014). Shooting for accuracy: Comparing data sources on mass murder. *Homicide Studies, 18,* 105–124.

Hymowitz, K. S. (2005, April 18). Zero tolerance policies are necessary to prevent school violence. In S. Barbour (Ed.), *How can school violence be prevented?* (pp. 24–26). New York, NY: Thomson-Gale.

International Association of Chiefs of Police. (1999). *Guidelines for preventing and responding to school violence.* VA: Alexandria.

Irigaray, L. (1985). *This sex which is not one* (C. Porter & C. Burke, Trans.). New York: Cornell University Press.

James, S. D. (2009, April 13). *Columbine shootings 10 years later: Students, teacher still haunted by post-traumatic stress.* ABC News. Retrieved May 23, 2019, from h https://web.archive.org/web/20130427102132/http://abcnews.go.com/Health/story?id=7300782&page=1.

Jenkins, M. (2019, February 20). *All California public schools may need to have school resource officers.* Retrieved June 12, 2019, from https://sacramento.cbslocal.com/2019/02/20/california-school-resource-officers/.

Jimerson, S. R., Brock, S. E., & Cowan, K. (2005). Threat assessment: An essential component of a comprehensive safe school program. *Principal Leadership, 6*(2), 11–15.

Johnson, E. S. (2019). Contemporary society and the phenomenon of school rampage shootings in the United States: A theoretical approach to understanding. In R. Papa (Ed.), *School violence in international contexts* (pp. 133–146). Thousand Oaks, CA: Sage.

Kalish, R., & Kimmel, M. (2010). Suicide by mass murder: Masculinity, aggrieved entitlement, and rampage school shootings. *Health Sociology Review, 19*(4), 451–464.

Karp, D. R., & Breslin, B. (2001). Restorative justice in school communities. *Youth & Society, 33*(2), 249–272.

Keppel, R. D. (2006). *Offender profiling*. Mason, OH: Thomson Custom Publishing.

Kiefer, H. M. (2005). *Public: Society powerless to stop school shootings*. Retrieved May 20, 2019, from http://www.gallup.com/poll/15511/Public-Society-Powerless-Stop-School-Shootings.aspx.

Kiilakoski, T., & Oksanen, A. (2011). Soundtrack of the school shootings: Cultural script. *Music and Male Rage. Young, 19*(3), 247–269.

Killingbeck, D. (2001). The role of television news in the construction of school violence as a "moral panic". *Journal of Criminal Justice and Popular Culture, 8*(3), 186–202.

Kim, C., Losen, D., & Hewitt, D. (2010). *The school-to-prison pipeline: Structuring legal reform*. New York: New York University Press.

Kimmel, M. S., & Mahler, M. (2003). Adolescent masculinity, homophobia, and violence. *American Behavioral Scientist, 46*, 1439–1458.

King, S., & Bracy, N. (2019). School security in the post-Columbine era: Trends, consequences, and future directions. *Journal of Contemporary Criminal Justice, 35*(3), 274–295.

King, S., Rusoja, A., & Peguero, A. (2018). The school-to-prison pipeline. In J. Deakin, E. Taylor, & A. Kupchik (Eds.), *The Palgrave international handbook of school discipline, surveillance, and social control* (pp. 269–290). New York, NY: Palgrave Macmillan.

Kinnally, K. (2018, April 12). *Maryland safe to learn act of 2018: What you need to know*. Retrieved June 12, 2019, from https://conduitstreet.mdcounties.org/2018/04/12/maryland-safe-to-learn-act-of-2018-what-you-need-to-know/.

Kissner, J. (2016). Are active shootings temporally contagious? An empirical assessment. *Journal of Police and Criminal Psychology, 31*, 48–58.

Klein, J. (2005). Teaching her a lesson: Media misses boys' rage relating to girls in school shootings. *Crime, Media, Culture, 1*(1), 90–97.

Klein, J. (2006a). An invisible problem: Everyday violence against girls in schools. *Theoretical Criminology, 10*(2), 147–177.

Klein, J. (2006b). Cultural capital and high school bullies: How social inequality impacts school violence. *Men and Masculinities, 9*(1), 53–75.

Klein, J. (2012). *The Bully Society: school shootings and the crisis of bullying in American schools.* New York: New York University Press.

Kleinman, S., Copp, M., & Henderson, K. (1997). Qualitatively different: Teaching fieldwork to graduate students. *Journal of Contemporary Ethnography, 25,* 469–499.

Kocsis, R. N. (2007). *Criminal profiling: International theory, research, and practice.* Totowa, NJ: Humana Press.

Kocsis, R. N., Irwin, H. J., Hayes, A. F., & Nunn, R. (2000). Expertise in psychological profiling: A comparative assessment. *Journal of Interpersonal Violence, 15*(3), 311–331.

Kohn, A. (2004). Rebuilding school culture to make schools safer. *The Education Digest, 70*(3), 23–30.

Kupchik, A. (2010). *Homeroom security: School discipline in an age of fear.* New York: New York University Press.

Kupchik, A., & Monahan, T. (2006). The new American school: Preparation for post-industrial discipline. *British Journal of Sociology of Education, 27*(5), 617–631.

Langman, P. (2005). Can school shootings be prevented? *Healing Magazine, 10*(2), 24–27.

Langman, P. (2009a). *Why kids kill: Inside the minds of school shooters.* New York, NY: Palgrave Macmillan.

Langman, P. (2009b). Rampage school shooters: A typology. *Aggression and Violent Behavior, 14*(1), 79–86.

Langman, P. (2017). *School shooters: Understanding high school, college, and adult perpetrators.* Lanham, MD: Rowman & Littlefield.

Langman, P. (2018). Different types of role model influence and fame seeking among mass killers and copycat offenders. *American Behavioral Scientist, 62*(2), 210–228.

Langman, P., & Straub, F. (2019). *A comparison of averted and completed school attacks from the Police Foundation's averted school violence database.* Washington, DC: Office of Community Oriented Policing Services.

Lankford, A. (2016). Fame-seeking rampage shooters: Initial findings and empirical predictions. *Aggression and Violent Behavior, 27*(1), 122–129.

Lankford, A. (2018). Do the media unintentionally make mass killers into celebrities? An assessment of free advertising and earned media value. *Celebrity Studies, 9*(3), 340–354.

Lankford, A., & Madfis, E. (2018a). Media coverage of mass killers: Content, consequences, and solutions. *American Behavioral Scientist, 62*(2), 151–162.

Lankford, A., & Madfis, E. (2018b). Don't name them, don't show them, but report everything else: A pragmatic proposal for denying mass killers the attention they seek and deterring future offenders. *American Behavioral Scientist, 62*(2), 260–279.

Lankford, A., Adkins, K. G., & Madfis, E. (2019). Are the deadliest mass shootings preventable? An assessment of leakage, information reported to law enforcement, and firearms acquisition prior to attacks in the United States. *Journal of Contemporary Criminal Justice, 35*(3), 315–341.

Larkin, R. W. (2007). *Comprehending Columbine*. Philadelphia, PA: Temple University Press.

Larkin, R. W. (2009). The Columbine legacy: Rampage shootings as political acts. *American Behavioral Scientist, 52*(9), 1309–1326.

Latané, B., & Darley, J. M. (1969). Bystander "apathy". *American Scientist, 57,* 244–268.

Lawrence, R. (2007). *School crime and juvenile justice*. New York, NY: Oxford University Press.

Lawrence, R. G., & Birkland, T. A. (2004). Guns, Hollywood, and school safety: Defining the school-shooting problem across the public arenas. *Social Science Quarterly, 85,* 1193–1207.

Leary, M. R., Kowalski, R. M., Smith, L., & Phillips, S. (2003). Teasing, rejection, and violence: Case studies of the school shootings. *Aggressive Behavior, 29,* 202–214.

Lee, S. (2019, June 7). How the good guy with a gun became a deadly American fantasy. *The Conversation*. Retrieved June 8, 2019, from https://theconversation.com/how-the-good-guy-with-a-gun-became-a-deadly-american-fantasy-117367.

Leitsinger, M. (2012, March 8). *When rumor, the Internet and school violence fears collide*. Retrieved May 4, 2012, from http://usnews.msnbc.msn.com/_news/2012/03/08/10604539-when-rumor-the-internet-and-school-violence-fears-collide?lite.

Levin, J., & Fox, J. A. (1999). Making sense of mass murder. In V. B. Van Hasselt & M. Hersen (Eds.), *Handbook of psychological approaches with violent offenders: Contemporary strategies and issues* (pp. 173–187). Norwell, MA: Kluwer Academic.

Levin, J., Fox J. A., & Mazaik, J. (2005). Blurring fame and infamy: A content analysis of cover-story trends in People Magazine. *Internet Journal of Criminology*, 1–17.

Levin, J., & Madfis, E. (2009). Mass murder at school and cumulative strain: A sequential model. *American Behavioral Scientist, 52*(9), 1227–1245.

Levin, J., & Madfis, E. (2018). Rampage school shootings. In A. J. Treviño (Ed.), *The Cambridge handbook of social problems* (pp. 253–267). New York, NY: Cambridge University Press.

Lickel, B., Schmader, T., & Hamilton, D. (2003). A case of collective responsibility: Who else was to blame for the Columbine high school shootings? *Personality & Social Psychology Bulletin, 29*, 194–204.

Lieberman, J. A. (2008). *School shootings: What every parent and educator needs to know to protect our children.* New York: Citadel Press.

Lincoln, Y., & Guba, E. (1985). *Naturalistic inquiry.* Beverly Hills, CA: Sage.

Lintott, J. (2004). Teaching and learning in the face of school violence. *Georgetown Journal on Poverty Law & Policy, 11*(3), 553–580.

List of School-Related Attacks—Foiled or Exposed Plots. (n.d.). Retrieved July 15, 2010, from http://en.wikipedia.org/wiki/List_of_school-related_attacks#Foiled_or_exposed_plots.

Livingston, M. D., Rossheim, M. E., & Hall, K. S. (2019). A descriptive analysis of school and school shooter characteristics and the severity of school shootings in the United States, 1999–2018. *Journal of Adolescent Health, 64*(6), 797–799.

Lockhart, P. R. (2019, February 6). *A black security guard caught a shooting suspect—Only to be shot by police minutes later.* Retrieved June 26, 2019, from https://www.vox.com/identities/2018/11/12/18088874/jemel-roberson-police-shooting-illinois-ian-covey-video.

Lodge, J., & Frydenberg, E. (2005). The role of peer bystanders in school bullying: Positive steps toward promoting peaceful schools. *Theory into Practice, 44*(4), 329–336.

Logan, C. (2002, May 2). Columbine jitters may cost a Kansas town millions. *The Pitch*. Retrieved July 5, 2010, from http://www.pitch.com/2002-05-02/news/tutu-careful/.

Lopez, G. (2017, November 6). *The Texas shooting shows why "a good guy with a gun" isn't enough.* Retrieved June 26, 2019, from https://www.vox.com/policy-and-politics/2017/11/6/16612014/sutherland-springs-shooting-good-guy-gun.

Lopez, G. (2018, June 21). *America's love for guns, in one chart*. Retrieved June 26, 2019, from https://www.vox.com/2018/6/21/17488024/gun-ownership-violence-shootings-us.

Lott, J. R. (2014, February 17). *Bloomberg's latest stats on school gun violence ignore reality*. Retrieved May 24, 2019, from https://www.foxnews.com/opinion/bloombergs-latest-stats-on-School-Gun-Violence-Ignore-Reality.

Lyons, W., & Drew, J. (2006). *Punishing schools: Fear and citizenship in American public education*. Ann Arbor, MI: University of Michigan Press.

MacDonald, I. M., & da Costa, J. L. (1996). *Exploring issues of school violence: The "code of silence."* Paper presented at the conference of the Canadian Association for the Study of Educational Administration, St. Catherines, ON, Canada.

Madfis, E. (2014a). Averting school rampage: Student intervention amid a persistent code of silence. *Youth Violence and Juvenile Justice, 12*(3), 229–249.

Madfis, E. (2014b). Triple entitlement and homicidal anger: An exploration of the intersectional identities of American mass murderers. *Men and Masculinities, 17*(1), 67–86.

Madfis, E. (2016). "It's better to overreact": School officials' fear and perceived risk of rampage attacks and the criminalization of American public schools. *Critical Criminology, 24*(1), 39–55.

Madfis, E. (2017). In search of meaning: Are school rampage shootings random and senseless violence? *The Journal of Psychology: Interdisciplinary and Applied, 151*(1), 21–35.

Madfis, E. (2018). Insight from averted mass shootings. In J. Schildkraut (Ed.), *Mass shootings in America: Understanding the debates, causes, and responses* (pp. 79–84). Santa Barbara, CA: Praeger Books.

Madfis, E., & Cohen, J. W. (2018). Female involvement in school rampage plots. *Violence and Gender, 5*(2), 81–86.

Madfis, E., & Levin, J. (2013). School rampage in international perspective: The salience of cumulative strain theory. In N. Böckler, W. Heitmeyer, P. Sitzer, & T. Seeger (Eds.), *School shootings: International research, case studies, and concepts for prevention* (pp. 79–104). New York, NY: Springer.

Mai, R., & Alpert, J. (2000). Separation and socialization: A feminist analysis of the school shootings at Columbine. *Journal for the Psychoanalysis of Culture and Society, 5*, 264–275.

Martins, L. (2019, March 13). *Inspired by Columbine, Brazil pair kill eight and themselves in school shooting*. Retrieved June 20, 2019, from https://www.reuters.com/article/us-brazil-violence-school/inspired-by-columbine-brazil-pair-kill-eight-and-themselves-in-school-shooting-idUSKBN1QU1TT.

Mathes, E. W., & Kahn, A. (1975). Diffusion of responsibility and extreme behavior. *Journal of Personality and Social Psychology, 31*(5), 881–886.

May, A. (2018, March 13). *Guns in school: It's not just an idea. Here's how some states are already doing it.* Retrieved June 8, 2019, from https://www.usatoday.com/story/news/nation-now/2018/03/13/can-guns-schools-save-students-during-shooting-heres-what-states-say/418965002/.

McCabe, K. A., & Martin, G. M. (2005). *School violence, the media, and criminal justice responses.* New York: Lang.

McCluskey, G. (2018). Restorative approaches in schools: Current practices, future directions. In J. Deakin, E. Taylor, & A. Kupchik (Eds.), *The Palgrave international handbook of school discipline, surveillance, and social control* (pp. 573–593). New York, NY: Palgrave Macmillan.

McCluskey, G., Lloyd, G., Kane, J., Riddell, S., Stead, J., & Weedon, E. (2008). Can restorative practices in schools make a difference? *Educational Review, 60*(4), 405–417.

McCrimmon, K. K. (2009). *The story of Safe2Tell.* Denver, CO: The Colorado Trust. Retrieved May 23, 2012, from http://safe2tell.org/wp-content/uploads/2009/03/storys2t.pdf.

McGee, J. P., & DeBernardo, C. R. (1999). The classroom avenger: A behavioral profile of school based shootings. *The Forensic Examiner, 8,* 16–18.

McMillin, S. (2009, April 18). *Getting teens to talk may be key to secure schools.* Retrieved May 23, 2019, from https://gazette.com/news/getting-teens-to-talk-may-be-key-to-secure-schools/article_11a0709c-80a6-5391-ab09-50755353d880.html.

Meindl, J. N., & Ivy, J. W. (2017). Mass shootings: The role of the media in promoting generalized imitation. *American Journal of Public Health, 107,* 368–370.

Meindl, J. N., & Ivy, J. W. (2018). Reducing media-induced mass killings: Lessons from suicide prevention. *American Behavioral Scientist, 62*(2), 242–259.

Meloy, J. R. (2015). Threat assessment: Scholars, operators, our past, our future. *Journal of Threat Assessment and Management, 2*(3–4), 231–242.

Meloy, J. R., Hempel, A. G., Gray, B. T., Mohandie, K., Shiva, A. A., & Richards, T. C. (2004). A comparative analysis of North American adolescent and adult mass murderers. *Behavioral Sciences and the Law, 22*(3), 291–309.

Meloy, J. R., Hempel, A. G., Mohandie, K., Shiva, A. A., & Gray, B. T. (2001). Offender and offense characteristics of a nonrandom sample of adolescent mass murders. *Journal of the American Academy of Child and Adolescent Psychiatry, 40*(6), 719–728.

Meloy, J. R., Mohandie, K., Knoll, J. L., & Hoffman, J. (2015). The concept of identification in threat assessment. *Behavioral Sciences and the Law, 33*(2–3), 213–237.

Meloy, J. R., & O'Toole, M. E. (2011). The concept of leakage in threat assessment. *Behavioral Sciences and the Law, 29*, 513–527.

Menninger, K. (1968). *The crime of punishment.* New York: Penguin Books.

Merelli, A. (2018, May 22). *What US guns rights advocates would like to ban instead of guns.* Retrieved April 19, 2019, from https://qz.com/1285430/all-the-things-gun-advocates-have-blamed-for-school-shootings/.

Merida, K. (1999, April 27). Fearful kids maintain code of silence. *Washington Post.* Retrieved May 3, 2019, from http://www.washingtonpost.com/wp-srv/national/daily/april99/snitch042799.htm.

Messerschmidt, J. W. (1993). *Masculinities and crime: Critique and reconceptualization of theory.* New York: Rowan & Littlefield.

Meyer, L. H., & Evans, I. M. (2012). *The teacher's guide to restorative classroom discipline.* Thousand Oaks, CA: Sage.

Mikkelson, D. (2015). *Rumor: A school shooter in Pearl, Mississippi, was stopped from killing additional victims by an assistant principal with a gun.* Retrieved June 24, 2019, from https://www.snopes.com/fact-check/full-stop/.

Mingus, W., & Zopf, B. (2010). White means never having to say you're sorry: The racial project in explaining mass shootings. *Social Thought and Research, 31,* 57–78.

Mirsky, L. (2003). *SaferSanerSchools: Transforming school culture with restorative practices.* International Institute for Restorative Practices. Retrieved February 18, 2019, from http://www.iirp.edu/pdf/ssspilots.pdf.

Moeller, T. G. (2001). *Youth aggression and violence: A psychological approach.* Mahwah, NJ: Lawrence Erlbaum Associates.

Monahan, T., & Torres, R. D. (Eds.). (2010). *Schools under surveillance: Cultures of control in public education.* New Brunswick, NJ: Rutgers University Press.

Moore, M. H., Petrie, C. V., Braga, A. A., & McLaughlin, B. L. (2003). *Deadly lessons: Understanding lethal school violence.* Washington, DC: National Academies Press.

Morris, E. W. (2010). "Snitches end up in ditches" and other cautionary tales. *Journal of Contemporary Criminal Justice, 26*(3), 254–272.

Morris, M. W. (2016). *Pushout: The criminalization of Black girls in schools.* New York, NY: The New Press.

Morrison, B. (2007). *Restoring safe school communities: A whole school response to bullying, violence and alienation*. Sidney, Australia: Federation Press.

Morrison, G. (2006). Deadly force programs among larger U.S. police departments. *Police Quarterly, 9*(3), 331–360.

Mossman, D. (1994). Assessing predictions of violence: Being accurate about accuracy. *Journal of Consulting and Clinical Psychology, 62*, 783–792.

Mossman, D. (2006). Critique of pure risk assessment or, Kant meets Tarasoff. *University of Cincinnati Law Review, 75*, 523–609.

Mullen, P. E. (2004). The autogenic (self-generated) massacre. *Behavioral Sciences and the Law, 22*, 311–323.

Muncie, J. (2008). The "punitive turn" in juvenile justice: Cultures of control and rights compliance in Western Europe and the USA. *Youth Justice, 8*(2), 107–121.

Murray, J. L. (2017). Mass media reporting and enabling of mass shootings. *Cultural Studies, Critical Methodologies, 17*, 114–124.

Muschert, G. W. (2002). *Media and massacre: The social construction of the Columbine story*. Unpublished doctoral dissertation, University of Colorado at Boulder, Boulder, CO.

Muschert, G. W. (2007). Research in school shootings. *Sociology Compass, 1*(1), 60–80.

Muschert, G. W., & Madfis, E. (2013). Fear of school violence in the post-Columbine era. In G. W. Muschert, S. Henry, N. L. Bracy, & A. A. Peguero (Eds.), *Responding to school violence: Confronting the Columbine effect* (pp. 13–34). Boulder, CO: Lynne Rienner.

Muschert, G. W., Henry, S., Bracy, N. L., & Peguero, A. A. (Eds.). (2013). *Responding to school violence: Confronting the Columbine effect*. Boulder, CO: Lynne Rienner.

Muschert, G. W., & Peguero, A. A. (2010). The Columbine effect and school anti-violence policy. *Research in Social Problems and Public Policy, 17*, 117–148.

Muschert, G. W., & Ragnedda, M. (2010). Media and control of violence: Communication in school shootings. In W. Heitmeyer, H. Haupt, A. Kirschner, & S. Malthaner (Eds.), *Control of violence: Historical and international perspectives on violence in modern societies* (pp. 345–361). New York, NY: Springer.

Muzzatti, S. L. (2004). Criminalising marginality and resistance: Marilyn Manson, Columbine, and cultural criminology. In J. Ferrell, K. Hayward, W. Morrison, & M. Presdee (Eds.), *Cultural criminology unleased* (pp. 143–154). London: Glasshouse Press.

Myketiak, C. (2016). Fragile masculinity: Social inequalities in the narrative frame and discursive construction of a mass shooter's autobiography/manifesto. *Contemporary Social Science, 11*(4), 289–303.
Mythen, G. (2008). Sociology and the art of risk. *Sociology Compass, 2*(1), 299–316.
National Association of School Resource Officers. (n.d.). *Frequently asked questions*. Retrieved June 12, 2019, from https://nasro.org/frequently-asked-questions/.
National Center for School Safety. (2006). *Serious violent crimes in schools*. Youth Violence Project.
Neroni, H. (2000). The men of Columbine: Violence and masculinity in American culture and film. *Journal for the Psychoanalysis of Culture and Society, 5*, 256–263.
Newman, K. S., & Fox, C. (2009). Repeat tragedy: Rampage shootings in American high school and college settings, 2002–2008. *American Behavioral Scientist, 52*(9), 1286–1308.
Newman, K. S., Fox, C., Roth, W., Mehta, J., & Harding, D. (2004). *Rampage: The social roots of school shooters*. New York: Perseus Books.
Noguera, P. A. (1995). Preventing and producing violence: A critical analysis of responses to school violence. *Harvard Education Review, 65*(2), 189–212.
Nolan, K. (2011). *Police in the hallways: Discipline in an urban school*. Minneapolis: University of Minnesota Press.
Nolan, K. (2018). Policing student behavior: Roles and responsibilities. In J. Deakin, E. Taylor, & A. Kupchik (Eds.), *The Palgrave international handbook of school discipline, surveillance, and social control* (pp. 309–326). New York, NY: Palgrave Macmillan.
No Notoriety. (n.d.). Retrieved June 7, 2019, from https://nonotoriety.com/.
Ogle, J. P., Eckman, M., & Leslie, C. A. (2003). Appearance cues and the shootings at Columbine High: Construction of a social problem in the print media. *Sociological Inquiry, 73*(1), 1–27.
Ohana, D. (2007). Desert and punishment for acts preparatory to the commission of a crime. *Canadian Journal of Law and Jurisprudence, 20*, 113–142.
O'Malley, P. (2008). Neoliberalism and risk in criminology. In T. Anthony & C. Cunneen (Eds.), *The critical criminology companion* (pp. 55–67). Sydney, Australia: Federation Press.
O'Toole, M. E. (2000). *The school shooter: A threat assessment perspective*. Critical Incident Response Group, National Center for the Analysis of Violent Crime, FBI Academy, Quantico, VA. Retrieved July 3, 2019,

from https://www.fbi.gov/file-repository/stats-services-publications-school-shooter-school-shooter.

Otto, R. K. (2000). Assessing and managing violence risk in outpatient settings. *Journal of Clinical Psychology, 56,* 1239–1262.

Owen, T. (2018, March 10). *Here's all the states where teachers already carry guns in the classroom.* Retrieved June 8, 2019, from https://news.vice.com/en_us/article/ywq8b5/teachers-armed-guns-classroom-state-laws.

Owen, T. (2019, March 26). *Owning a bump stock can now get you 10 years in prison.* Retrieved June 7, 2019, from https://news.vice.com/en_us/article/3kg9bv/owning-a-bump-stock-can-now-get-you-10-years-in-prison.

Palermo, G. B., & Kocsis, R. N. (2005). *Offender profiling: An introduction to the sociopsychological analysis of violent crime.* Springfield, IL: Charles C. Thomas Publisher.

Palermo, G. B., & Ross, L. E. (1999). Mass murder, suicide, and moral development: Can we separate the adults from the juveniles? *International Journal of Offender Therapy and Comparative Criminology, 43*(1), 8–20.

Parsons, C. (2018). Looking for strategic alternatives to school exclusion. In J. Deakin, E. Taylor, & A. Kupchik (Eds.), *The Palgrave international handbook of school discipline, surveillance, and social control* (pp. 529–552). New York, NY: Palgrave Macmillan.

Pattillo, M., Weiman, D., & Western, B. (2004). *Imprisoning America: The social effects of mass incarceration.* New York: Russell Sage Foundation Publications.

Payne, S., & Elliott, D. S. (2011). Safe2Tell®: An anonymous, 24/7 reporting system for preventing school violence. *New Directions in Youth Development, 129,* 103–111.

Perez, S. (2011, March 5). *Where is the Santana shooter now?* Retrieved April 13, 2019, from http://santee.patch.com/articles/where-is-the-santana-shooter-now.

Perrin, P. B. (2016). Translating psychological science: Highlighting the media's contribution to contagion in mass shootings: Comment on Kaslow (2015). *American Psychologist, 71,* 71–72.

Petherick, W. (2006). *Serial crime: Theoretical and practical issues in behavioral profiling.* Burlington, MA: Academic Press.

Petee, T. A., Padgett, K. G., & York, T. S. (1997). Debunking the stereotype: An examination of mass murder in public places. *Homicide Studies, 1*(4), 317–337.

Pinizzotto, A., & Finkel, N. J. (1990). Criminal personality profiling: An outcome and process study. *Law & Human Behavior, 14,* 215–233.

Pollack, W. S., Modzeleski, W., & Rooney, G. (2008). *Prior knowledge of potential school-based violence: Information students learn may prevent a targeted attack*. Washington, DC: United States Secret Service and United States Department of Education.

Pratt, J., Brown, D., Brown, M., Hallsworth, S., & Morrison, W. (2005). *The new punitiveness: Trends, theories, perspectives*. Portland: Willan Publishing.

Public Agenda. (2004). *Teaching interrupted: Do discipline policies in today's public schools foster the common good?* New York: Public Agenda. Retrieved June 12, 2019, from https://files.eric.ed.gov/fulltext/ED485312.pdf.

Rafa, A. (2019). *The status of school discipline in state policy*. Education Commission of the States. Retrieved May 22, 2019, from https://www.ecs.org/wp-content/uploads/The-Status-of-School-Discipline-in-State-Policy.pdf.

Raitanen, J., & Oksanen, A. (2018). Global online subculture surrounding school shootings. *American Behavioral Scientist, 62*(2), 195–209.

Rajan, S., & Branas, C. C. (2018). Arming schoolteachers: What do we know? Where do we go from here? *American Journal of Public Health., 108*, 860–862.

Randazzo, M. R., Borum, R., Vossekuil, B., Fein, R., Modzeleski, W., & Pollack, W. (2006). Threat assessment in schools: Empirical support and comparison with other approaches. In S. R. Jimerson & M. J. Furlong (Eds.), *The handbook of school violence and school safety: From research to practice* (pp. 147–156). Mahwah, NJ: Lawrence J. Erlbaum Associates.

Rappaport, N., & Barrett, J. G. (2009). Under the gun: Threat assessment in schools. *American Medical Association Journal of Ethics, 11*(2), 149–154.

Reddy, M., Borum, R., Berglund, J., Vossekuil, B., Fein, R., & Modzeleski, W. (2001). Evaluating risk for targeted violence in schools: Comparing risk assessment, threat assessment, and other approaches. *Psychology in the Schools, 38*(2), 157–172.

Rigakos, G. S., & Hadden, R. W. (2001). Crime, capitalism and the "risk society": Towards the same olde modernity? *Theoretical Criminology, 5*(1), 61–84.

Robbins, C. (2005). Zero tolerance and the politics of racial injustice. *The Journal of Negro Education, 74*(1), 2–17.

Robins, L. N. (1966). *Deviant children grown up: A sociological and psychiatric study of sociopathic personality*. Baltimore, MD: The Williams & Wilkins Company.

Robertson, T. (2001, December 16). Across the nation, school attack plots pose legal challenge. *Boston Globe*, pp. A1, A26.

Rocque, M. (2012). Exploring school rampage shootings: Research, theory, and policy. *The Social Science Journal, 49*(3), 304–313.

Rosenbaum, D. P., Lurigio, A. J., & Davis, R. C. (Eds.). (1998). *The prevention of crime: Social and situational strategies.* Belmont, CA: Wadsworth.

Rosenfeld, R., Jacobs, B. A., & Wright, R. (2003). Snitching and the code of the street. *British Journal of Criminology, 43,* 291–309.

Ruddy, S. A., Neiman, S., Hryczaniuk, C., Thomas, T. L., Parmer, R. J., & Hill, M. R. (2010). *2007–08 School Survey on Crime and Safety (SSOCS): Survey documentation for public-use data file users.* Washington, DC: National Center for Education Statistics, Institute of Education Sciences, U.S. Department of Education. Retrieved April 13, 2019, from http://nces.ed.gov/pubs2010/2010307.pdf.

Sacco, F. C., & Larsen, R. (2003). Threat assessment in schools: A critique of an ongoing intervention. *Journal of Applied Psychoanalytic Studies, 5*(2), 171–188.

Sachsman, S. (1997, September 8). Prof stalkers beware: MOSAIC is here. *Yale Daily News.*

Sanders, C. (2004). Forward. In A. Arluke, *Brute force: Animal police and the challenge of cruelty* (pp. vii–xiii). West Lafayette, IN: Purdue University Press.

Sarteschi, C. (2016). An examination of thwarted mass homicide plots and threateners. *Aggression and Violent Behavior, 30*(1), 88–93.

Saul, S. (2018, February 21) An armed principal detained a campus gunman. But he's against arming school staff. *The New York Times.* Retrieved June 8, 2019, from https://www.nytimes.com/2018/02/21/us/school-shootings-teachers.html.

Savage, C. (2018, December 18). *Trump administration imposes ban on bump stocks.* Retrieved June 7, 2019, from https://www.nytimes.com/2018/12/18/us/politics/trump-bump-stocks-ban.html.

Schiele, J. H., & Stewart, R. (2001). When white boys kill: An Afrocentric analysis. *Journal of Human Behavior in the Social Environment, 4*(4), 253–273.

Schiff, M. (2013). Dignity, disparity, and desistance: Effective restorative justice strategies to plus the school-to-prison pipeline. In *Center for Civil Rights Remedies National Conference. Closing the School to Research Gap: Research to Remedies Conference.* Washington, DC.

Schlafly, P. (2003, April 23). Zero tolerance or zero common sense. *Eagle Forum.* Retrieved June 25, 2019, from http://www.eagleforum.org/column/2003/apr03/03-04-23.shtml.

Schofield, J. W. (2002). Increasing the generalizability of qualitative research. In A. M. Huberman & M. Miles (Eds.), *The qualitative researcher's companion* (pp. 171–203). Thousand Oaks, CA: Sage Publications.

Schutt, R. K. (2004). *Investigating the social world: The process and practice of research*. Thousand Oaks: Pine Forge Press.

Schwarz, E., & Kowalski, J. (1991). Malignant memories: Posttraumatic stress disorder in children and adults following a school shooting. *Journal of the American Academy of Child and Adolescent Psychiatry, 30*, 937–944.

Seletan, W. (2011, January 11). *Friendly firearms: Gabrielle Giffords and the perils of guns: How an armed hero nearly shot the wrong man*. Retrieved June 24, 2019, from https://slate.com/technology/2011/01/joe-zamudio-and-the-gabrielle-giffords-shooting-how-an-armed-hero-nearly-shot-the-wrong-man.html.

Sewell, K. W., & Mendelsohn, M. (2000). Profiling potentially violent youth: Statistical and conceptual problems. *Children's Services: Social Policy, Research, and Practice, 3*(3), 147–169.

Shapiro, J., Dorman, R. L., & Burkey, W. M. (1997). Development and factor analysis of a measure of youth attitudes toward guns and violence. *Journal of Clinical Child Psychology, 26*(3), 311–320.

Shepard, S. (2018, February 28). *Gun control support surges in polls*. Retrieved June 26, 2019, from https://www.politico.com/story/2018/02/28/gun-control-polling-parkland-430099.

Sherman, L. W., Farrington, D. P., Welsh, B. C., & MacKenzie, D. L. (Eds.). (2002). *Evidence-based crime prevention*. New York: Routledge.

Sherman, L. W., & Strang, H. (2007). *Restorative justice: The evidence*. London: The Smith Institute.

Sidhu, S. S. (2017). Name no names: The role of the media in reporting mass shootings. *Journal of the American Academy of Child & Adolescent Psychiatry, 56*, 3–4.

Siebel, B., & Roston, A. (2007). *No gun left behind—The gun lobby's campaign to push guns into colleges and schools*. Brady Center to Prevent Gun Violence. Retrieved June 24, 2019, from https://papers.ssrn.com/sol3/papers.cfm?abstract_id=987861.

Simon, J. (2006). *Governing through crime: How the war on crime transformed American democracy and created a culture of fear*. Oxford: Oxford University Press.

Silver, J., Horgan, J., & Gill, P. (2018). Shared struggles? Cumulative strain theory and public mass murderers from 1990 to 2014. *Homicide Studies, 23*(1), 64–84.

Skiba, R. (2000). *Zero tolerance, zero evidence: An analysis of school disciplinary practice*. Policy Research Report. Indiana Education Policy Center.

Skiba, R., Arredondo, M. I., Gray, C., & Rausch, M. K. (2018). Discipline disparities: New and emerging research in the United States. In J. Deakin, E. Taylor, & A. Kupchik (Eds.), *The Palgrave international handbook of school discipline, surveillance, and social control* (pp. 235–252). New York, NY: Palgrave Macmillan.

Skiba, R., Michael, R. S., Nardo, A. C., & Peterson, R. L. (2002). The color of discipline: Source of racial and gender disproportionality in school punishment. *The Urban Review, 34*(4), 317–342.

Skiba, R., & Peterson, R. L. (1999). The dark side of zero tolerance: Can punishment lead to safe schools? *Phi Delta Kappan, 80*(5), 372–382.

Sommer, F., Leuschner, V., & Scheithauer, H. (2014). Bullying, romantic rejection, and conflicts with teachers: The crucial role of social dynamics in the development of school shootings—A systematic review. *International Journal of Developmental Science, 8*, 3–24.

Spitalli, S. J. (2003). Breaking the code of silence. *American School Board Journal, 190*(9), 56–58.

Spjut, R. J. (1987). When is an attempt to commit an impossible crime a criminal act. *Arizona Law Review, 29*(2), 247–279.

Stancato, F. A. (2001). The Columbine tragedy: Adolescent identity and future recommendations. *The Clearing House, 77*(1), 19–22.

Steiker, C. S. (1998). Forward: The limits of the preventive state. *Journal of Criminal Law & Criminology, 88*(3), 771–808.

Strong, K., & Cornell, D. (2008). Student threat assessment in Memphis City schools: A descriptive report. *Behavioral Disorders, 34*, 42–54.

Student Suspended After Finger Gun Incident. (2010, April 18). Abclocal.go.com. Retrieved October 3, 2010, from http://abclocal.go.com/ktrk/story?section=news/local&id=7392273.

Stueve, A., Dash, K., O'Donnell, L., Tehranifar, P., Wilson-Simmons, R., Slaby, R. G., & Link, B. G. (2006). Rethinking the bystander role in school violence prevention. *Health Promotion Practice, 7*(1), 117–124.

Sulkowski, M. L. (2011). An investigation of students' willingness to report threats of violence in campus communities. *Psychology of Violence, 1*(1), 53–65.

Sullivan, M. L., & Guerette, R. T. (2003). The copycat factor: Mental illness, guns, and the shooting incident at Heritage high school, Rockdale County,

Georgia. In M. H. Moore (Ed.), *Deadly lessons: Understanding lethal school violence* (pp. 25–69). Washington, DC: National Academies Press.

Sumner, M. D., Silverman, C. J., & Frampton, M. L. (2010). *School-based restorative justice as an alternative to zero-tolerance policies: Lessons from West Oakland.* Henderson Center for Social Justice, University of California, Berkeley, School of Law.

Syvertsen, A. K., Flanagan, C. A., & Stout, M. D. (2009). Code of silence: Students' perceptions of school climate and willingness to intervene in a peer's dangerous plan. *Journal of Educational Psychology, 101*(1), 219–232.

Teicher, S. A. (2006, October 19). How students can break the 'code of silence': A number of resources let students anonymously voice their concerns about troubling issues at school. *The Christian Science Monitor.* Received April 13, 2019, from http://www.csmonitor.com/2006/1019/p15s01-legn.html.

Thurau, L. H., & Wald, J. (2010). Controlling partners: When law enforcement meets discipline in public schools. *New York Law School Law Review, 54,* 977–1020.

Times Wire Reports. (2001, February 1). *Child suspended for brandishing chicken.* Retrieved June 20, 2019, from http://articles.latimes.com/2001/feb/01/news/mn-19819.

Towers, S., Gomez-Lievano, A., Khan, M., Mubayi, A., & Castillo-Chavez, C. (2015). Contagion in mass killings and school shootings. *PLoS One, 10*(7), e0117259.

Trembley, R. E., & Craig, W. M. (1995). Developmental crime prevention. *Crime and Justice, 19,* 151–236.

Turvey, B. E. (2008). *Criminal profiling: An introduction to behavioral evidence analysis* (3rd ed.). Burlington, MA: Academic Press.

Twemlow, S. W., Fonagy, P., & Sacco, F. C. (2004). The role of the bystander in the social architecture of bullying and violence in schools and communities. *Annals of the New York Academy of Sciences, 1036,* 215–232.

Twemlow, S. W., Fonagy, P., Sacco, F. C., O'Toole, M. E., & Vernberg, E. (2002). premeditated mass shootings in schools: Threat assessment. *Journal of the American Academy of Child and Adolescent Psychiatry, 41*(4), 475–477.

Urbina, I. (2009, October 11). It's a fork, it's a spoon, it's a…weapon. *New York Times.* Retrieved May 3, 2019, from http://www.nytimes.com/2009/10/12/education/12discipline.html?_r=2.

Van Ness, D. W., & Strong, K. H. (2010). *Restoring justice: An introduction to restorative justice.* New Providence, NJ: Anderson.

Verhovek, S. H. (1999, November 11). *Teenager to spend life in prison for shootings*. Retrieved April 13, 2019, from http://www.nytimes.com/1999/11/11/us/teenager-to-spend-life-in-prison-for-shootings.html?ref=kiplandfkinkel.

Verlinden, S., Hersen, M., & Thomas, J. (2000). Risk factors in school shootings. *Clinical Psychology Review, 20*(1), 3–56.

Vincent, G. M., Terry, A. M., & Maney, S. M. (2009). Risk/needs tools for antisocial behavior and violence among youthful populations. In J. T. Andrade (Ed.), *Handbook of violence risk assessment and treatment: New approaches for mental health professionals* (pp. 377–424). New York, NY: Springer.

Virginia Tech Review Panel. (2007). *Mass shootings at Virginia Tech April 16, 2007: Report of the Virginia Tech Review Panel presented to Timothy M. Kaine, Governor, Commonwealth of Virginia*. Retrieved April 11, 2019, from https://scholar.lib.vt.edu/prevail/docs/VTReviewPanelReport.pdf.

Volokh, A. (2000). A brief guide to school-violence prevention. *Journal of Law and Family Studies, 2*(2), 99–152.

Vossekuil, B., Fein, R., Reddy, M., Borum, R., & Modzeleski, W. (2002). *The final report and findings of the safe school initiative: Implications for the prevention of school attacks in the United States*. Washington, DC: U.S. Secret Service and U.S. Department of Education.

Wacquant, L. (2009). *Punishing the poor: The neoliberal government of social insecurity*. Durham, NC: Duke University Press.

Wakefield, M. A., Loken, B., & Hornik, R. C. (2010). Use of mass media campaigns to change health behaviour. *The Lancet, 376*(9748), 1261–1271.

Wald, J., & Losen, D. J. (2003). Editors' notes. In J. Wald & D. J. Losen (Eds.), *New directions for youth development: Deconstructing the school-to-prison pipeline* (pp. 1–2). San Francisco, CA: Jossey-Bass.

Wamsley, L. (2019, May 2). *Florida approves bill allowing classroom teachers to be armed*. Retrieved June 17, 2019 from https://www.npr.org/2019/05/02/719585295/florida-approves-bill-allowing-classroom-teachers-to-be-armed.

Watkins, A. M. (2005). Examining the disparity between juvenile and adult victims in notifying the police: A study of mediating variables. *Journal of Research in Crime and Delinquency, 42*(3), 333–353.

Watts, I. E., & Erevelles, N. (2004). These deadly times: Reconceptualizing school violence by using critical race theory and disability studies. *American Educational Research Journal, 41*(2), 271–299.

Webber, J. A. (2003). *Failure to hold: The politics of school violence*. New York: Rowman & Littlefield.

Welch, K., & Payne, A. A. (2018). Zero tolerance school policies. In J. Deakin, E. Taylor, & A. Kupchik (Eds.), *The Palgrave international handbook of school discipline, surveillance, and social control* (pp. 215–234). New York, NY: Palgrave Macmillan.

Western, B. (2007). *Punishment and inequality in America.* New York: Russell Sage.

White-Hamon, L. S. (2000). *Mass murder and attempted mass murder: An examination of the perpetrator with an empirical analysis of typologies.* Unpublished doctoral dissertation, California School of Professional Psychology, Fresno, CA.

Whitehead, J. W. (2001, January 23). *Zero common sense school discipline rules cheapen students' humanity.* The Rutherford Institute. Retrieved July 26, 2019, from https://www.rutherford.org/publications_resources/john_whiteheads_commentary/zero_common_sense_school_discipline_rules_cheapen_students_humanity.

Wilson-Simmons, R., Dash, K., Tehranifar, P., O'Donnell, L., & Stueve, A. (2006). What can student bystanders do to prevent school violence? Perceptions of students and staff. *Journal of School Violence, 5*(1), 43–62.

Winn, Z. (2018, March 13). *Explaining Florida's new school safety law.* Retrieved June 12, 2019 from https://www.campussafetymagazine.com/safety/explaining-floridas-new-school-safety-law/.

Wise, T. (2001). School shootings and white denial. *Multicultural Perspectives, 3*(4), 3–4.

Wrangham, R., & Peterson, D. (1996). *Demonic males: Apes and the origins of human violence.* New York, NY: Houghton Mifflin.

Wylie, L. E., Gibson, C. L., Brank, E. M., Fondacaro, M. R., Smith, S. W., Brown, V. E., & Miller, S. A. (2010). Assessing school and student predictors of weapons reporting. *Youth Violence and Juvenile Justice, 8*(4), 351–372.

Yaffe, G. (2010). *Attempts: In the philosophy of action and the criminal law.* New York: Oxford University Press.

Young, J. (1994). Incessant chatter: Recent paradigms in criminology. In M. Maguire, R. Morgan, & R. Reiner (Eds.), *The Oxford handbook of criminology* (pp. 69–124). Oxford: Oxford University Press.

Youth Justice Board. (2004). *National evaluation of the restorative justice in schools programme.* Retrieved July 17, 2019, from http://www.creducation.net/resources/National_Eval_RJ_in_Schools_Full.pdf.

Index

A

Actuarial justice 25, 27–29, 98, 99, 144
American Bar Association 16, 44
American Psychological Association (APA) 16, 21, 44
Arming faculty members 148
Attempted crime 158
Automated decision-making 19, 21, 22
Averted school rampage 2, 3, 10, 11, 46, 47, 68, 79, 107, 155, 157, 171, 172, 174, 176

B

Bombs 3, 12, 49, 54, 57–59, 61, 63, 64, 76, 78, 120, 170
Breaking the code of silence 106, 113, 121, 124, 130, 131
Bullying 10, 45, 75, 129
Bystander inaction 119
Bystander intervention 113, 125, 129, 139, 141

C

Chardon High School massacre 143
Columbine High School massacre 4, 8, 9, 59, 64, 76, 78, 104, 106, 124, 144, 150, 151, 157, 170
Columbine Report 77
Copycat effect 78, 151
Crime prevention through environmental design (CPTED) 18
Criminal attempts 158

D

Depression/suicidal thinking 10, 71–73
Deterrence 29, 123, 129, 158
Deviant group/subcultural affiliation 65, 75, 79
Directly informed confidants 114, 130

E

Extreme risk protection orders. *See* Red flag laws

F

False accusations 143, 144
Fame 11, 150, 152, 153
Fascination with rampage violence 78
Firearms, access to 62, 146, 147
Foucault, Michel 27, 142, 143
Friday the 13th 76

G

Gender 65–69, 79, 91, 140
Generalizability 179, 180
Gonzalez, Emma 145
Goth subculture 75, 77
Grounded theory 179
Group characteristics 53, 65, 75, 97, 140
Guided professional judgment. *See* Warning signs
Gun availability 156
Gun control 9, 145, 147, 156, 157

H

Harcourt, Bernard 25, 27, 46
Hit list 5–7, 48, 50, 51, 54, 56, 57, 89–92, 113, 114, 177
Homogeneous communities 10
Hymowitz, Kay 43, 44

I

Indirectly informed bystanders 113
Individual characteristics. *See* Personal characteristics
International comparative research 157
Involved co-conspirators 116

K

Killer duos 157, 170

L

Leakage 105, 113, 116, 121–126, 128, 130, 154, 157, 158
Lockdown drills 109
Louisiana Technical College massacre 68

M

Marginalization 73–75, 79
Marjory Stoneman Douglas High School massacre 8, 144, 145, 156
Masculinity 10, 66, 69

Mass murder 8, 14, 28, 53, 60, 62, 65, 68, 99, 115, 139, 151, 154, 157, 158, 168–170, 176, 177
Media coverage 8, 28, 51, 125, 146, 150, 151, 153
Mental illness/mental health issue 10, 71, 72, 75, 79, 91
Metal detectors 14, 18, 29, 104, 105, 111, 123, 141, 144

N

Natural Born Killers 78
Nazi skinhead subculture 75
Neoliberal penality 25, 27

P

Personal characteristics 69, 71
Planning a rampage attack 4, 24, 53, 54, 57, 68
Positive school climate 110, 111, 117, 124, 129
Previous history of misbehavior 22, 69, 91
Profiling 19, 20, 29, 53, 65, 66, 91, 94, 95, 99, 140

Q

Qualitative methodology 178

R

Race/ethnicity 14, 66, 79
Red flag laws 147
Red Lake Senior High School massacre 66, 105

Restorative classroom discipline 129
Restorative justice 129
Risk 1–3, 7, 15, 19–29, 45–48, 50–54, 57, 60, 62, 64, 66, 67, 69–72, 79, 87–91, 93, 97, 98, 109, 115, 139–141, 143, 147, 148, 150, 153, 155, 158, 178
  levels of, 47, 50
  risk society, 27, 28

S

Sandy Hook Elementary School massacre 8, 104, 144, 151, 156
School criminalization 2, 25, 127, 142
  causes of, 25
  definition of, 1, 128
School rampage 1, 2, 6, 7, 9, 10, 12, 14, 28, 29, 44, 46, 47, 51–55, 60, 63, 65, 70, 73, 74, 76–78, 80, 87–90, 93, 96, 98, 100, 103–109, 113, 116, 118, 120, 126, 127, 129–131, 139, 141–146, 156, 157, 167, 168, 172, 178
  causes of, 5, 9–11, 45, 69, 74
  definition of, 55, 67, 169–171
School resource officers (SROs) 1, 5, 17, 56–59, 61, 64, 70, 72, 78, 89, 93, 104, 108, 112–114, 116–119, 121–123
School-to-prison pipeline 143
Social status at school 65, 73, 75, 79, 140
Sociology of risk 143

Student code of silence 107, 109, 110, 113, 115, 121, 124–126, 130, 131, 141–143, 158
Student/faculty rapport 112
Substantive threats 23, 51, 93, 96
Surveillance cameras 15, 141
Suspicious clothing 66, 142

T

Tasso da Silveira Municipal School massacre 66
Threat 8, 12, 13, 22–24, 43, 44, 46–48
 forms of (verbal, written, and electronic), 5, 48–50, 53, 87
Threat assessment approach 22, 24, 29, 48, 50–53, 60, 65, 92, 93, 98, 99, 140, 155
Threatened targets 115
Transferability 180
Transient threats 23, 50
Trench coats 13, 75–77

V

Victims, targeted vs. random 54, 55, 170, 171, 177

Violence risk assessment 2, 11, 19, 29, 45–47, 65, 79, 87, 98, 140, 155
Violent media/music 75, 78
Virginia Tech massacre 50, 66

W

Warning signs 2, 20–22, 29, 53, 64, 65, 71, 73, 75, 78, 97, 147, 148, 153, 154
Weapons
 acquisition 88, 89
 fascination with, 60, 64, 65, 78
 manufacture of, 60, 140
 possession, 61, 90, 99, 123
 training with, 62
Westside Middle School massacre 157

Z

Zero tolerance policies 1, 15, 16, 29, 44, 45, 61, 92, 99, 104, 105, 127, 128, 141, 144

Ingram Content Group UK Ltd.
Milton Keynes UK
UKHW011101060723
424579UK00016B/438